HISTORY AND LIBERTY

The Historical Writings of
Benedetto Croce

by

A. ROBERT CAPONIGRI

ROUTLEDGE AND KEGAN PAUL
London

First Published 1955
by Routledge & Kegan Paul Ltd
Broadway House, 68–74 Carter Lane
London E.C.4
Printed in Great Britain
by Butler & Tanner Ltd
Frome and London

HISTORY AND LIBERTY

TO

PROFESSOR HERBERT W. SCHNEIDER

with esteem and gratitude

τοῦτο γὰρ ἀθάνατον φωνᾶεν
ἕρπει
εἴ τις εὖ Ϝείπῃ τι

PINDAR: Isthmian IV

CONTENTS

CONTENTS

APPENDICES

PREFACE

THE thought and achievement of Benedetto Croce surely need no introduction in the English-speaking world. During the past half-century his fame and reputation have spread, quite literally, to the farthest reaches of the world. Translations of his writings and discussion of his ideas are to be found, not only in the principal, and even the lesser, languages of Europe, but in the tongues of the Middle and Far East, in Russian and in Japanese. Greater testimony to the universal resonance of his ideas could scarcely be asked. The English-speaking world, however, anticipated all others —even Germany, from which he drew so much inspiration—in appreciation of this universal relevance of his thought. His impress, moreover, was not only early, but deep. Certain of his ideas have entered into the permanent intellectual patrimony of English-speaking culture. That expressionism is now the point of departure of aesthetic theory, in England and America, as well as in Italy, is principally the effect of that impress. To speak of an introduction would, consequently, be both anachronistic and superfluous.

There would, however, seem to be ample occasion for, and fruit to be hoped from, a discussion of Croce's historical writings. This persuasion has its roots in a variety of reasons, both immanent to these works and circumstantial to the mutual receptivity between continental and English-speaking culture. A fresh interest in, and appreciation of, the problems of history, both as the theory of historical process and as historiography, has become one of the marked characteristics of twentieth-century thought. In general, the source of this interest is humanistic and stems from a diffidence toward the human potential of a science unguided by human sympathy and ethical insight. This interest has been felt with special force in the English-speaking world, in which both humanism and scientism have profound attachments. It has received its most vigorous logical development, however, in Italy, precisely in the historiographic practice of Croce. As in the case of aesthetics, a profound community reveals itself between the preoccupations of the two cultural spheres, and many English scholars have been concerned to secure the common fruits thus promised. In the last analysis, however, the occasion and the justification for the discussion of Croce's historical works reside in those works themselves. The inner quality of the vision of man's life in time which pervades them, and not any circumstantial criterion, must ultimately measure their stature and justify their claim upon the attention of reflective men. The purpose of the present essay has kept in view both of these factors. It seeks to minister, in a small way, to the cultural and intellectual understanding between the Italian and the English-speaking spheres; but it is concerned above all to present this inner and pervasive vision of Croce's histories in its true lineaments, to be judged by its own quality.

What is the ultimate quality of this vision of history in Croce? It may be expressed in a single phrase: history is the history of liberty. The phrase itself is not new, any more than that vision itself. It is rather the immemorial vision of history which has evoked the profoundest movement of the spirit of western man. The particular achievement of Croce as an historian and as a theorist of history (and these roles are one, for his reflections upon history have their origin in his commitments as an historian) is the clarity and force with which he has apprehended and stated this immemorial vision in terms conclusively cogent in the twentieth century. His apprehension, moreover, possesses the dimensions of human reality itself. He sees the meaning of liberty, of human liberty in history, in its pure idea. Thus his affirmation of the spirituality and the essential creativity of the human agent is unfaltering. At the same time, however, he apprehends with almost microscopic clarity the existential labour of the spirit in the creative process of history, the almost Sisyphean labour by which that image of liberty is converted into the historical reality of human institutions. Finally, his historical writings are permeated with a profound appreciation of the *ethos* and the *pathos* of the labour of the human spirit in history. This vision, once glimpsed, needs no apology. It transcends all cultural limits and addresses itself directly to the profoundest interest of men in all times and in all circumstances.

ACKNOWLEDGEMENT

N<small>OT</small> the least pleasure accompanying the completion of any work is the expression of one's gratitude to all who have contributed to its accomplishment. The author's gratitude goes out, before all, to the late Senator Croce; he not only opened the vast resources of his private library to the writer, but, despite advanced age and great illness, favoured him with personal counsel. His appreciation is very nearly as keen for the courtesy and aid extended by the staff of the Italian Institute for Historical Studies in Naples and especially by its director, Prof. Federico Chabod. Prof. Raffaelle Franchini, of the Nunziatella in Naples, Profs. Paul Bosco and Paul E. McLane of the University of Notre Dame, and Prof. Carlo Antoni of the University of Rome have offered him assistance too great to be measured. His wife, Winifred, by her encouragement and care has contributed daily to the work. His thanks must go also to his assistant, Mr. John Haddox, for his painstaking work on manuscript and proofs. Finally, he expresses his gratitude to the Committee on Publications of the University of Notre Dame.

A. ROBERT CAPONIGRI

Notre Dame
Christmas, 1954

PART ONE

THE REALM OF NAPLES
AND THE ETHICO-POLITICAL
CONCEPT OF HISTORY

I

ETHOS AND IDYLL IN HISTORY

AFTER a quarter of a century of intellectual activity which witnessed, not only the penetrating and now classical studies on Hegel and Vico, but the speculative achievement of the 'Philosophy of the Spirit' as well, Croce wrote that at the centre of his activity, as, in his own words, its 'heart within a heart,'[1] lay history. When again a similar period had passed and the opportunity presented itself, in the preface to a collection of historical and critical essays, to review its work, he wrote, 'I have dedicated to history the greater portion of my efforts during these last years, thus closing, in a certain sense, the circle which I had initiated in my youth when, from historical researches, I passed to philosophy, only to return again to history as to the only concrete mode of philosophizing.'[2] At the beginning and at the end stands history. His vast speculative work, which by any other standard may well stand by itself, is placed in the perspective in which he viewed it: as the effort to penetrate theoretically to the basis of historiography.

Croce's interest as an historian has ranged wide, as wide, almost, as the limits of European culture itself. One object, however, before all others, has been its most constant concern. The history of Naples, first to solicit the inquiry of his youth, occupied again the last nostalgic studies of his declining years. The reason for this lifelong pre-occupation did not lie in the dignity or grandeur of its object, for this history exhibited no heroic argument. Rather, as he was to write, this is a history which is not history, which cannot sustain comparison with that of the other states of Italy, Rome or Venice or Florence, which has aroused in those who have undertaken to narrate it either pity or disdain, and not admiration.[3] That reason must be sought elsewhere; in the remark, for instance, which he was to repeat many times, that there can be no history without participation, without commitment.[4] Naples is the first object of such

---

[1] CCMS in FPS, p. 1140. (For key to references confer Appendix A.)
[2] US, preface.   [3] SRN, 256.   [4] CFM, 61.

historical participation and commitment for Croce. With it he achieved an identity so complete as to impart to his narrative an almost autobiographical tone. This identity it is which sustains the brooding concern of seventy years for the city and the realm; which renders no detail too insignificant to draw his eye, endows every personality which walked its streets or partook in any degree of its tumultuous life with an attractive spark, permits no inscription or monument, however obscure, to elude his quest. As a result, that portion of his work devoted to this history, though perhaps surpassed in profundity or range, is unequalled in humanity and nobility, the simple nobility and the profound humanity of a Cato narrating the history of his Rome.

Quite apart from such considerations as the stature of its object and the commitment of its narrator, the history of Naples holds a unique position among Croce's historical writings. The 'matter of Naples' (as with an epic resonance it may be called) is the matrix within which Croce first achieved his proper vision of history and attained his full stature as an historian. This is the vision, as he expresses it, of history as moral drama[1] with more of tragedy than of idyll in it.[2] This is the vision which is crystallized into the ideal and the method of ethico-political history.

The vision of human history as moral drama is certainly not new; it is rather the first, the immediate and spontaneous intuition of western man concerning history, and the most constant. Mere originality, however, could never be the mark of a culture so thoroughly, so profoundly classical as that of Croce. His achievement lay rather in the re-evocation of this vision of history at a juncture when it had all but vanished and when western man was most in need of it to revive in himself the sense of his own humanity and spirituality. The quality and character of this achievement is, consequently, to be measured and assayed, not by reference to the vulgar norm of novelty, but to the clarity and power of his expression of that constant vision of history and by the magnitude of the forces against which he reasserted it.

These forces Croce tends to group generically under the name 'positivism'. Though heterogeneous, these forces exhibited one common feature: they tended to reduce man to the level of nature. The characteristic of the nature to which positivism tended to reduce man was alienation, the same character which Hegel had recognized as the mark of nature in all its many forms. The specific form of this

[1] SRN, 272.   [2] FPS, 634.

alienation was the denial of liberty to man and his enclosure within the determinate and determined complex of natural forces and processes. Denied liberty, man was made alien to the moral struggle or drama which is the existential form of that liberty, its living actuality, and to that creation and creativity which is the inner principle of that drama. Finally, this alienation dissevered man from the consciousness of his own character as spirit, the character under which liberty, morality, creativity are all to be subsumed.[1]

With respect to history the impact of these forces and the alienation they induced was ambiguous. They seemed, at first glance, to confirm and even to extend the domain of the concept of history, by subsuming under it the realm of nature itself. The form of nature, heretofore conceived as static, was asserted to be processive and evolutionary and hence, apparently, historical. History in this context appears to have an ontological sense. From the point of view of historiography, the transfer and extension seems equally effective; it gives rise to a concept of a natural history or of a science of history. This would consist, in the active, historiographical sense, in retracing the paths of those forces in the processive movement of nature, while, in the more formal, methodological sense it would mean the formulation of the 'laws' of that movement, reflecting thus the classical legalism of science and the definitiveness of the 'philosophy of history'. Little reflection is needed, however, to discern that this extension of the concept of history and this reconstruction of historiographic method are specious. They are lacking one element of that history in which man is involved and which is the very form and structure of his presence to himself, liberty and alternality. And the pure form of this liberty is moral drama. Nature cannot be rendered historical simply by endowing it with the external form or mark of temporal process, for the essence of history lies not in mere temporal succession but in the spiritual transactions which inform that succession. Historiography, consequently, cannot be merely the retracing of the temporal path of natural forces, but must consist in the penetration and comprehension of that inward moral dynamism.[2]

It is with reference to this dual alienation, the reduction of man to nature and the specious transfer of the historical character to natural process, that Croce's reassertion of history as moral drama in

[1] FPS, 5, 16, 21, 23, 46, 89, 118, 124, 130-1, 143, 189-90, 199, 222-3, 384, 469-70, 1160.
[2] TSS, 53 sqq., 70 sqq., 81 sqq., 112 sqq., 265 sqq.; SPA, 1-51, 203 sqq., 283 sqq., 287 sqq.; SH, 89 sqq., 99 sqq., 127 sqq.; CFM, 1 sqq., 248 sqq.

the ethico-political conception of history must be measured. That conception of history is elaborated, in the first instance, not in abstract, methodological terms, but concretely, in the actual narrative of histories and, most specifically, in the matrix of the 'matter of Naples'.

His achievement is revealed in a stronger light when that 'matter of Naples' is considered in its most general character. No other matter in the history of Europe would seem more readily to justify the historian's acquiescence to a naturalistic conception of history. All of the positivistic and naturalistic dogmas seem to find here their supremely plausible application. How might that essential failure, which, on Croce's own recognizance,[1] is the most intimate character of that history, more readily and plausibly be explained than by reference to the poverty of economic resources—the arid, inarable land, the rocky formation of terrain, the scarcity of mineral deposits; or to the ethnic factor—the complex hybrid population, into the formation of which there entered all of those strains which, in the catalogues of nineteenth-century ethnicism were judged most 'inferior'; or to psychological factors—that quality of 'dolce far niente' which the nineteenth century, through a confused veil of sentimental romanticism and hard-souled scientism, mistook for a 'natural' phenomenon and not for the moral reality it was. And the roll-call might be extended indefinitely, through all the favoured 'factors' of naturalistic theory. And this mode of explanation, in addition to its facility and plausibility, has the added attraction of permitting the historian to assume a sympathetic attitude toward the Neapolitans, exonerating them from the responsibility of an historical pattern which they had neither wrought nor chosen, or investing them with a romantic aura by depicting them in essential revolt against historic necessity.[2] Croce has been more concerned, perhaps, than any earlier historian of Naples, to place the natural conditions of its history in the clearest light, only, however, to place in even greater relief its essential moral drama. He confronts the naturalistic myths one by one and confutes them; the myth of the natural exuberance of the Neapolitan realm, which supposedly had made it an irresistible object of greed and the victim of numberless invasions, by pointing out its natural poverty, and by rehabilitating the reputation of the one man (Antonio Serra) who had pierced that illusion of natural richness and had suffered obloquy and prison for his pains;[3] that of race, by pointing out that racially the Neapolitan

[1] SRN, 256.   [2] SRN, 256 sqq., 269 sqq.   [3] SRN, 148–52.

people was compounded of strains which had proved their prowess repeatedly in history[1] and by laying bare the logical and historical fallacies of nineteenth-century ethnicism. His conclusion, historically and logically inescapable, is simply that natural conditions are neutral; they are the theatre, but they in no wise determine the drama which is enacted on their boards. The fallacy of the naturalists is to have substituted a mythical history of nature for the history of men. History, to borrow for an instant the terminology of the naturalists and positivists, is not a 'natural phenomenon' but a 'moral phenomenon'. History is to be explained neither by a single nor by a multiplicity of natural causes, but only by reference to the spiritual force at work within it.[2]

The opposition to positivism constitutes only the negative aspect of the vision of history as moral drama, of the ethico-political conception of history. Its positive aspect is to be discerned clearly first in the conception Croce entertains of the moral life of man and, secondly, in the methodological inferences he draws from this concept.

The ethico-political conception of history is Croce's reply to the logical demand in the theory of history for a universal history. Previously, this universality had been conceived transcendentally and holistically, or quantitatively, by romantic and positivistic historiography respectively. Romantic philosophy had sought to construct universal history in principle by finding a *point d'appui* outside the historical process, referring that process to an absolute subject to which it might be present in its entirety. (It may be remarked, parenthetically, that the difficulties and contradictions inherent in this effort form the basis of Croce's criticism of romantic historiography.)[3] Positivism escaped this transcendentalism and holism, but substituted for them a quantitative notion of universal history, the ideal of which was an exhaustive compilation of the human record. On the other hand, it reflected a transcendentalism of its own when it aspired to formulate the abstract laws of historical process; while recognizing the inexhaustible novelty of the content of history, it sought to restrain this content within the abstract boundaries of those laws. The one and the other, from Croce's point of view, is fallacious; romanticism, because it fails to recognize man's historical situation in all its implications and, by projecting a transcendental point of view, opens the way to the classical pitfalls of the 'philosophy of history', terminalism, eschatology, utopianism;

[1] SRN, 270. [2] SRN, 272-3. [3] TSS, 41 sqq., 243 sqq.

7

positivism, because it fails to find any living centre of unity within history, offering only the dualism of abstract processive laws and the ceaseless accumulation of inexhaustible historical 'fact'.[1] While rejecting romanticism and positivism alike, Croce recognizes the claims of universalism in historical theory. He meets these claims by the suggestion that the universality of history is neither transcendental and holistic, nor quantitative, but qualitative; that it resides in the immanence of the totality of the human spirit in every moment of its concrete history.[2]

It is possible for Croce to assign this qualitative universality to history, because he discerns at the centre of historical process the ethical life of man; and the ethical life of man can sustain this universality only because of the office he assigns it in the total economy of the human spirit. The ethical life, for Croce, consists in the human effort to achieve totality, qualitative wholeness in every temporal moment of its existence and to move toward this integrity through a continuous effort, however distended through time. This wholeness or plenitude of the spirit is conceived against the background of the distinct moments into which the life of spirit may logically be categorized. Croce had suggested an analysis in which these distinct moments appear first as the dichotomy between theoretical and practical and again as the subdistinction of each member of this dichotomy, the theoretical into the aesthetic and the logical, the practical into the economic and the ethical. The ethical moment appears first as one in which the limits of utility are transcended and the spirit attains to some degree of ideality and universality in the practical life. The ethical life in this limited sense is transcended in its second form. The distinctions he has suggested are logical or categorical. In its historical existentiality, spirit is always one. The moral life is the effort to secure a qualitative universality, in terms of the synthesis of the logical moments of spirit within each of the existential moments of spirit; an inward, qualitative universality commensurate with the concrete universality of mere existence (which itself, of course, must be an abstraction, since it is only logically distinct from the moral effort to qualify it). To speak of history as moral drama is to see historical existence in this inward term of the moral effort toward qualitative, human universality which informs it. To speak of universal history can only be to speak of history which is human, in the degree to which it exhibits this moral effort. This is the sense of his claim at the end of the *History of the Realm of Naples*

[1] TSS, loc. cit. and 265 sqq. [2] TSS, 81 sqq.

that he has rendered that history a bit more human. The moral drama of history and its qualitative universality are therefore one and the same; they complement and sustain and in a certain sense define each other. And they define at the same time the object of the historian's quest, whatever be the matter of his history; he seeks always the human spirit seeking to realize this qualitative universality in a moment of time, in a concrete mode of historical existence.[1]

Because it is possible to distinguish the structure of the human spirit logically into moments such as these, it is also possible, Croce believes,[2] to constrain historical concern and inquiry within the limits of these distinctions and to compose authentic histories of art, of philosophy, of politics and economics and of human mores. These diverse types constitute the 'genres' of history, as the lyric and the novel, the drama and the satire are conceived to be the 'genres' of art. As the 'genres' of art are, however, readily revealed to be but abstract fictions convenient and useful for the organization of the matter of the history of art for didactic and expository ends, but useless for the comprehension of art in itself and even less so for the regulation of art as to content or form,[3] so the 'genres' of history reveal themselves as abstract and unilateral, when viewed apart from the history of the spirit in its totality, that is to say, its qualitative universality. The parallel may be pressed further. As the totality, the qualitative universality, the simple and consummate humanity of the spirit are present in every concrete existential moment of history, and as the criticism and history of art seek in every work of art the fullness of the idea of art, and do not rest content with abstractions like the 'genres', so too does history in the fullest sense of the term seek the fullness of the spirit, that is, its ethical effort and character in every concrete moment of history. This is what ethico-political history is: the effort to seize the totality, the qualitative universality of the spirit, in every one of its historical moments. At the same time, however, Croce recognizes that care must be taken lest this idea degenerate into another and cryptic form of transcendental history; as though it would be possible to write a history of man which would not be the history of art, of politics, of mores. The human spirit does not achieve its qualitative universality over and above, but in and through the actuality of its diverse moments. Ethico-political history, correspondingly, is not a history which in any way transcends the concrete histories; for such a transcendent history would be vacuous. It is the history precisely of this effort toward qualitative

[1] FPS, 519–20, 997–8.   [2] FPS, 513–14.   [3] FPS, 209–11, 690, 1090.

totality in and through the unity and dialectic of the distinct moments. And ethico-political history, while it speaks of all these diverse moments, has only one subject, the human spirit in its historical unity.

This exposition of the vision of history as moral drama and of the ethico-political conception of historiography based upon it has been abstract and formal; and Croce has expounded it in this manner at considerable length. Such exposition does not, however, correctly reveal the true character of the doctrine; it is not a doctrine which was formulated speculatively and then imposed, 'a priori', upon the matters of his histories. On the contrary, it is a doctrine which was formulated directly in response to the problems and exigencies of historiography itself, drawn from the matter of the histories, rather than imposed upon them from without. Specifically, the ethico-political conception of history was born of Croce's struggle, as it may well be called, with the matter of the history of Naples. It is conceived as the only manner in which that history may be narrated in its humanity, and in it, the essential history of man, which is present in every historical argument. A poignant note is added by the fact that this conception of history is solicited not by a pageant of power and achievement but by a vision of human failure. It would be easier, perhaps, to recognize history as the work of man's ethical will, if history were all glory and achievement; the moral drama of history would then be essentially comic in the Dantean sense and the historian would be sustained through all vicissitudes by the knowledge and assurance of eventual triumph. The recognition of the actuality of the ethical will in the weak and in the failure is more difficult and, it might be added, a more Christian insight. And it is upon such an insight as this, evoked by the matter of the history of Naples, that the Crocean conception of ethico-political history rests.

The gradual formation of this conception is itself the inward drama of the history of Naples which Croce composed. His address to this matter passes through a number of phases in which the gradual crystallization of the ethico-political conception of history is reflected. The first of the phases might well be called the idyllic. In it, Croce addresses that history as an idyll; his chief effort is imaginative recall, the re-evocation of its matter and its spirit. In this phase, the historiographical effort comes closest to that of poetry and art and it is instructive that at about the same time Croce was engaged in the speculative effort to bring history under the general con-

ception of art.[1] The fruit of this period and attitude is a series of
evocations, each substantially autonomous, of places, of persons, of
events incidental to that history and presented to the eye of the
imagination in an aura of poetry and even of romance. It is also a fact
that Croce was encouraged in this approach by his association,
through the 'Società napoletana per storia patria' with such men as
Giuseppe de Blasiis, Bartolomeo Capasso and Michelangelo Schipa.
These men, despite their formidable erudition and their lofty ideals
of scientific (that is philological) scholarship in historiography, were
essentially idyllic in their approach to the matter of Naples. It is for
this reason that his spiritual break with these men signalizes his own
passage to a second phase in his address to this same matter, which
must be called tragic. This separation is expressed most clearly in the
eulogy which Croce pronounced on the death of Capasso.[2] With a
directness almost too harsh for the occasion, Croce avers that with
Capasso an era in the historiography of Naples had passed, the
regionalistic. That this regionalism was essentially idyllic was witnessed by the mere fact of its existence. For it could be maintained
only by closing one's eyes to the actual state of Naples, and to the
impossibility any longer of thinking of it save in the larger terms of
the history of Italy and of Europe. In this statement, Croce was not
criticizing Capasso so much as he was announcing the fresh orientation of his own thought. In his efforts to come to grips with the
actuality of Neapolitan history, he had come to see that its centre lay
in the struggle of the Neapolitan people for historical existence as an
autonomous nation. Here was the moral drama in direct and immediate terms, and he set himself to trace it, fragmentarily at first, but
in greater and greater organic unity. In the process, the tragic aspect
of this drama became clear: the inevitable frustration, the radical
failure to which that aspiration was doomed, not by any external or
'natural' force, but by the inward flaw in the subject of that history.
But this tragic phase is not definitive; it is in turn succeeded by a
third, in which hope and moral exhortation are the dominant notes.
This hope was born of Croce's perception that there opened a path of
salvation for Naples: incorporation as a living and organic part of
the new Italy created by the Risorgimento. In a certain sense, this
attitude might be called anachronistic; for that incorporation had
been a physical fact for thirty-odd years at this juncture of Croce's
career. It was far, however, from a spiritual fact. Spiritual unity,

[1] Cf. FSP, 197–8; PS, *sub titulo*.
[2] NN, IX (1900), 3, 42 sqq.; cf. *Arch.* of same year.

which alone could breathe life into the physical union which had already been accomplished was the task, not of the Risorgimento, but of the generation which followed it, the generation of Croce himself. His attitude, consequently, was not anachronistic, but actual.[1]

The aphorism which Croce was to repeat so often—history is in its essence more tragedy than idyll,[2]—is thus not the mere echo of a classical sentiment as old as Thucydides, but the record of his own experience as an historian. His first approach to the history of Naples was idyllic. His purpose was pure re-evocation and contemplation of a past whose bond with the present was not vital but sentimental. Nor was this idyllic character altered by its union with an impeccable sense of scholarship; the idyllic character was simply extended to the scholarship. Gradually, however, a transformation was to be effected. The reality of the moral drama which is the substance of that history began to reveal itself and to reveal, at the same time, the inner sources of defeat which were to resolve that drama in tragic fashion. The images of pure recall gave way to the tensions of moral struggle, rendered more terrible by the ever present sense of imminent defeat, threatening, not from without, but from within. The witness of this drama could not remain unmoved. Aesthetic distance surrendered to moral participation and the sense of tragedy communicated itself as well to narrative and narrator.

The sources of this initial idyllicism, this 'arcadianism' (though Croce would not permit without qualification this sense of the term[3]), lay deep within Croce. It was imparted to him first perhaps by his mother whom he recalls, in a passage reminiscent of Vico,[4] in his own short autobiography.[5] Devout and romantic, it was she who first awakened in him the love of romances and first guided him on those pilgrimages through the streets and churches of Naples which were to become a life-time devotion. The maladventures which succeeded the tragedy of Casamicciola[6] contributed to the idyllic mood. The sojourn at Rome, where he was to be repelled, on the

---

[1] On this point, cf. the writer's article 'Ethical and Sociological Bases of Italian Politics' in *Ethics*, LIX, no. 1 (Oct. 1948), pp. 35–48.

[2] Cf. FPS, 634, 1056.

[3] Cf. LI'700, 1 sq.

[4] Cf. Vico, *Autobigrafia*, ed. Croce, 1911, p. 3; A. R. Caponigri, *Time and Idea*, London, 1953, p. 13.

[5] FPS, 1139 sqq.

[6] FPS, 1143 sqq.; cf. R. Franchini, *Note Biografiche di Benedetto Croce*, Torino, 1953, pp. 15 ff.

one hand, by the aridity of the university teaching and, on the other, by the tone of political disillusionment, drove him in upon himself and back upon the past. Returning to Naples with both the leisure and the means to indulge his tastes, he formed the associations which were to direct, or redirect, this idyllic tendency upon the history of Naples.

Among the earliest and the most profound in its effects was the association formed at this time and destined to be life long, with the 'Società napoletana per storia patria'. This society had been established originally by the neoguelf historian Carlo Troya.[1] His efforts had failed, due to political vicissitudes, but were renewed by Paolo Emilio Imbriani, of the patriotic family whose history Croce was, in part, to compose.[2] This start was in turn abortive, but a third, under Bart. Capasso, in 1874, succeeded. The society had the double purpose of gathering the unpublished records of the realm (continuing thus, in a restricted area, the work of Muratori) and of publishing a journal and monographs on relevant topics. To its efforts are to be referred the *Monumenta Neapolitani Ducatus* of Capasso (1881–4) and the *Chronicum Siculum* of de Blasiis (1887), as well as Croce's own *Teatri di Napoli* (1889–91). Croce's name appears in the records of the society for the first time as 'socius' in 1886; from that time forward his name is never absent; in 1893, with Capasso as president, he appears as secretary; in 1914, he became president.

The profound effect of this association upon Croce's historical interests and upon his approach to history is readily discernible. The pages of the *Archivio storico per le provincie napoletane*, the official organ of the society, witness the stimulus provided by the conversation of such men as Capasso and de Blasiis; they report the first form of researches which were to provide the bases for Croce's entire reconstruction of Neapolitan history as well as for the wider area of the baroque era in Italy and the liberal transformation of Italy and of Europe. To cite but a few examples, Croce's most extensive early work, the *Teatri di Napoli*, appeared first in these pages, as well as the study of Pulcinella, the first of his excursions into the important field of dialect literature.[3] His interest in the topography and the art history of Naples is indicated and adumbrated in such articles as 'Napoli nelle descrizioni dei poeti',[4] while the essay, 'Di alcuni artisti spagnuoli che lavoravano a Napoli'[5] indicates the direction of studies which were to take more extensive form in *La*

---

[1] For whom cf. SSI, *passim*.　　　　　　　　　[2] Cf. UFP.
[3] *Arch.*, XIV, XV, XVI (1889–90–1); XXIII (1898), 605–68, 702–42.
[4] *Arch.*, XXI (1896).　　　　　　　　[5] Ibid., XXI (1896).

Spagna nella vita italiana durante la Rinascenza, itself in many ways the direct prelude to the mature statement of the history of the baroque era in Italy. An adumbration of the liberal theme which in time was to grow out of and to overshadow all lesser themes is to be found in the 'Studi storici sulla rivoluzione di '99'.[1] This association also provided stimulus to Croce's theoretical interests, for in its pages appeared such essays as 'Giambattista Vico primo scopritore della scienza estetica' as well as that on the reduction of history to the general concept of art.[2]

The influence of this association on the character of Croce's historiography is no less apparent. Its effect was to confirm and to fortify him in that idyllicism to which, as we have seen, he was already inclined. This effect was achieved not by argumentation but by example, the example of Capasso, of de Blasiis, of Schipa, in whom this attitude, wedded to the most rigid ideals of scholarship, was dominant. Indeed, an accurate depiction of the spirit of this society as embodied in these men and as it operated by example on Croce might indicate precisely this union of idyllicism with methodological scrupulousness. These are traits which readily complement each other in minds which are sincere but basically uncritical. Only slowly was Croce's awakening critical acumen to release him from this spell, from the dreams these old men dreamed. The document of this emancipation has already been noted. In it Croce sharply distinguishes these elements, retaining the methodological ideal, but repudiating the idyllicism. The regionalism which he excoriates (given the state of Neapolitan history) is but a specific form of that idyllicism. But much experience and reflection as an historian separated the mature Croce who pronounced this commemoration from the young Croce working under the example of those courtly scholars whose memories were always to remain among his fondest.

The mood of idyll expresses itself with least alloy of the awakening sense of tragedy in the studies of physical Naples and of the history of art in the Neapolitan provinces which form a chief concern of Croce's early years. So great was his interest in this area that, with a group of associates, he founded a special medium for its expression, *Napoli Nobilissima* an illustrated journal of topography and art history. *Napoli Nobilissima* was published continuously from 1892 until 1906, when it ceased to appear because its collaborators were persuaded that its occasion had passed.[3] Its publication was renewed in 1920; political events intervened to bring this new series to an early

[1] *Arch.*, XXIII (1898). [2] Cf. PS, *passim*. [3] NN, XV (1906), Proe.

end in 1922. During both periods, its format was the same. Designed to appeal to the eye, it was profuse in illustrations drawn from both public and private resources. Many of these illustrations are induplicable; they present a panorama of the city during the two millennia of its existence and lend to the pages of the review a restricted, but abiding, value and interest.

The circle about Croce in the publication of *Napoli Nobilissima*, while sharing sentiments, and even members, with the 'Società napoletana per storia patria', was quite different in spirit. The chief difference was age; all of the collaborators in *Napoli Nobilissima* were young men, Croce's contemporaries. This difference was reflected in the quality of the idyllism each displayed. That of the older group was nostalgic, defensive, retrospective; that of the younger, buoyant, ebullient, filled with youthful curiosity. It was without ulterior or profounder preoccupations, immersed in the detail, even the 'superficia' of its subject. While surrendering nothing of the scholarly ideals learned from the older circle, this younger idyllism transformed the whole matter of the physical and artistic history of the city and the realm into a bright and flowing mosaic, all colour and life, idyllic even in its depiction of tragedy (when tragedy forced itself upon its attention), transmuting it wholly into heroism, melodrama and romance. The motives which impelled this group in this undertaking also reflect its youth; these motives are both practical and 'spiritual', as the introductory statement declares. The practical object was to stir their fellow citizens to an interest in the monuments which literally 'are strewn through the streets of the city' and in their preservation. The 'spiritual' purpose is to lay the foundations of a history of art in the 'Napoletano', the whole region embraced by the Neapolitan realm.[1]

Croce's devotion to the practical aim of the review is reflected in the locally celebrated case of the 'broken vases' in which he caused the utter discomfiture of the curator of the local museum.[2] His adherence to its 'spiritual' or scholarly purposes is admirably reflected in the extensive investigation of the field of Neapolitan art history which he undertook, comprising a considerable number of individual studies and entitled 'Sommario critico della storia dell'arte nel Napoletano'. Croce prefaces this series with two articles criticizing the manner in which the history of Neapolitan art had been treated by the one historian who had dominated that field.[3] Bernardo

[1] NN, I (1892), Proe.　　　　　　[2] NN, XII (1903); XIII (1904).
[3] NN, I (1892), 122-6, 140-4; cf. AVL, II, 200.

de Domenicis, born in 1684, had published the work on which his authority rested, *Vite dei pittori, scultori ed architetti napoletani*, between 1742 and 1743. He had already, Croce notes, drawn the censure of Burckhardt and Schulz, but he feels this censure had been too merciful. De Domenicis had shown himself entirely innocent of any sense of history or even of truth. He names and identifies artists for whom there exists no evidence; he endows these fictions with psychological and artistic personalities, and distributes among them the art-monuments of the region according to canons known to himself alone. Yet his authority, the censure of Burckhardt and Schulz notwithstanding, remained unchallenged. Croce's own revision of this history makes claim to no originality; it relies heavily upon materials already collected and upon critical monographs in which the preceding half-century had been prolific. But he succeeds in laying down, on this basis, the critical frame of reference within which the programme of *Napoli Nobilissima* might be unfolded, free from the shadow of de Domenicis.

The question of the Spanish influence upon Italian life and culture very early attracts Croce's interest. It was under Spanish rule, he notes, that Naples reached the extent and assumed the form which it preserves without substantial alteration. In a number of early contributions to *Napoli Nobilissima* he recreates the larger phases of this influence, noting especially that it was through Spanish efforts that the centre of the city was shifted westward and northward from its earlier Angevine site. In the time of Robert of Anjou, the western wall had lain along a line eastward of the present Via Toledo (Roma) while the vital centre lay to the east about the 'Mercato'. Under the Spaniards the whole arch of the city extending toward Posillipo was brought into being.[1] This interest is summarized in the articles appended to the volume *Spagna nella vita italiana*, in which the traces of the Spanish influence are recalled in detail, from the half-legendary founding of S. Leonardo in Insula Maris to the creation of the aristocratic section about the noble streets Toledo and Medina.[2]

Croce is endlessly fertile in discovering fresh angles of vision from which the inexhaustible beauty of the city might be approached. One such he discovers in the vision of Naples as it presented itself to poetic sentiment over the centuries;[3] another, in the accounts of the city given by visitors and travellers from foreign

[1] NN, III (1894), 92–5, 102–12, 122–6, 156–9, 172–6; VII (1897).
[2] SVI, 263 sqq.; cf. NN, I (1892), 2–11, 35–9, 51–3.
[3] NN, II (1893); III (1894); IV (1895).

lands, and especially the earliest of these on record, Bernardo de Falco.[1] The vision which de Falco evokes is one which the modern eye might recognize only with difficulty; the city he describes is not a metropolis, but still a mediaeval fortress. To the testimony of de Falco Croce adds a fascinating study of the views of Naples printed and etched during the fifteenth century; the reproductions of the views constitute one of the most charming features of the volumes.[2]

Croce's passionate and exacting preoccupation with the physical beauties of Naples and its memories reaches its most intense and almost lyrical expression in one essay, that which is called 'Un Angolo di Napoli'. and which opens the collection *Storie e leggende napoletane*.[3] Although composed later than the essays mentioned above, it is of their spirit. A short time before its composition Croce had taken up residence in an ancient 'palazzo' in the seventeenth-century square of Trinità Maggiore. This 'palazzo', once the Neapolitan seat of the feudal family Sanseverino di Bisignano, and later, while occupied by the Rocca family, frequently visited by Vico,[4] stands at the very heart of the most ancient city. Taking his stand upon one of its numerous balconies, Croce directs the reader's gaze out over the city and one by one calls the roll of the magnificent and venerable monuments which rise up to meet the gaze on every hand: Santa Chiara, beloved of the Neapolitans, first, with its peerless tower raised by the pious Sancia, wife of Robert, and its bells, to Neapolitan ears, sweeter than any others on earth; the vaulted monastery of the same name beyond, a structure of pure design; thence by a natural and irresistible movement of the eye, to the convent of S. Francesco le monache opposite, and up the narrow street to the devotional shrine of S. Marta, where the same Sancia worshipped. Confronting the stern façade of the Jesuit church which dominates the adjacent square—it is the façade of a fortress rather than of a place of worship—he recalls its ancient history; once the seat of one of the most powerful feudal families of the region, the Sanseverini of Salerno, it had been girdled with gardens shaded with orange trees, filled at dusk with the shaken silver of olive branches and murmurous through the day with the fretful breezes from the gulf. Upon the foundations of this fortress-palace, the modern structure of the church arose, the spacious chambers and halls and the lordly 'cortile' readily lending themselves to renovation in the florid 'Jesuit' style.

---

[1] NN, 2a series, I (1920); cf. AVL, I, 223.

[2] NN, XIV (1905); cf. AVL, I, 217.   [3] SLN, I sqq.

[4] Cf. *Il concetto moderno della storia*, Bari, 1947, 7.

Farther beyond, to the street of S. Anna dei Lombardi, rich with
secular associations, the remains of the ancient city walls which the
diligent research of Capasso had reconstructed, the mosque-like
tower of the 'Carmine', the eye passes until the circle is complete
and there has been evoked a world of forms in which past and present
mingle. But this city evoked by the historical imagination is not left
tenantless; Croce peoples those streets and palaces, those monasteries
and churches, towers and 'piazze' with a thousand souls, who here
knew the full range of human sorrow and desire, meagre joy and
endless hope: Sancia passing from her tower to her church, the
passionate and imperious Sanseverini, plotting rebellion and their
own destruction, while beyond the orange groves within their
whitewashed cells the nuns of S. Francesco in sandalled feet moved
noiselessly to prayer; the merchants of S. Anna dei Lombardi, hawk-
ing their wares under the contemptuous gaze of the indolent Neapolitans whom they exploited. Here, in this essay, Croce has distilled
two decades of devoted inquiry; even more, he has transmuted that
dead matter into a vision and a living song, so that with justice these
pages have been called the most lyrical, the nearest to poetry, of any
he composed. If poetry, this essay is also a 'swan song'. It brings to
a close, effectively, if not deliberately, that whole phase of Croce's
activity as an historian which we have called idyllic. For even before
its composition, a change had been transpiring in his vision and conception of history, a change which was to bring him constantly
closer to its vital centre, the moral drama.

II

NAPLES, 1799:
EDUCATION BY REVOLUTION

THE transition from the mood of idyll and of contemplative re-evocation to the view of history as moral drama begins with Croce's studies on the Neapolitan revolution of 1799. This transition is complex. Together with and within the movement from the idyllic to the moral-dramatic view of history, it involves a growth in his sense of the inner, organic structure of Neapolitan history and marks, consequently, a decisive step forward in the ethico-political conception of history. Croce himself recognizes the importance of these studies; in the bibliographical appendix to the anthology of his writings, whose preparation was among his last literary activities,[1] he remarks that the prolegomenon to the history of the realm of Naples is to be found precisely here in these early studies on the revolution of 1799, and that not merely as to matter, but, even more importantly, as to form and treatment.

These studies on the Neapolitan revolution of 1799 include in the first instance the volume of that title. It is composed for the most part of early essays and researches, written and conducted contemporaneously with the idyllic contributions to *Napoli Nobilissima*. Thus it is clear that the transition from the idyllic to the ethico-political view of history was not a sudden conversion, but a gradual process, growing simultaneously with and within the idyllic mood of evocation. In addition these studies include the important monographs in the volume entitled *Una Famiglia di Patrioti*, as well as a number of the most striking essays in the *Vite di Fede di Avventura e di Passione*, and *Uomini e Cose della Vecchia Italia*. Some of these studies are subsequent to the definitive work in which the Neapolitan theme culminates and in which the ethico-political conception appears for the first time as a completely formed and effective principle of interpretation and organization, the *Storia del Regno di Napoli*. These later compositions on the subject of the revolution,

[1] FPS, II, 816.

its particular events or dominant personalities, in turn constitute a fresh application of that ethico-political conception; whereas in the *Storia del Regno di Napoli* that conception is synoptic, so to say, enabling Croce to encompass and inclose in one unifying and unitary study the whole complex matter of six centuries, in these monographic studies that conception enables him to analyse and portray the historical will in its ultimate existential unit, the person. In a certain sense, these studies bring that conception to new fruition and afford it fresh corroboration; for without this extension to the concrete person and the group who are the ultimate moral agents in the drama of human history, the ethico-political conception might have remained, theoretically, and despite the effective, synoptic employment, one of those pseudo-metaphysical theories which place the moral will in history outside its only possible existential situs, the human person, individual or collective. The monographic studies of these latter collections constitute, therefore, not only a material, but a logical extension of the ethico-political insight.

In literary form, consequently, Croce's treatment of the theme of the Neapolitan revolution is anything but formal and unified. It is, rather, episodic and monographic; and these studies of limited compass tend, as has been suggested, to fall into two classes: an earlier, brought together in the volume of that title, and a later, distributed through the other volumes already mentioned. The real principle of demarcation between these two groups, however, is qualitative; it is the achievement of the ethico-political conception of history in its first, effective form. The earlier essays mark the first emergence of that conception; the latter its ripe extension to the human personal agent in history. From the point of view of the formation of the ethico-political conception of history, the earlier, though lesser in stature, are the more relevant and illuminating, while the latter serve rather to illustrate the logical terminus of the ethico-political theory in a vision of the stature of the person as the real existential moral agent in history.

The volume entitled *La rivoluzione napoletana* comprises a series of studies composed at various times during the last decade and a half of the nineteenth century. Of these essays some are biographical,[1] a form to which Croce was from the first attracted and to which he was with time to attach greater, rather than less, importance, since it is the natural form which historical narrative based on the insight into the moral agency of the person in history tends to take. Others

[1] RN'99, 'Eleonora de Fonseca-Pimentel', sqq.; 'Luisa San Felice', pp. 115 sqq.

are clearly polemical, such as that concerned with the ambiguous role of the great Lord Nelson in the intricate events of those fateful months.[1] Others again are philological or documentary, such as the paraphrase and presentation of extracts from contemporary diaries, that, for example, of the young soldier who in a three days' Odyssey braved the terrors of the aroused mobs of the San Fedists and of the scarcely less horrendous exaltation and enthusiasm of the republicans immured in Sant'Elmo (where they awaited the Messianic advent of the French troops under Championnet), only to be brought into the baleful presence of Cardinal Ruffo himself, and to escape death only by the merest of accidents.[2] In all of these forms, Croce displays one constant characteristic of style, a tense incisiveness which was to grow with the growth of the sense of the moral drama in history.

Beneath this external fragmentary form, however, there is clearly discernible, in process of formation, a new, more organic and dynamic view of the history of Naples and a decisive movement closer to the dramatic, moral and personal heart of history. In his study of this event, Croce, assisting for the first time at history 'in the making', is afforded his first glimpse of the historical reality of that Naples on which his historical imagination had so fondly and idyllic-ally dwelt. Heretofore, Naples had been this city by the bay; it had been these streets and squares, these monuments, viewed indeed, in the dim process of their formation in a dream-like past, but detached from the living and vital struggle of which they had been born, much as the shell of some fabulous form of marine life, cast up upon the shore, and empty of the life which had produced it and which it had sheltered, might be held in the hand for inspection, turned this way and that in the sun to bring out the facets of its form and colour. With the address to the history of the revolution, however, the shell, so to say, burst in his hand, and from the dry dead fragments the life within sprang up anew. He caught his first glimpse of Naples as a nation, as that moral entity which he was more and more to under-stand the nation to be. And this glimpse was afforded him when that nation was engaged in a bitter action welling up from the very depths of its being as a moral entity. He found himself in the presence of this nation seeking to emerge into a new state of moral, political and social ideality amid the awful turmoil of titantic and conflicting passions, amid the 'vipers' tangle' of lofty but twisted motivations, amid scenes of human carnage more Dantesque than the images of the Inferno itself. The ambitions of kings, the cupidity of ministers,

[1] RN'99, 251. [2] RN'99, 'Nel furore della reazione', 231.

insensate egotism and selfless idealism, selfless almost to the point of inanity; the fate of a city and a nation written between the lines of a foolish and dissolute woman's billet-doux to an illicit love, a cardinal of the Church scouring the countryside to arouse the lowest elements of the people to defend, in the name of religion, a king who cowered in a guarded palace half a thousand miles away; these and others of like human and ambiguous character revealed themselves to him as the living motive principals of the history which had inhabited the streets and palaces, which had raised the monuments among which he had loved to pass and linger. In a word, the city which he had heretofore loved to depict in its physical aspect now was revealed to him as the theatre of the human drama of history. Passage was effected from the outer to the inner life of history.

This vision or insight into the Neapolitan nation as a moral entity, whose very life consisted in its moral effort to realize in its life an inner idea, even through the cataclysmic events of revolution, was not the product of an instantial intuition. It was the product of a laborious process, the examination of the documents, and was built up, piece by piece, as Croce moved among the welter of testaments to the event. Among these witnesses he was to pass like a new Socrates, questioning motive and fact, analysing, synthesizing; arrested now by the dynamism of a woman, Fonseca-Pimentel, in whom the goddess of liberty would seem to have become incarnate, now by the pathetic image of another woman, Luisa San Felice, who in the midst of revolutionary passion could think only of her lover's safety; questioning now a king, now a prince of the Church, now the haughty and contemptuous Lord Admiral of the English fleet, now a humble soldier, bewildered, but observant. Slowly the impression and the conviction arose; here, in this moral turmoil, was the reality of Naples, and the reality of history itself. This was the irreducible in history, the moral action of man in his existential plight.

What gives unity, organic structure and dynamic movement to his superficially fragmentary study of the revolution of 1799 is Croce's clear discernment of the moral principals active in this event. These he identifies, each in its specific character and reality, and relates them in the swift movements of events. Identification and relation are but the matrix of evaluation or judgment which is itself ultimately moral and, for this reason, the historian's real participation in the history which he is composing. In this evaluation and judgment of the forces of the revolution Croce reveals for the first time the central force and power of his historiography.

The first of these forces is the Neapolitan monarchy against which the revolution was immediately directed. The role which this monarchy played was at once the most ambiguous and the most tragic in the entire drama, whose denouement was the dissolution of this institution in the unification of Italy. The ambiguity attaching to the monarchy was not wholly intrinsic to it. It springs, in part at least, from the role or the position forced upon or attributed to that monarchy by the revolutionary forces themselves. The essential myth of the revolution demanded that it appear in a Messianic and soteric role, as the salvation of the people which it awakened. A complementary demand places its opponent in a role essentially diabolic. This mythology the Neapolitan revolution of 1799 inherited from its parent movement, the great revolution of 1789, of which it was the southernmost resonance. It sought to dispose the forces within its own orbit according to the inner demands of this myth. And according to this economy, the role of the Neapolitan monarchy was predestined: it had to appear in the satanic role of oppressor.

The initial attraction of Croce was to the revolutionary element of this transaction, the republican and jacobin element, as is attested by his sympathetic treatment of Eleanora de Fonseca-Pimentel, as well as by his conviction that this revolution was the preparation for the Risorgimento.[1] This woman of impeccable ancestry and of great personal beauty, charm and talent, became, as it was earlier remarked, the incarnation of the goddess of liberty; the embodiment and the voice, through the journal she was to found on the Parisian model, the *Monitore*, of extreme jacobinism. The attraction of Croce is essentially idealistic, that is to say, he views her person and activity in the first instance through the veil of the myth which she embodied. In the moral evaluation of the revolution, however, he was able to pierce this veil and to dissipate this myth, with respect precisely to the Neapolitan monarchy. The role which the myth of the revolution imposed upon the monarchy did not, he perceived, correspond to its historical and moral character nor to the line of policy it had pursued, hesitantly no doubt, on the very eve of the jacobin uprising which was to turn the city and the realm into a nightmare charnel house of blood and passion, and set the monarchy on the path to its ultimate dissolution.

What was the role which the myth of the revolution imposed upon the monarchy of Naples regnant at the end of the eighteenth

[1] Cf. RN'99, ch. XIII.

century? It was the role of oppressor, marked by obscurantism and servitude; the role, in a word, which would make this institution the foil for the messianism and the soterism of the revolution and provide its historical justification. But Croce finds it possible to demand, on the basis of the documents which he sets himself to examine, whether one can accept this essentially moral judgment, to accept that is to say, the moral testimony of the revolutionary myth. His answer is negative; and its substance is the recollection of the nascent liberalism of the Bourbon policy in the decades preceding the revolution, and the open character of that monarchy toward the 'wave of the future' of the time, that is to say, toward constitutional and liberal reform.

The monarchy which ruled in Naples at the end of the eighteenth century was that of the Spanish branch of the house of Bourbon. The initiation of this phase of the well-nigh millennial monarchical institution of Naples had occurred in 1734 with the end of the Austrian vice-regency; an event due, Croce remarks, almost entirely to the determination of one woman, an Italian, Elisabetta Farnese, to place her son upon a throne worthy, in her view, of the family's past.[1] In order to support the romantic illusion of the revolutionary myth, this monarchy should have exhibited the oppressive character which would make it the historical analogue of the Bourbon regime against which the parent revolutionary movement in France was directed. The facts, however, Croce notes, do not bear out this analogy; the imposition of this role was arbitrary. In actuality, the regime of the Bourbon kings in Naples in the decades preceding the revolution of 1799 was one of the most enlightened and progressive which modern Europe had seen.[2] The revolution directed its force against an institution and a regime which, in his own words, 'had more than half a century earlier resolutely entered upon the path of reform constitutional, juridical, economic and social alike'.[3] The seventy-odd years of its pre-revolutionary existence had marked an era of vital renaissance in the 'Regno'. Culturally, this revitalization was signalized by such achievements as the renewal of the life of the theatre and the opera with the residence of Metastasio and the building of San Carlo,[4] as well as by the extensive programme of embellishment of the city, including the completion of the Villa di Chiaia, which, beginning as a royal or rather vice-regal pleasure-walk was now extended to its full length along the bay and opened to the public's

[1] SRN, 181. [2] Cf. 'Sentenze e giudizi di Bernardo Tanucci', in UCVI, II.
[3] RN'99, X. [4] Cf. TN, ed. Pierro Napoli, 1891, 322.

pleasure.[1] These initiations had been inspired by Don Carlo; but succeeding rulers had extended them into every area of civic life, not excluding those touching most closely the royal administrative power itself. Measured by later standards, or for that matter by any absolute standards which might be invoked, Croce notes, the progress projected and achieved whether in the economic, the juridical or the administrative areas might seem paltry to a degree.[2] But, he adds, can the measure of such advances in any earlier era be that of later accomplishment? Must one not rather be, as a simple command of common sense and rudimentary historical justice, mindful of the painful advance of man in history, the actual ideals and the effective possibilities of the time? By this standard, much was accomplished and even more projected during this period under the monarchical aegis, so that the reputation of Naples for enlightened self-rule never stood higher in the general esteem of Europe. It might be averred, he notes, that the real source of this vitality lay not in the monarchy or the monarch but rather in certain other foci of the national life; specifically, in that 'ceto medio', that middle class (the non-economic intention of this term in Croce's employment, which will later be considered more fully, must here be noted) which had rapidly been rising during the period under consideration.[3] This is surely not to be denied; and this 'ceto medio' will presently occupy Croce's attention more fully, for it introduces a fresh moral dimension into this entire drama. The recognition of this fact, however, can in no wise be used to lessen the prestige of the monarchy or to call into question the genuineness of its liberal will; this union between the monarchy and the 'ceto medio', which was the liberalizing force of the regime, could only have been a reciprocal bond, for the 'ceto medio' was in no position to impose its mind or will. The figure of a Tanucci, in whom this union becomes substantial and effective, cannot be minimized; nor can it be employed to displace the monarch's will, as Tanucci's own testimony establishes.[4] Further evidence of this fact is that the monarchy, even after the intriguing will of Maria Carolina had forced Tanucci from his position of influence, did not leave the path of reform.

It was against this monarchy (a despotism in its basic idea, to be sure, but within which the wider will of the people in the form of the influence of the 'ceto medio' had begun to make an impression and

[1] Croce, 'La Villa di Chiaia', cf. NN, I (1892).   [2] SRN, 180 sqq.
[3] Cf. SRN, 176. Cf. also 211, 'La Minoranza come il vero Soggetto Storico'.
[4] UCVI, loc. cit.

which in terms of its own monarchical consciousness had shown every sign of envisaging a common good wider than its own dynastic interests, and more elevated by the general recognition of Europe than the ideal universally prevalent) that the revolutionary myth was invoked and the revolutionary force directed. And it was upon this monarchy that the revolution was to work its most devastating moral effects, revealing at the same time the moral limits of its own claims as well as the fatal moral flaw of the Bourbon monarchy itself. What was the effect of the revolution upon the liberalizing Bourbon monarchy of Naples? It was not its extinction. That institution was too strongly rooted and entrenched for that. It was not, in the first place, a political effect at all. It was a moral effect. It was the transformation of that institution from a liberalizing, reforming agency, pregnant with authentic though limited vision of a common good, into a retrogressive, reactionary, oppressive police state, in which every glimmer of the common good was gradually to be extinguished—gradually, for even as late as the neoguelf movement for Italian unification, the Neapolitan monarchy was to show its power to rise to the moral vision, though not to the effective will, of the new Italy.[1] Its effect was to break the bond which was the living moral sinew of that monarchy as a liberal and reforming agency, the bond between the monarchy and the 'ceto medio'; and to force upon the monarchy a reorientation of its policy to seek its support among the least enlightened, the rural peasantry and the urban proletariat, and the least disinterested, the clerical, faction of its subjects.[2] The effect of the revolution was to turn the steps of the monarchy from that path of reform on which, as Croce notes, it had set its feet, into a path of moral and spiritual dissolution which was to grow more precipitous under the pressure of the events of the first decades of the nineteenth century until that monarchy was to disappear from the historical theatre under the successive blows of the revolution of 1848 and of Garibaldi's advance.

While this analysis, by throwing into relief certain actualities which the traditional accounts had tended to obscure, enabled Croce to deliver himself from the spell of the romantic illusion of the revolution, by revealing its moral ambiguity as measured by its effects upon the monarchy, it enabled him at the same time to penetrate to the moral weakness, the fatal flaw which lay concealed within the liberal attitude of the monarchical institution. Since in the drama of history we are confronted by the interplay not of physical but of

[1] SRN, 255 sqq.   [2] SRN, 205 sqq.

moral forces and idealities, it is not possible to fall into the naturalistic fallacy of treating these agencies as though they were purely determinate and determined. It is not possible, therefore, to lay the failure of the Neapolitan monarchy, that is, its despotic reaction and its abandonment of the policy of reform, even under the pressure of the revolution, wholly at the door of there volutionary forces. Being a moral agency, the monarchy retains its moral character even under that terrible pressure, retains, that is, its freedom and its historic responsibility. That transformation must therefore be traced to an inner source; to a fatal flaw of the spiritual order. What was this flaw, in Croce's view? His reply is neither hesitant nor ambiguous. And it is consonant with the radical personalism which his ethico-political conception is to throw into ever greater and greater relief. He recognizes the seat of this moral flaw in the monarch and in his consort, in Ferdinand and in Maria Carolina. His judgment upon these personages is not moral in the limited sense of an evaluation of the modes of personal conduct or the disposition of their wills on the level of their personal interests. It is an ethico-political judgment; that is to say a judgment passed upon their persons from the point of view of their status as the bearers of the ethico-political consciousness of the nation. And it is precisely here that the flaw reveals itself: in the incommensuration within those royal minds and wills between their ethico-political status and their mere restricted personal status. Their essential error and their moral failing lay in the contraction of the ethico-political field of judgment and action to the limited area of their personal interests. This was a retrogressive step, transacted within the forum of their personal conscience, which had its effect in the outer world of political reality because of the position they occupied. By reason of this fatal constriction they could not see through and beyond the revolution to its real meaning even after they had mastered its physical violence. They could not make it a stepping stone to a more exalted and inclusive consideration of the basic problems of their kingdom. This flaw was to blind them to the possibility which the immediate future was to offer them, namely, the opportunity of overcoming once and for all the central problem of the Neapolitan kingdom (its inability to achieve total coherence on a regional basis) by taking up the vision of the united Italy, and the leadership of that movement of unification which at more than one juncture was within its grasp. It was this fatal flaw which doomed this dynasty to extinction, an extinction which was artificially retarded at a number of points during the next half-century, but which was inevitable, not through some external determination, but through this inner failure, this 'gran rifiuto'.

The Neapolitan monarchy, it was suggested, presents in Croce's analysis and account a profoundly ambiguous character; a moral ambiguity in which he discovers its fatal flaw. A similar flaw afflicts the second major moral agent in that pathetic drama of the revolution of '99, namely that 'ceto medio' which in unity with the monarchy had constituted the strength and hope of the reform movement of the half-century preceding the revolution. In a certain sense, this 'ceto medio' is not the secondary, but the primary protagonist of the revolution, beside which even the monarchy loses stature in the perspective of events. For it was this 'ceto medio' which furnished the leadership of the revolution, which was the matrix in which was formed that jacobin spirit which inflamed the city in those fateful years. And as it moves into the centre of that stage, the ambiguous character of this class appears more baffling, posing a moral problem whose terms elude capture, or once captured, resist intelligible correlation.

The basic ambiguity of the 'ceto medio' is simple in the extreme with respect to the concrete problem which it presents. It is the problem of how this class could have placed itself at the head of the revolutionary movement. Nothing in the history of that class,[1] in its formation or in its previous alignment of power prepares one for this jacobin transformation. On the contrary, that history prepares one to assert, on moral grounds, only the antecedent improbability of such a transformation, and to predict, with a degree of assurance, only its final discomfiture. What was the history of that 'ceto medio'?

To understand this, it is necessary to indicate at once that while 'ceto medio' may be correctly translated as 'middle class', this translation carries with it certain risks, because of the association of the English terms. The chief association is economic; the middle class has always denominated a class whose basis of identification and historical coherence has been economic.[2] This is not true of the 'ceto medio' as Croce meets it in the study of the revolution of '99. If it is possible to fix its character in a single term, that class must be called rather an intellectual and moral unit, its chief identifying quality and the principle of its coherence being, not economic interest, but intellectual criticism turned in a social and political direction. This 'ceto medio' makes its voice clearly heard for the first time perhaps in the writings of Pietro Giannone, whose *Storia civile del regno di*

[1] Cf. RN'99, ch. IV, 194 sqq., and SRN, 212 sqq.　　　[2] SE'900, 260.

Napoli may justly be thought of as the 'magna carta' of the 'ceto medio'. From the character of this document it is readily apparent that in its basic principles and orientation and in the depths of its moral will, the 'ceto medio' was not revolutionary; on the contrary it evinces from the beginning that abhorrence of revolution which is the mark of the true intellectual and which rests ultimately upon the appreciation of historical movement and on the intuition of the historical form of the moral will. Despite the depth and the breadth, the sometimes truculent and always trenchant character, of Giannone's criticism—and the *Storia civile* is critical in the most radical sense of the term a document intended not for the consolation of national pride but for the awakening of the national and civil conscience—it can in no wise be called a revolutionary document, if any breath of jacobinism be attached to the term revolution. It is a criticism which recommends historical and moral action, and not revolutionary and antihistorical violence and subversion. The positive marks of the Neapolitan 'ceto medio' appear most clearly in Giannone himself, intellectualism tempered by moral will, directed to and orientated toward progressive and transformist social and political action, within limits historically effective.

In line with these lineaments of its earliest protagonist and its 'magna carta' the 'ceto medio' had entered, during the half-century or more preceding the revolution of '99, upon an effective course of historical action. Finding its support in the enlightened regime of the new Bourbon dynasty, it had entered upon an effective programme of co-operation with the monarchy in a programme of reform within the 'Regno' which, Croce had indicated, had won the recognition of the most enlightened and advanced sectors of European opinion. On this path of reform the union of the monarchy and the 'ceto medio' had taken significant steps and even more importantly perhaps had established a pattern of co-operative action which gave every promise of becoming historically determinative, not only for the 'Regno' but perhaps for the whole of Italy.[1] When, however, that co-operative effort was in full tide and there was every reason to think, despite such setbacks as the dismissal of Tanucci, that it was upon the eve of achieving its most significant advances, the 'ceto medio' turned from that pattern of reformism which it had established to embrace the model of the French revolution in certain of its most extreme characteristics. From Reformism to jacobinism, from co-operativism to revolution, from monarchy to republicanism,

[1] Cf. SRN, 176 sqq.

from liberal anti-clericalism to free thought, these were the termini of that sudden and perplexing conversion of the Neapolitan 'ceto medio', with effects, as Croce has noted, fatal for the country it sought to serve, and nugatory of all of the efforts and achievements of half a century. The question which must transcend all others concerning the 'ceto medio' and its part in the revolution must, therefore, in Croce's view, be the question of the moral roots of this transformation. How was it possible that this transformation should take place? What was its moral spring and its moral character? And what did it bode for the 'Regno' and for the 'ceto medio' itself?

The first of these questions, that concerning the moral root or spring, he addresses in the manner which is to become characteristic of the ethico-political conception of history. Recognizing that the 'ceto medio' taken in its mere collectivity must remain always something of an abstraction, and that in this character historical action must be attributed to it only obliquely, Croce turns to the individual person, in which that collectivity is existentially rooted. For while he recognizes that to the individual no more than to the collectivity can historical action be attributed directly, but that to the one and the other alike this attribution can only be oblique and reciprocal, nevertheless, his nascent personalism, which enters so clearly into the ontology of his later liberalism, leads him to believe that the collective process of that conversion might be more clearly grasped in the individual, the person. For the purposes of replying to this question, consequently, he selects for study a number of individuals who had lived through the whole process of that conversion and were to experience presently in their persons the further stage of that process, the reconversion of the 'ceto medio' from jacobin revolutionarism to moderate liberalism. The first of these is Giuseppe Poerio, the founder of the family which was to win acclaim in both the literary and the patriotic annals of the 'Regno' and which was later to be one of the vital forces knitting the 'Regno' to the new kingdom of Italy into which it was absorbed.[1]

The value of the example of Giuseppe Poerio lay in the fact that he had traversed in his own person the entire career of the 'ceto medio'. Coming to Naples in his youth from his native Calabria, he had quickly acclimated himself to the atmosphere of the city. He established himself as a lawyer—a profession second to none under the Bourbons and destined to increase rather than to decrease in importance and, in Naples especially, always the avenue to higher

[1] UFP, ch. I; cf. also ch. II, 141.

opportunities. His interests, however, quickly passed the limits of his private career; he identified himself with the most advanced elements of reformism, while maintaining complete loyalty to the monarchy. Nothing about his early career suggests the revolutionary. On the contrary, the logic of his life and career—if a life or a career may be said to have a logic—elicits the opposite expectations. Yet in the hectic days of the revolution Poerio was among the first touched by the jacobin mania, among the readiest to resort to extreme measures. The nadir of this transformation was marked by his support of the appeal to French arms when the revolutionary hope of arousing the Neapolitan populace proved illusory. It was an action, this invitation of alien, armed intervention, which only a mind profoundly disturbed and disorientated could contemplate; thus was Poerio to pass judgment on himself when that mania had passed. In the reaction under Cardinal Ruffo, he was to bear the full brunt and force of the transformation which the revolutionary experience worked in the monarchy. The remaining years of his life, with but short periods of respite, he spent in exile. Exile afforded a period of reflection; Poerio came to look with amazement (and not a little horror) upon the revolutionary fever which had consumed him and his contemporaries and undone the work of half a century, replacing it by foreign domination and the oppression of a monarchy in reaction. Out of this period of reflection was born a fresh attitude and orientation, that which Croce calls 'moderate liberalism'. It is based on a rejection of the revolution, in principle and as a method, as fundamentally inconsonant with genuine progress and reform and as historically without justification. Its more positive basis is a fresh dedication to the cause of civil, political and social reform, within a far wider horizon than it was possible to achieve within the limits of the Neapolitan problem. Poerio is to be numbered among the first of these Neapolitans who by their contact and experience outside the 'Regno' were to come to the melancholy but salutary conclusion that the problems of the 'Regno' could be solved only by merging Neapolitan aspirations with the growing sentiment for a united Italy. This was a heroic insight, not readily come by or accepted, involving, as it did, the sunset of the 'Regno' in the hope that it would rise again in the larger dawn of the new Italy; yet it was the insight which Poerio together with many of his contemporaries achieved. The moderate liberalism for which the name of Poerio came to stand could thus be called the finest fruit of the revolution, at the same time that it was a rejection of the revolution. It was a reaffirmation of the creed of liberty which the 'ceto medio' had slowly been formulating, in reaction against the abstract ideals and methods of revolution and jacobin dogmatism.[1]

While the career of Giuseppe Poerio illustrates the entire process of the revolutionary conversion and liberal reconversion of the 'ceto medio' in Naples, it still does not answer the central question which Croce had put concerning that process. It does not solve, in ethico-political terms, the problem: why had the liberal and reformist movement to pass through the revolutionary experience? Croce finds a more satisfactorily relevant reply in the reflections of another figure who had shared the same experience of Poerio but who had brought to his reflection upon that experience a more acute power of psychological analysis as well as a trained and penetrating historical sense. This was Vincenzo Cuoco. He put the question and answered it in the terms which Croce recognizes as basic; and with which he finds himself in complete agreement.[2] The jacobin episode in the career of the 'ceto medio' of Naples, Cuoco believes, is to be traced to the moral and psychological necessity of living through an error in order to overcome and to pass beyond it. The substance of the error lay in the abstract adherence to the idea of republicanism, an idea which appeared to impose itself, in its abstract form, with peremptory authority and to compel moral acceptance of revolutionary methods. The error was magnified by the delusion of the Neapolitan republicans that the idea could be imposed upon the country by alien force when it failed to awaken a spontaneous response in the people. The real psychological danger, however, lay in the affinity between the revolutionary ideal and the ideals to which the 'ceto medio' of the 'Regno' was already committed. The revolutionary programme seemed to be the logical extension of the reformist ideas of the previous decades; it was, of course, their negation. This, however, could not be discerned abstractly. It had to be discovered through experience. Cuoco, as his own thought matured, came to deny all correspondence between the French Revolution, its ideals and method, and the historical aspirations of Naples and Italy. He was to ally himself definitively with the 'moderate liberalism' of Poerio.[3]

---

[1] For contrast cf. Croce's study of a 'typical' reactionary, the Prince of Canosa, UCVI, II, 18.

[2] Cf. RN'99, *passim*; SRN, 214–15 and *passim*; AVL, III, 12–14.

[3] With reference to Cuoco a romantic digression might be permitted. Reference was made earlier to the fact that the fate of Naples was to be read, at the height of the revolution, between the lines of a *billet-doux*. This letter was composed by

It is Cuoco who introduces to Croce the third of the moral agents in the drama of revolution: the people. Jacobin republicanism, Croce notes, had as its basic dogma the occult correspondence of the republican idea with popular aspirations. It was sustained in this persuasion, as Cuoco also notes, by the myth of a natural justice inhabiting the minds and the hearts of the people at a level too deep to be affected by the course of institutional history and needing only direct appeal to awaken it. Developing this argument in another direction, Cuoco finds in this myth or dogma a mark of the Gallican character and hence the intrinsic limit of the ideas of the great revolution of '89. This dogma was accepted without criticism as the very heart of their creed by the Neapolitan republicans, the 'ceto medio' which had undergone the strange alchemy of the revolutionary conversion.[1] Nowhere, perhaps, as Croce indicates, is this article of faith set forth with greater concentration of fervour and eloquence than in the pages of the 'Monitore' which Fonseca-Pimentel continued to publish until the very moment when the waters of the reaction, or rather its waves of blood, were to engulf her. And it was to this illusion, in the first stage of the uprising, that the revolutionary leaders addressed themselves; their first strategy was a direct appeal to the 'people' to shake off the years and the centuries, to release the flame of republicanism which lay enclosed within their hearts, or better in their 'nature'. Having made this appeal they paused, in a moment of great silence, confidently awaiting the great response which would in one moment fulfil millennial longings.

The degree of blindness into which that 'ceto medio' had fallen by that psychological necessity which Cuoco had analysed is nowhere illustrated better than by this fatuous expectation. At this moment, that 'ceto medio' reached the extreme of alienation from its historic centre. Had those leaders in that hour been capable of that historical judgment which is the basis of all effective historical action, as Croce writes, they would have seen that by that strategy they were denying the historical principle which had distinguished them as an effective agent group in the liberalizing movements of the previous decades.

Luisa San Felice, a woman of romantic mores and many lovers. One of these, in his concern for her safety, communicated to her the plans of the revolutionaries. She in turn, anxious for the safety of another, passed on this information indiscreetly, thus contributing directly to the discovery of the revolutionary conspiracy. Of these lovers, one or the other, the legend goes, was Vincenzo Cuoco. Cf. RN'99, 'Luisa San Felice', etc.

[1] V. Cuoco, *Saggio Storico*, ed. Nicolini, Bari, 1913.

The 'ceto medio', which had entered into the alliance for reform with the monarchy, was intellectualistic and selective in instinct and on principle. Its instinctive aristocracy was fortified by several careful distinctions which its severe intellectual culture had enabled it to make, and which, by contrast, the facile combination of abstract reason and impulsive sentiment, which marked the revolutionary mentality in France, had failed to grasp.[1] Most basic was the distinction that while all reform should have as its ultimate beneficiaries the people, the instruments and agents of reform had to be the historically existent and effective agencies of social organization, which precisely to the degree to which they became agents of reform and progress, would themselves be transformed. The 'ceto medio' had been, therefore, essentially anti-revolutionary and anti-popularist on grounds which, in the context, were historically and logically sound. The direct appeal to the people by the revolutionary committee, consequently, was in direct violation of that historical logic, the measure of the distance which the 'ceto medio' had travelled from its historical and ideal centre. The response to that appeal was such as the historical consciousness of the 'ceto medio' should have admonished it to expect. It was Sanfedism. And once it had been invoked, the revolutionists were to learn, that terrible power, the people, could not be laid by such expedients as the invocation of alien arms—the second desperate step in the revolutionary strategy. Awakened, that power worked out its historic effect according to the inner logic of its moral character. For this reason, consequently, Croce turns to the task of describing this third and perhaps most powerful of all the moral agents of the revolution, the people.

What was this 'people' which the revolution had invoked but from which, on confrontation, it had withdrawn in terror? The answer could be had only from history itself. Thence alone could be derived an understanding of its character and potential as an historic agent and, consequently, some clue to the part it played in the revolution and the succeeding reaction.

The origins of the people were to be sought first of all in the type of vassalage which had existed under the harsh Neapolitan baronage, even before the introduction of the 'great feudalism' of the north by the Norman invaders.[2] The gradual transformation of the system of feuds into allodial fiefs had not acted to the benefit of that class of vassals; on the contrary, it had only rendered their relation to the

---

[1] For this question of aristocracy and liberalism cf. AVL, III, 331-8.

[2] AVL, II, ch. XV, 428-40, 'I Lazzari'; cf. also RN'99, 231 sqq.; SRN, 223-5.

land, already tenuous, more tenuous still. The simultaneous decline of the 'commune' (which had known in southern Italy an earlier and stronger florescence than in the north of which it was later to be thought so typical and for which in fact the southern 'commune' had served as model) dissolved the only other social structure into which the serfs, disengaged from the first feudal relation to the land, might have been assimilated, and which might have served as a preparation and discipline, however remote and rudimentary, for the reception of liberal ideas a thousand years later. The flow of the serfs, detached from the land by the transformation of the feudal system, toward the urban centre of the region, Naples, in which the decline of the primitive commune structure might be said to be most marked, brought together these two factors in the first formation of the people. The city was without the institutional, social or economic structure and dynamism to absorb this influx, or to offer to these persons a way of life, or to generate new social relations to replace those from which they were recently released. The city had cultivated no commercial or manufacturing activities of its own. Its commerce and industry were almost without exception in foreign hands, Castilian, Genovese, Florentine. The local feudal nobility, who made the city their seat, had nothing but contempt for these pursuits and preferred to live in constant dependence on these foreign agents.[1] Thus the formation of a middle class in the economic sense was impeded from the start. The new arrival from the countryside could find no outlet for his energies either in the arts and crafts or in commerce, for these were closed to him, guaranteed to foreign elements by concessions granted by or wrung from the nobility of the city. To these factors must be added the almost entire illiteracy of this new element, as well as the complete absence of any means of remedying this lack, for the educational tradition of the region was military or clerical. Finally, there must be noted the millennial social and political conditioning of these people for whom power could only be from above and who recognized its symbols only in the persons and the agents of transcendent representation.

This was the situation of those who, released from feudal bonds to the land, had drifted to the city. The case of those who had remained behind was no better; it was, if anything, more debased. From tillers of land which in a certain, though most restricted, sense had been theirs, they were transformed into landless day-workers in

---

[1] Cf. SVI, *passim*.

the fields of others, living with no commitment save the daily stint of toil and its meagre wage and no attachment which was not merely a memory. Needless to say, no social provision existed for their betterment and there was no force which could prevent them from sinking constantly to a more debased level, deprived of all human dignity and without the minimal security necessary to the human person.

The people thus in historical perspective comprised two elements, both of which were to be effective agents in the revolutionary drama. These elements, though superficially diverse, possessed profound affinities which guaranteed a common pattern of political action under the provocation of the revolution. In the provinces were the vast numbers of detached agricultural workers. These people were literally without any provision for life, without the minimal social guarantees. Yet they possessed one idea which, however deluded. was to be effectively invoked by the counter-revolutionary forces: reverence for the king, his person and his agents, as the only substantial political authority. This reverence was born, of course, of the action which the kings, for their own purposes, had taken to release these people from the local tyrannies of the barons. It was an empty release. The relations which had existed under the barons, however onerous, had nevertheless been real relations and had carried real guarantees.[1] The freedom which now came to them was completely devoid of even such minimal assurances. The kings made no provision to replace those older and effective relations. This was a fact, however, which only generations of experience could impress upon the peasants, and even then not wholly, for the memory of the barons' oppression was kept green by the ever-present signs of their power in local castle and keep. Constituting the second element of the 'people' was the vast fluid mass of the urban population. In status below even the miserable artisan who by the practice of some small trade or craft could win a slight assurance of livelihood, this portion of the people lived from day to day and from hand to mouth, with the assurance neither of bread nor of shelter. Their culture, if such a term can be applied to them, was even lower than that of their provincial counterparts, for in the city they were exposed to the corroding presence of unattainable wealth and refinement. This corruption expressed itself in more than one form. Directly, it appeared in the manner in which these people passed without reflection (and

---

[1] Cf. Croce's remarks, SRN, 61.

without defiance, for it was all a matter of circumstance) into a pattern of lawlessness in which theft and ruffianism, beggary and every manner of craftiness became the normal means of life. Less directly, but even more forcefully, it appeared in the attitude which they developed toward their superiors and in the social and political notions which they formed and exhibited. These might be characterized either subjectively or objectively, that is to say, in the social dispositions they exhibited and in the social ideals they cherished; in both, their essential servility and the moral degradation of their state were documented. The objective ideal was synthesized in the notion of the 'buon signor'; this was the nobleman, of wealth incalculable (from the point of view of the 'lazzarone') dispensed with heedless largess; of manners elegant, perhaps a bit effeminate, and laced with a certain brutality and insensitivity; careless of the economies of life and substance, so that he could be cheated with impunity, even while he was flattered to his face, and subjected to petty frauds which his exalted station forbade him even to notice, much less to vindicate; who spent his time in ceaseless diversion, in sports and in amorous intrigue, without thought of the serious business of politics or government; in a word, an ambiguous idol whom the 'lazzerone' could adulate even as he exploited, and whom, in his miserable heart, he could even despise as a weaker creature than himself, a victim and not a master of life. The subjective character of the man of the people was the perfect complement of this. It was blended of equal parts of servility and duplicity, of meanness and craftiness. His fundamental view of life, fundamental though unspoken save in the daily strategies of existence, was egotistic and savage; he lived for himself alone by means of the exploitation of superiors secretly despised. The ideal was to have a master whom one could serve and exploit, adulate and commiserate in one complex pattern. Lacking such attachment, one lived by chance, by transient substitutes, but on the same principles. Beyond this there was one thing only, the millennial reverence and dread of power and authority from above. Such power must take the form of the 'buon signor' who was too great to be tricked, too lavish to be exploited, too good to be abused, in whose presence, ideally at least, the divergent tensions of the 'lazzarone's' soul might be relaxed. This was the populace to which the name of 'lazzarone', itself of dubious origin, was to become attached; and who exercised so strong an influence, by its mere presence, that its unspoken ideals infiltrated the consciousness of the whole city, and even the unbending viceroys of Spain and the Bourbon kings who succeeded them did not scorn the image of the 'buon signor' with all its ambiguities, or disdain to model themselves upon it.[1]

This then was the 'people' which was to enter so dramatically and so decisively into the drama of the revolution. This analysis of its genesis and character makes it possible to understand how great was the delusion of the revolutionary jacobins in their appeal to this 'people', how great the seduction effected by the abstractions of revolutionary oratory, divorced from the realities of history; how intrinsically impossible it was morally for the people to respond to the revolutionary invocation, for which it was without historical and moral preparation, and finally, to comprehend the character of its reaction, Sanfedism. Such a convergence of historical delusion and historical inevitability must have proved cataclysmic, and places the issue beyond praise or blame, beyond every emotion but dismay. The revolutionary leaders, in their blind enthusiasm, were placing an unconscionable responsibility upon the people in thus invoking their alliance in the work of revolution; it was a burden which historically no one had the right to ask them to assume and which no one, historically advised, could possibly expect them to take up. Moral action in history cannot spring full-born from the native endowment of men; it is the flower of education in civility, and cannot reasonably be asked of those to whom that education has been denied. The failure of the people to respond to the challenge of the revolutionary invocation is simply, therefore, fact. It cannot be attributed to them as a fault. Such exoneration, however, cannot be extended to the revolutionary leaders themselves. They were not, like the people, historically unprepared. Their civil education was much advanced, so advanced as to have earned, as Croce had noted before, the admiration of Europe. They were historically guilty of a double moral failing, first, in the fatuous invocation of the people to the jacobin ideals, and secondly, in the strategy to which they had recourse, when this invocation, inevitably, failed. This strategy, as already indicated, was to invite the arms of France to lend to the ideals of the republic from without the support which they could not evoke within. Such an action only increased the historical futility of the revolutionary pattern of action. It was patent treason, to be speciously justified only by an appeal to jacobin ideas of internationalism, and it was tactically erroneous, for it could only provoke with greater force that reaction against which the foreign arms were invited to intervene.

[1] Cf. SRN, 121 sqq.

By contrast, Sanfedism could be understood most clearly as the expression of the historical preparation of the people for political action in such a crisis as the revolution. It was the only mode of action for which the people were historically prepared and of which, consequently, they were morally capable. The basic principle of Sanfedism was the appeal to the sanctity of transcendent authority. This was an appeal the people were prepared to heed, so deeply burned into their souls was the ultimate conviction that the mark of authority was transcendent representation. It was a double appeal, the appeal first of that authority mocked by the revolution and in the second of that authority to be vindicated and to be returned to its central place in the pattern of life they knew. Against these convictions of the blood and of the bowels, the airy abstractions of the revolutionaries, their appeals to equality, fraternity and liberty could only be futile; even more, they inevitably incited resentment, as beyond comprehension. To these facts was added the skill of the appeal of Ruffo, who knew, far better than did the deluded revolutionaries, the temper of the people—not abstractions, but concrete reasons and tangible objectives. And finally, the appeal of Sanfedism touched profound springs of resentment and hatred in the tortured soul of the 'lazzarone' and of his provincial brother, hatred which had seethed for generations, without direction, feeding upon itself, and now released toward objects indicated to it by an authority which it could not question.

What then was the result of the revolution, its 'meaning' in history, to Croce's view? It was not simple, any more than the event itself. From the point of view of the revolutionary party, it was an immediate defeat and an ultimate triumph; in a word, it was part of the civil education of the 'ceto medio', that civil education without which historical action is impossible. It compelled that group to return to its earlier pattern of social and political action, with a broadened and deepened understanding of the historical and moral bases of that pattern. Out of it was to come the liberalism which was in the following century to prove the historically effective means of the triumph of Italian unity. From the point of view of the Bourbon monarchy, it was ultimate defeat, though immediate and temporary triumph. It revealed the historical and moral inadequacy of that regime which made it incapable of rising to the highest demands of its historical task. By the movement of reaction, the Bourbons of Naples effectively removed themselves from history. Some time must elapse before this fact stood completely revealed, but it was a fact from the moment of the king's return from Palermo. The succeeding stages were but a 'coda', lending aesthetic unity, but adding nothing substantial. And with respect to the people, what was the revolution? Its effect upon them was nearer to its effect upon the revolutionaries, than upon the monarchy; it was a step, and a great step, in their civil education. Most saliently, it was the first stage in their basic reorientation away from the vestigial feudal loyalties of the eighteenth century toward the emerging liberal ideals of the nineteenth. It was but a stage, however, and by no means a complete readjustment; the role of the people was to continue ambiguous, a moral factor whose value even the politically most astute could not readily divine.

Such was the historical meaning of the Neapolitan revolution of 1799, taken, so to say, in its objectivity; but that revolution had profound and transforming meaning also for Croce as an historian and as a philosopher. This meaning was the transformation worked by his study of this complex of events, first, in his conception of the history of Naples and secondly in his conception of history and of historiography. The latter, of course, can be stated and understood only in terms of the former. The transformation takes place entirely within the transformed approach to the concrete history of Naples. Any effort to separate these elements, to render them extraneous to each other, would falsify them, and falsify the most important phase of Croce's career as an historian and as a theorist of historiography. Both elements of this meaning of the revolution of 1799 are therefore best rendered in terms of the history of Naples itself.

The overall transformation was one of dimension. What had before been superficial, two-dimensional, now acquired depth and perspective. This depth and perspective was above all human. The perception of human perspective in this history meant the complete transcendence of the idyllic mood in historiography. Human depth and its appreciation by the historian precludes that aesthetic and psychological distance which the idyllic mood engenders, or which, more accurately, engenders the idyllic mood. To perceive that human depth, that human dimension, is to become involved in it; the simple act of perception is the primary and basic involvement. Where before he had seen monuments and towers, about which the spiritual eye could weave what dreams and images it would, he now saw the open and undisguised struggle of human ideals and volitions. The participants in that struggle, that drama, were completely committed; this is the historical, and not merely the psychological fact.

This commitment is their historical reality, for what they are for history and in history is the reality of their implication in that drama. As those actors are committed, so too is the historian. He cannot take up his position at a distance, because he would distort the vision he has achieved, by mistaking those human principals for natural factors. The central questions could, from that distance, no longer be put. The meaningful questions are those which arise directly from commitment, the commitment of the principals and of the historian. Every question is, consequently, a question of 'value', for the human struggle and commitment in history is both itself a value and the matrix of all values; and history itself becomes value, and a fabric of value, by the simple fact that it is woven of human committed effort. This is the basic principle of the ethico-political conception of history as it touches both the historical principals and the historian. It would be the gravest error and misinterpretation of Croce's insight to conceive this ethico-political conception of history as merely the substitution of certain qualitatively diverse factors, for other factors; the 'factors' of the human drama for the 'factors' of natural force. No such substitution is possible; the differentiation is too radical. The ethico-political conception imports above all this depth of vision and commitment and it is in the matter of the revolution of '99 that Croce achieves it.

This vision in depth embraces as well the time-structure of the history of Naples. As a result of the studies of the revolution, the history of Naples is grasped for the first time by Croce in its depth in historical time. This is not of course a perception superimposed on the human vision; it is achieved only in and through it. It is as though, by his studies of the revolution of '99, Croce had opened a door, and found himself in the central salon of one of those apartments of infinite vistas so characteristic of Italian 'palazzi', for example of his own Palazzo Filomarino. In those apartments, wherever one might stand, the eye is carried irresistibly, and by the magic of the artist's will, to range the whole sweep of chambers opening one upon the other. In this way, involved in the complex events of the revolution, his historian's vision was irresistibly forced backward in time and forward, back into the dim origins of this present complex, forward to its consequence and meaning. Thus the history of Naples arose before his eye as a complex time-form, reaching back to the dim centuries of the middle ages and forward to the moment, which had transpired finally in his own life-time, when the identity of Naples was taken up into the larger identity of the new Italy. That history arose as a whole, as it were, but still as a problem, as a question, complex, organic, but in its depths still a mystery. In the effort to state and solve this problem as evoked by the moral issues of the revolution, Croce achieves the full vision and statement of his ethico-political theory of history.

III

NAPLES, THE REALM:
A STUDY IN HISTORICAL FAILURE

THE study of the revolution of 1799 in Naples, and of the groups and individuals who appeared as its moral protagonists, exercised a profound influence, then, upon Croce's conception of history, of its objects, of its problems, of its method, and finally of the historian's office and role. This influence is discernible first of all in transformation effected in his view of the scope and form of the history of Naples. Those studies on the revolution had begun as curious inquiries, directed toward the illumination of certain moot points: to explore the fascination of the character of Fonseca-Pimentel, to linger over the pathos and the irony of the role and fate of Luisa San Felice, to present the diary of an eye-witness, observant but little comprehending, of the paradoxes and the terrors of those days. Now they quickly underwent a profound change; it was as though, thinking to improve with the chisel the contours of a statue carved by another, he had suddenly cut into living flesh. The revolution leaped to life beneath his hand; he saw it now, not as an isolated congeries of events and persons, but as a moment, a vital moment, in a living process which extended backward in time to the very origins of Naples as a 'realm', as a political, cultural unit striving for historical reality and existence, and coming forward in time, to the very threshold of his own life when that realm passed away, taken up into a life larger and more capable of effective historical existence than itself. The scattered, fragmentary, isolated images gave way to the historical image of Naples as an organic whole, its life deployed over seven centuries, the image of the 'realm of Naples' as an historical moral entity.

When seized thus in its totality, that is, as a time-form, the realm of Naples is revealed in its essentially problematical character. That realm, and its history, do not constitute a 'fact' to be established, or more accurately, re-established, in its 'objectivity'. They constitute a problem, to be stated in its proper terms and resolved. The revolution supplies the terms both for the positing and for the resolution of this problem. In the revolution the inner quality of history is first revealed. Since the revolution was but an episode in the centuries-long drama of Neapolitan history, its terms irresistibly enlarge and extend themselves to the whole. The revolution was the whole history of Naples 'writ small', or conversely the history of Naples is the revolution 'writ large'. The same constitutive and qualitative terms are proper to both, the terms of the ethico-political struggle which is the reality of man's historical existence.

The perception of the problemicity of the history of the realm of Naples, and by implication of history as such, induces in Croce the attitude concerning the role of the historian which will become proper to him. For whom is the history of Naples, history itself therefore, a problem? Not indeed for history; that is, not for history as transpired. The past had its problems, to be sure; it is at once the statement and the solution of those problems, within the terms of its transpired existence. That is a problemicity, however, over and done with. The historian who would set himself the task of restating it and resolving it anew would fall into an attitude of pure redundancy. The problemicity of history in its inward qualitative character is ethico-political; but that redundant manner of conceiving that problemicity and resolution cannot be ethico-political, or simply moral, because the attitude of the historian cannot be participation, but only detachment. The problemicity of the history of Naples, consequently, is real only in the sense and to the degree that it is a problem for the present; that is to say, is an element in the ethico-political situation in which the existent moral agents of history are called upon to act. It is, therefore, a problem for the present. All history is this, a problem for the present. If this be true, then it also becomes clear in what sense it is possible to speak of a resolution of the problemicity of history. Historical inquiry must participate; and this participation is not merely existential, but qualitative; it must renew the ethico-political quality of historical action. The resolution of the problem of the history of Naples, and by implication, of problemicity of history as such, is to be found only in present action, predicated upon the past as an element of the problemicity of the present. History demands of the historian an attitude directly opposed to that idyllicism of Croce's early period; it demands participation. His is the function of determining the status of the past in the problemicity of the present; he directly prepares the ethico-political action of the present. He neither reconstructs a past which is over and done with, nor seeks to foretell the future on the basis of a 'scientific' knowledge of the 'laws' of history. He is man acting historically, ethico-politically, in his own proper qualitative sphere. He stands at the vital centre, where past, present and future converge. The historical judgment is the form of present action.

The first evidence of this influence of the revolution, and the first intimations of the form his treatment of the history of Naples must take, appear in the eulogy of the historian of mediaeval and Norman Naples, Bartolomeo Capasso.[1] His praise for the historical work which Capasso had achieved is unfeigned and unstinted; it is, he notes, a work which must remain a constant point of reference for all subsequent inquiry. At the same time, the point of view from which that vast achievement was projected has now been transcended. Capasso's attention was focused upon Naples; the 'Regno' lay at the centre of his universe. Its history might be developed with respect to other historical structures, with respect to Spain, or the papacy. Naples, however, had the source of its historical life within itself, so that these points of reference appeared only upon its periphery, even when, as happened more than once during the centuries to which Capasso devoted his best attention, Naples lay subject to alien powers. His primary object was the contemplation of Naples itself; all other objects he perceived only as they passed across or impinged upon this central visual field. This concentration, there could be no doubt, was the source of Capasso's power as an historian. Yet it could not, Croce argues, be maintained. It rested upon an illusion, and could in turn breed nothing but illusion. Capasso mistook the problem of the history of Naples for its solution. He had assumed the historicity of the realm of Naples. He had taken it for granted that Naples was an historical actuality, that this realm of Naples, of which he wrote with such muted reverence and almost religious awe, was a 'fact'. As a result, he could ask questions concerning that 'fact'; but he could not put the fundamental question, he could not question that fact itself. But, Croce perceives, it is precisely the 'fact' which must be questioned. It can, however, be questioned only from a point of view which transcended it. That point of view had been provided Croce's generation by the Risorgimento. For Capasso, though he lived through it, the Risorgimento could never be, in the full sense of the term, a reality, the historical centre. For Croce, no other centre is possible.

Croce's history of Naples, when at last it was written, would

[1] Cf. NN, IX (1900), 3, 42 and *supra*.

seem, by his own account, to have been undertaken almost by chance. Occupied one day in reordering his books, and especially, in bringing together all those which referred to the history of Naples, he chanced to lay his hand on the work of Enrico Cenni, the juridical historian of the 'Regno'. With an inconsequence which every scholar and book-lover would understand, he put aside his original task and read the book afresh from cover to cover.[1] To the interest which the topic held for him, both in itself and because it was integral to his interest in the history of Naples, there accrued another. He had in his youth known Cenni. He recalled him as he had seen him many times, a venerable figure, erect and proud, as were all the men of that heroic age of the Risorgimento, his head crowned by a magnificent mane of white hair, his every look imperious and commanding.[2] Cenni had belonged to that group of Catholic liberals who, for a time, had promised to play such a decisive part in the history of Italy and for whose difficult and ambiguous position, though it was never his own, Croce entertained a profound respect. The roots of this regard lay in the central effort of the Catholic liberals to embrace in one effective historical ideal both the concept of liberty and the historical faith, in its institutional form, which had played so great and memorable a part in the history not only of Italy but of the whole of Europe and of the world. It was an effort which Croce respected because he himself would fain have seen this union effected, as many aspects of his thought reveal. He felt it to be logically and historically impossible; but for those who had made it the central moral effort of their lives, he could entertain nothing but respect.

It was not, however, with Cenni the Catholic liberal, with whom, in this chance encounter, he now became engaged. It was with Cenni, the Neapolitan and the historian of Naples, and with the vision of the history of Naples which he evoked. It was an idyllic vision, redolent of an historical idyllism of which Croce could not absolve himself, in which history was transmuted and transformed. The terms of the transformation were those closest to Cenni's heart and understanding: liberty and law. He set about, with an effort of the imagination essentially poetic, to rediscover in that history the ideal moral and juridical values which he held to be absolute. In the midst of a Europe which was still semi-barbaric, the realm of Naples rose before the eye of his imagination as a civil monarchy, as a modern state, in which the feudal baronacy had been restrained,

[1] SRN, 1.   [2] SRN, 5.

liberty and justice guaranteed to the people, and the whole of society ruled by a sovereign conscience, guided by noble concepts both political and moral. Its chief glory, in Cenni's view, was not political, but civil; for while, in the rest of Europe, the struggle with the feudal system proceeded slowly, with difficulty and revolution, with recourse to violence, in the realm of Naples, by his account, that system was defeated early and with recourse to no other arms than reason and law. This early and pacific defeat of the feudal system was, in Cenni's view, the result of the superiority of Neapolitan jurisprudence; it was in essence a juridical triumph. Neapolitan jurisprudence had first discerned the distinction in feudal investiture between *jurisdictio* and *dominium*; in the realm, there was no need for a declaration of the rights of man, because these rights were alive and present in the common conscience, which the jurists articulated by their formulation of the *jura civitatis*, and which the kings vindicated by their policy against the barons. The juridical school of Naples appeared, in his view, as the 'teacher of Europe in civil equity'. And as Neapolitan jurisprudence had defended that notion from the harsh encroachments of the barons so, without ever incurring the taint of heresy, it defended it against the jurisdictional claims of the Roman curia, the encroachments of the Holy Office upon the liberty of conscience which that ideal of civil equity implied. The history of the realm of Naples was, by Cenni's account, the uninterrupted progress of civil consciousness articulated in juridical terms, clarifying and elevating the entire life of the realm, rendering it normative for the whole of Italy and of Europe.[1]

Croce's emotions, as he set the work aside, were mixed. The commanding authority of Cenni did not relax its hold easily. Recalling that venerable figure, he felt a stab of guilt as objections to that idyllic vision crowded in upon his mind. But neither would these be stilled. If this were indeed the history of Naples, this its privileged place in the record of civil and political effort and achievement, this the outstanding virtue and wisdom of its rulers and its people, why is that history, that record, so little known? Or why, rather, is it everywhere challenged and denied? Cenni had foreseen this objection; his reply was ready and characteristic. It was the baleful influence of French thought and the French example which blinded the general vision to the glories of the Neapolitan record.[2] The Italian consciousness, losing itself in a servile imitation of French ideas, failed to see that those very ideas and values were to be found in a

[1] RN'99, 3-5. [2] SRN, 4.

purer form in their own historical experience. But this was an *ad hoc* reply, not truly worthy of its author; for history is not explained by the invocation of demons, not even the demon of jacobinism.

This idyllization of the history of the realm is a material failing in Cenni's account, but it has its origin and root in another, methodological fault. Cenni is infected by the 'boria dei dotti' which Vico had recognized and stigmatized; the 'conceit of the learned', which, in Vico's words, leads them to imagine that whatever they know and understand, their wisdom, must be as ancient as the world itself.[1] It is a strange conceit, working always for the denigration of the present, concealing the achievement of history by projecting it back upon the past. Thus Cenni had inverted the whole juridical and political movement of five hundred years by reading back into the history of the Neapolitan monarchy and its struggles with the barons and the Church juridical distinctions which had been won only laboriously. This is, however, not his gravest fault; it is overshadowed by another, the 'factorial' fallacy. Cenni had treated the history of Naples as an illustration of juridical theory. He had assigned to the juridical structure a determining influence upon all other dimensions of its life. Inevitably, he had distorted historical reality. No nation exists to illustrate a theory. No element of social life determines the whole. Nations, like individuals, seek first and above all, as the condition of all else, existence. Every nation (and the term is employed in a large sense, to indicate simply the group subjectivites which reach the level of historical articulation), every nation strives to achieve effective historical existence within the terms allotted it by fate, or history itself.[2] It strives, not to be this or that, to illustrate this or that abstract ideal or notion, but to secure its own historical existence and within the matrix of that existence, which is the condition of all else, to bring to fruition whatever idealities it perceives within itself. This effort to achieve effective historical existence is a profoundly ethical effort, free and holistic. It is free, and hence creative, because it is not determined from within or from without. There is no force, no principle within itself or without the nation which will guarantee this existence to it, under whatever formality, whether of dialectical materialism or of providence. It is a creative freedom within the conditions which history itself dictates, 'ipsis rebus dictantibus' in Vico's phrase. The authentic object, consequently, of the historian's concern is this ethical creative effort to achieve historical existence, and the qualitative character of the exist-

[1] *Scienza Nuova Seconda* (ed. Nicolini), Bari, 1942, para. 127, 128.   [2] SI'71, 4.

ence which is achieved. The reality of the history of Naples is the effort of the Neapolitans to achieve authentic historical existence as a nation, in the conditions and with the resources allotted them. This is what Cenni failed to see; as a consequence, he missed the very subject of his history. And his failure aids Croce to posit the problem of the history of Naples in the only relevant terms. What was the quality of the Neapolitan effort to achieve historical existence as a nation and what the results that it achieved? If this question can be answered, the historical reality of Naples will have been seized in its creative principle and in its qualitative form.

The vision which Cenni had invoked of a nation, a civil monarchy, paramount in the political and ethical virtues proper to a state is not, Croce notes, without historical verisimilitude.[1] There had indeed existed, in the very theatre in which the history of Naples itself was to be enacted, a state, an empire, in which many of the exalted traits of the Cenni catalogue had at least been approximated. This state was not, however, the realm of Naples. It was rather that chivalric empire which the Norman-Swabian kings had established, with its base and fulcrum in Sicily and its seat at Palermo. Of this empire, Croce recognizes, the lofty epithets of Cenni's account might with great justice be predicated. Cenni's patriotism, his profound love of Naples and his pride in its history, had induced him to transfer to the object of his passion the traits and character which belonged rather to another. The transfer was not indeed difficult. It was to be achieved by the simple figure of speech which takes the whole for the part, and then by interpreting the figure literally. For Naples had been, in a certain sense, a part of that vast empire of the Norman and Swabian kings; it had been numbered among the tributaries which fed that empire's greatness and had received by participation a portion of the benefits which flowed from its suzerainty. It was possible, consequently, by an inclusive metaphor to speak of Naples and that empire as one. But in no sense was it possible to conceive of Naples as the true subject of that history. That history was enacted on a plane superior to the history of Naples; that empire had its springs of power, its dawn and its sunset elsewhere; and its epic might include the tale of Naples only as an episode, a minor episode recounted to relax the tension of mightier events.

Yet the bond between that empire and the realm of Naples is real and intimate, as real and as intimate as the relation between life and death. For it was of the death throes of that empire that the realm

[1] SRN, 5 sqq.

49

of Naples was born. From its southern centre in the rich and strategically placed island of Sicily, the Norman-Swabian power had extended its sway in every direction, west and south and east; and in this movement Naples had been among the first to fall beneath its influence and, as most proximate, had shared most extensively in the life which the empire represented. But there came a moment, common to all human structures of power, when that extended sway could no longer be maintained; when the power which had flowed out so freely and so abundantly turned back upon its centre. In the wake of that receding tide lay the wreckage of empire, cities, regions and provinces cut off from the whole which had given them their life; *dejecta membra*, they strew the shores of the Mediterranean and the hills of southern Italy, Benevento, Taranto, a hundred more—and Naples. Here then must the true origins of that realm be sought, in the wreck of that empire. *Mors tua vita mea*: this must be the motto which forever binds the history of Naples to that of the empire from which it sprang. And that birth was for Naples no easy thing. It was indeed a being cast down into existence, into '*Dasein*', traumatic as every birth must be. Here must the history of the realm of Naples begin, with this *dejectum membrum* of a mighty corporate empire, plunged by its violent origin into the ambiguous and hostile medium of historical existence, with no alternative before it save to validate that existence for itself or in its turn to perish. A more unpropitious birth of empire could scarcely be imagined. Empires which in history have achieved effective existence have been, without exception, born of strength; but the realm of Naples was born of weakness. Those empires have sprung from seed which from their internal resources have articulated their complex corporate structure; but this realm of Naples has its source in the mutilation of a great imperial body, and enters historical life with the scars of that mutilation upon it.[1]

This realm of Naples, ejected thus into the '*Dasein*' of historical existence, appears then at the first moment of its life as pure problemicity. The essential problem may be stated in a variety of ways, but whatever the form it assumes it is still the same problem: whether out of that mutilated member there might be formed a body politic and civil, capable of historical existence as an autonomous nation, as a corporate moral entity embodying itself and its idea in a system of institutions capable of sustaining identity and of promoting effective action in the face of innumerable historical pressures. This is the problem which the historian of the realm of Naples must propose to

[1] SRN, 41.

himself, and not that other, otiose task of depicting a realm that never was, that answers only to the patriot's desire. In the solution of this problem, in the answer to this question, the authentic history of Naples will be contained; and in it in germ, all human history, qualitatively present.

This is the problem, the question to whose solution Croce addresses himself; it is only as a response to this problem that the *Storia del Regno di Napoli* can be read. It cannot be read as a source of information, though it is rich in that, massing detail with an easy skill which conceals itself in its operation. It cannot be read as 'philosophical reflection', for it issues in none of those philosophemes, which are thought by many to comprise the fruit of the philosophy of history. Nor can it be read as a paradigm of any abstract theory of history. It is wholly existential, wholly, that is to say, a response to a question or problem of existence, and itself wholly the existential act of historical inquiry, based solely on the ethico-political insight. And its purely existential character is established finally by the attitude which pervades it. For it is not an abstract answer to a rhetorical question; it is an existential reply to a problem which is existential for the historian himself. The quality of participation pervades it completely. For Croce does not set this problem in the character of an abstract or detached historian to whom the character of his subject is indifferent and his method all. He posits the problem as one for whom the problem is still actual. Concretely, he posits the problem and suggests his answer as a Neapolitan of the post-Risorgimento generation in Italy. In this character he was confronted by a situation which was, so to say, the *de facto* reply to his problem; by the fact, that is to say, that the realm of Naples had ceased to enjoy an autonomous status, however labile and ambiguous, but had been taken up into the larger unity of the new Italy. This was the fact; and on a certain level, it was a reply to and a solution of that millennial problem. But not on the historiographic level, that is to say, on the ethico-political level. There that fact was still a problem, as Croce could readily read in the faces of many about him, who rejected that fact. In setting himself that problem, consequently, Croce, is in his own person and as an historian, continuing the life of Naples itself, for its union with the life of the new Italy could never remain a mere fact, but must become in its turn an ethical and historical decision, a decision which had to be made in the historical consciousness of which, in this work, Croce is an eloquent spokesman.[1]

[1] SRN, 53.

Read in this manner, as an existential response to an existential and historical problem, and as itself an act of historical decision, the work is unambiguous. It is a sentence of death upon the realm of Naples; or rather, it is an elegy for a life which never could be born, whose image or ghost hovered above six centuries of history, hungering, so to say, for historical corporalization, but doomed, in the absence of any effective agency, to retreat finally into the realm of dreams, the ghost of the realm of Naples. It is the recognition that that 'dejectum membrum' could never of its mutilated state engender a body civil and political whole in principle and in action, and capable of historical existence, but that its only hope of life lay in reunion with some greater whole, in this case a whole which still lay in the womb of time, awaiting birth, the new Italy. And it is the recognition that the record of the realm of Naples, when read in these basic problematic and existential terms, is but the record of successive attempts to find the greater whole to which it might be united and from which it might draw the life which of itself it could not sustain. But this response to that basic problem of the history of the realm of Naples is incorrectly read, if it be interpreted as a recognition of a fore-ordained fate, from which there was no escape; such a response would contravene completely the ethico-political conception of history by which the work is motivated. It is rather (paradoxical as this may seem) the recognition that this impotence of the realm of Naples to be born to history is an ethico-political impotence, a moral impotence, therefore, and a moral failure, which may find alleviation and mitigation, to a degree, in reflection upon the unpropitious natural conditions which accompanied and qualified that historic effort, but which can never be resolved without residue into the determinate action of those natural forces. Surely this history can be nothing but a dolorous record, a tragic record; but Croce's oft-repeated statement that history holds more of tragedy than of comedy is not an aphorism but a conviction, whose force he does not hesitate to recognize in the instance in which his participation is most immediate and most complete.

In order that the ethical quality and character of this history may be set in unambiguous relief, Croce is careful to review and to place in proper perspective the natural conditioning factors whose influence is integral to that history.[1] And on this score also his position is without equivocation. Those natural conditions were unpropitious in the extreme to the probable success of the effort of the realm of

---

[1] SRN, 72 sqq., 145–52, 272.

Naples to achieve historical existence; but they cannot be thought decisive. Even when recorded to their full sum, they yet fall far short of determinate force, they still but delineate the theatre for the ethical action in which that history must essentially consist. For in the face of this summation of the natural factors, nothing can be concluded concerning that basic problem; it is still left unanswered, still remains, that is to say, a problem. It is still possible, nay, even necessary, to say that another ethical will might in the same natural theatre, under the same natural conditions, have worked another end. This is simply to recognize anew, in a specific instance, this general persuasion that natural factors can never provide the true principles of historical solution.

Since the natural forces are neutral, merely delineating the theatre of the moral drama of Neapolitan history, Croce turns his attention to these ethical resources. What promise did the ethical endowment of this new realm, detached from the parent stem, hold for the success of its effort to achieve autonomous historical existence? Mutilated member, rather than germinal form, though it was, the ethical endowment of the new political entity was not inconsiderable. It possessed, in Croce's view, two principles of inner consistency and coherence which, at first glance at least, promised much for the formation of a national consciousness solidly founded and free of elements of illusion. The first of these was territorial unity,[1] a certain natural, geographical wholeness, which eliminated the problem of boundaries, or at least made it so remote as to be immediately irrelevant, and which provided a natural framework for the ethico-political effort. This territorial integrity was a product of the extension of Norman power; moving north-eastward from its Mediterranean centre in the island of Sicily, the Norman arms and policy had reduced to a certain unity and homogeneity the highly complex and heterogeneous elements which had occupied the area. Among these elements were to be numbered the longobardian duchies—of which that of Benevento was the most powerful, for a long time contesting the leadership of the area with Naples and strengthened in this contest by its central position—the coastal communes such as Amalfi and Ravello, the Napoletano, the city of Naples, that is, and its dependent environs, as well as numerous smaller formations, all enjoying autonomous or semi-autonomous status. This work of unification had, it is true, already begun in such adventures as the reduction of Amalfi by the Genovese naval power; but in its definitive

[1] SRN, 42.

form it was the work of Norman arms. This task of territorial unification would have been the first task of an emerging national consciousness, whether its centre were to be at Benevento or at Naples, just as six centuries later it was to prove the first problem in the national unification of the peninsula. It was, consequently, no mean advantage for the nascent political entity to find itself in undisputed possession of boundaries, from the southernmost coasts to the line of demarcation with the papal territories, which were to remain constant for the whole of its historical existence.

The second element of unity and consistency with which the new realm, fragmentary though it was, began its historical career was the monarchical form of government.[1] This too was part of its Norman-Swabian patrimony, and embraced not only the character of a state governed from its natural centre, with equal institutions and laws, and organized magistracy and administration, but also the more formalistic element of monarchy, a personal and hereditary sovereign. This character, like its territorial unity, was to remain constant throughout its historical career, the basis of a tradition of fact and idea to which the republican episodes of the revolution of Masaniello in 1647 and of the jacobin revolution of 1799 can be considered only sportive deviations. So great was the reputation of this monarchical and administrative structure, resting so solidly upon a territorial constant, that throughout the whole of Italy, broken into innumerable fragments and subject to every kind of pressure, internal and external, the term 'The Realm', came, without adjectives, to designate Naples, and Naples, in turn, to represent an ideal to which subconsciously the whole of Italy subscribed and aspired. The earliest Angevine rulers did nothing to weaken or impair this inheritance. They guarded that territorial integrity jealously and maintained both the governmental form and the administrative apparatus, and thus would seem to have set foot on a secure path toward historically effective national consciousness.

A third factor which Croce notes, while not on the same plane as those already mentioned, still contributed to the promise they offered. This was the alliance with the papacy.[2] This alliance was, in a sense, the very basis of the Angevine rule; for it was at the invitation of the pope that Charles of Anjou had entered this theatre. Its importance at this juncture was, so to say, the international leverage with which it endowed the new realm, enabling it to exercise a certain transcendent freedom in affairs even within its own borders.

[1] SRN, 44.   [2] SRN, 46.

This was to prove especially effective in the question of baronial disputes; for a monarchy without such leverage beyond its borders proved without exception helpless before the baronial power. These factors together, and despite the unfavourable historical origins of the realm and the unpredisposing character of its natural endowment, held out fair promise of success in its effort to achieve historical existence as a nation.

Against these propitious factors there were, however, to be set a number of others whose effect was to lessen, if not altogether to neutralize that first promise. The status of the monarchy as an institution, and more specifically of the Angevine dynasty, was the first of these. The monarchical institution, it is clear, was the real locus for the formation of a national consciousness; here, if anywhere, that consciousness might find the conditions proper to its culture and growth. The condition of the monarchical institution itself, however, was somewhat ambiguous, if not precarious. This ambiguity has a double source, embracing both conditions inherent to the institution as it had been formed historically and the manner and condition of the Angevine advent to power. The effect of this ambiguity was to threaten the inherent and, so to say, natural power of the monarchical institution to effect the inner conscious and ethical unity of the realm.

The radical and inherent weakness of the monarchical institution in the Neapolitan theatre had already been indicated in principle by Croce when he had pointed out the fallacy of Cenni's assimilation, without residue, of the history of Naples to that of the Norman-Swabian hegemony in the Mediterranean.[1] That assimilation was without justification, because the Norman rule, despite the numerous and indubitable advantages it had brought to the region, still remained something over and above the intimate life of the lands it ruled. It transpired principally on another plane, it had its centre in another place. For these reasons, it must remain intrinsically alien and hence at root rejected. This alienation must remain unobtrusive in period of relative stability; in periods of transition and readjustment, however, precisely such as the present juncture, in which an older order was dying and a new struggling for birth, that alienation could not fail to reveal itself in all its force and bring to the fore latent causes of discord and insurrection. Under this aspect, consequently, the monarchy, far from guaranteeing order, became in its turn a principle of tension.

[1] SRN, 25.

The manner of the introduction of the Angevine dynasty did little to strengthen this inherent weakness of the monarchy. That dynasty possessed little power to foster, at least immediately, the sense of identity with the other elements upon which an authentic national consciousness must rest. The Angevine power had entered this theatre under guelf influence, as a counterpoise to the ghibelline leanings of the later Swabian rulers, if not simply to displace them.[1] In this way, it appeared in immediate contrast and opposition to the political tradition. Its alliance with the papacy, under one aspect an undoubted source of strength, thus became a hindrance and impediment. The feudal rights over the realm, not of southern Italy only, but of Sicily as well, in virtue of which the papacy offered the territories to the house of Anjou in vassalage, were ancient, if not always undisputed. Nevertheless, the new regime had about it a character of usurpation, deriving from the ghibelline sentiment widespread in the area. As a result, it encountered the gravest difficulty in establishing the character of legitimacy and of claiming that unquestioning allegiance which must be the basis of any monarchical influence and above all of its power to assume moral leadership and express the moral consciousness of the nation.

All of the weakness of the Angevine monarchy, and above all its inability to assume and to express the moral leadership and consciousness of the nascent realm, stood revealed as it confronted the second force of that society, the baronage. This weakness might, in fact, have been counterbalanced and converted into strength had that dynasty possessed the power to reduce the baronage of the realm to a state of submission and domestication similar to that which was being imposed upon the same estate in other parts of Europe. But this was not the case. It has been remarked before that the real base of the Norman-Swabian power, the fulcrum from which it had been able to subdue and dominate the southern reaches of the Italian peninsula, had been Sicily. From this island the Norman empire had drawn both the actual resources of power and the tremendous advantage of a base outside of the territory which it had sought to reduce. This was the situation not only at the beginning but also at the end of its long period of dominance, when most of its activities had become continental; for the island remained the seat of its power and Palermo its capital. With the Angevines, however, an entirely contrary situation prevailed. They were present within, and restricted to, the very area which it was their political task to reduce and subdue, and

[1] SRN, 46.

present there on anything but unambiguous terms, whether of representation or of power. As a result, the Angevine power was never in a position to exercise over the barons of the realm the kind of power which would have been necessary to establish an unambiguous moral and political leadership and thus enable it to give expression to a unity of life of the realm. On the contrary, it was compelled to pursue, with respect to the barons, the most disastrous policy, given the character of its adversary, that might be imagined, namely, a policy of suasion and concession—signs in the limited but infallible heraldry of the baronage, only of weakness. In addition, the Sicily from which the realm of Naples had been dismembered, and to which, in its first stages, it had sought to reunite itself by force, had now, under an alien and hostile dominion, become an ever-present threat; for it was entirely conceivable that a fresh attempt to annex the territory of the realm from the Sicilian centre would be as successful as the first had been, and the barons did not hesitate to invoke this possibility in their contests with the Angevine power. For this reason, the monarchy did not and could not become the effective centre of the national consciousness as the same institution had become in other regions where analogous conditions had prevailed. The fact was that while the name and symbols of power lay with the monarchy, its effective preponderance lay with the barons, who were very numerous and, for the most part, rich. If anywhere in the realm, the conditions of a heightened sense of a common good and of a national consciousness might be supposed to exist among this privileged and richly endowed minority. It is even possible to imagine, as Croce allows himself for a moment to do, that through the agency of the baronage the realm might have been transformed into an aristocratic republic the model for which existed both in classical and in Italian experience. This was, however, but a dream. The apparent promise of the baronage was to prove but another delusion for the realm in the first phase of its autonomous life. The baronage showed itself, in the event, completely incapable of becoming the seat of a genuine national consciousness even in germ or of developing a policy, not for the common good, but even of enlightened self-interest.[1] Machiavelli was later to sum up the character and quality of these barons in one sentence—a class of persons averse to all civility; and, as was his custom, he appended to this estimate a practical injunction that the good of the realm and the power of the king could be assured only by their complete repression.[2] In this judgment,

[1] SRN, 65. [2] *Discorsi*, I, 55; cf. SRN, 59, 69.

history was to sustain the astute Florentine. With time, it became axiomatic that the baronacy was without political and civil value; progressive atrophy was to be its history, and extinction as an effective historical principle its unlamented fate.

To what effective policy, Croce inquires, did the barons lend their preponderance of power? The answer is, none. There was in their counsels and in their actions no trace or hint of political ideas or ideals. To speak of political policy or ideals, one must extravagantly dignify the particularistic, centrifugal and frequently inwardly contradictory interests which they pursued by impulsive and unpremeditated devices. It never occurred to them, even as they held a preponderance of power in their hands, to effect a renewal of the constitution of the realm in the direction of that aristocratic republic on which Croce had permitted his imagination to linger for a moment; this would have demanded a degree of class cohesion and co-operation which was beyond their sentiment or moral power. Nor did any of the baronial families, utilizing the immense power and possessions which many of them had accumulated, set its hand to the great enterprise of constituting itself an indigenous monarchical principle in the realm, a feat which lay within the effective power, it would seem, of at least three of them, the Caracciolo, the Sanseverini and the di Sangro. Rather, they seemed drawn by the image of the greater baronial anarchy which existed under Pedro of Aragon in Sicily; so that at one time, when a league had been formed among a number of them, the rumour spread that it was the design of this league to deliver the realm into the hands of the popes and to rule in their name as vicars, portioning the realm among them, and in this way effectively destroying even that minimal internal cohesion which the realm had acquired under the Norman and Swabian hegemony and through the resistance to the papal expansionism. These particularistic and anarchistic tendencies were, moreover, completely materialistic, governed only by the will to preserve and to acquire, and relieved occasionally only by vague and sentimental and unrealistic expressions of attachment to one or another of the houses which pretended to power over the realm, such as the attachment expressed by the Sanseverini to the house of Guise. Whenever it becomes possible to discern a pattern in their decisions and actions sufficiently clear to be called, not indeed a policy, but a tendency, this tendency manifests itself as directly opposed to the formation of an effective organ of national consciousness, such as the very historical existence of the realm demanded.

One such pattern does seem to Croce to recur with notable persistence. It is composed of three elements which interweave to form a single theme, the tenacious defence of ancient rights and the ruthless extension of possession and power. The first and central element is the deliberate maintenance and even the aggravation of a state of anarchy within the realm, as the basic condition for the deployment and the increment of their feudal privileges. The hard cores of these privileges or 'rights' are recounted in the processes of the last great conspiracy of the barons, that which was brought to a bloody end in the Hall of the Barons of the Castelnuovo: they are the rights of anarchism: the right to maintain their fortified 'castelli' and thus to exercise the direct authority of force in their domains; the right over the persons of their vassals, of *ad hoc* taxation, or better, exaction, and so forth, and they demanded above all their 'pristine liberty', that is their primeval anarchy. The nearest thing to a pronouncement of policy which might be extracted from their expressions was the proposal of the Sanseverini and the Orsini so to divide the power of the rival claimants to the monarchy (Angevine and Durazzo), that each might preserve what he held, but gain no more, and thus to insure baronial control of all that remained; or the maxim expressed by the brothers Petrucci in the last rebellion, to the effect that so long as the king was distracted and preoccupied by wars and troubles, the barons could hope to continue 'secure and prosperous'.[1]

This policy of sustained anarchy, if policy it can be called, was directed toward two adversaries, toward the two centres whence a restrictive principle of order might conceivably emerge: the monarchy and the vassalage (it would be but another misnomer, Croce notes, to speak in this context, of the 'people'). Croce has already enumerated the difficulties under which the monarchy laboured. All of these, it remains to note, were weapons prompt to the hands and designs of the barons. By their adroit employment, they were able, not only to prevent any effective extension of the monarch's power, but themselves to usurp a considerable portion of it. Their purpose, so to say, was to keep the monarchy constantly off balance. By dint of constant threat of conspiracy and rebellion they wrung from the king concessions which in effect dissolved the ancient constitution of the realm. This dissolution was, in Croce's view, ultimately beneficial; but this effect cannot be ascribed to the counsel or intention of the barons. And its immediate noxious effect, the frustration of the emergence of a national consciousness, in the context, outweighed

[1] SRN, 67.

the ultimate good. Among these concessions were freedom of marriage, inheritance, limitation of the power of regal magistrates (which had been so important in securing unity and organization under the Norman rule), of the regal administrative officials, and of the obligations to military service. The effect of all was the same: to prevent the monarchy from becoming a centre upon which all elements of the realm might converge.

The attitude or policy of the barons toward their vassals may be said to have been guided by a political instinct which saw in the wretched populace the possible ally of the monarch. The legendary cruelty of the barons' conduct, though not without considerable documentation, may to a great degree be discounted, since, as Croce notes, master and serf did reach an effective *modus vivendi*, based on reciprocal need.[1] The guiding motive of the lord's conduct cannot, however, be mistaken; it was to keep the vassal safely within his own power, an exclusive object of exploitation, as it were. To this end his operative axiom was, the poorer the vassal, the harder he worked and the easier for him to resist political temptation. He was loaded down with taxes and exactions of every kind, and constricted by such economic measures as those which forbade him to offer his harvest for sale until the lord's had been disposed of, or which commanded him to sell it to the lord at the latter's price. To the same end, the barons clung tenaciously to their rights of jurisdiction as the surest way of keeping the vassal within their own power and out of contact with the king and his justice, so that between populace and monarch no vital rapport could be established which might have political fruit. The whole position of the barons was strengthened, finally, by the fact that there existed no mediatorial class which could operate to relieve the great, categorical distinctions of that society. The class which was in time to take up this function, the 'ceto medio', of which Croce speaks, had scarcely begun to emerge and to achieve self-consciousness.

In this situation, Croce remarks, it is necessary to look away from the monarchy in its purely political character and to attend rather to its educative and ameliorative force.[2] Though impotent to effect an immediate improvement, he discovers, the monarchy of this first phase of the autonomous life of the realm was not without importance and effect for the civil education of the Neapolitan people. In this direction, it showed itself both active and effective, and though its efforts were not to manifest their chief fruits for a long time, it

[1] SRN, 61-2.   [2] SRN, 74 sqq.

presently becomes clear, in Croce's opinion, that the national consciousness, however limited, which Naples was finally to achieve
received here its first impulse and form. The educative work of the
monarchy lay principally in its remote preparation of the 'ceto
medio'. This it did in the first place by the support which it gave to
the communes in their struggle with the barons. The growth of the
communes in southern Italy was slow; at every stage of their development, however, they opposed an effective limit to the expansive
tendencies of the barons and even more importantly provided the
environment within which the 'ceto medio', destined to be the real
organ of national consciousness and the real carrier of national character, might emerge and grow. The communal form had its origin
in the simple administrative needs of the peasants, such, perhaps, as
strategy for meeting the exactions imposed by the barons. From this
it grew, very gradually, into a more regular mode of organization,
exercising functions of debate and administration, and within its own
framework developed the distinction between the middle class and
the workers and artisans. While the monarchy did not give the
initial impetus to the formation of the commune, it looked with
great favour upon this social and administrative organ and endowed
it with many privileges and granted it many concessions. When it
lay within its power, it accepted the communes into the royal
demesne. The growth of the communal power was especially con-
spicuous under Ferrante I of Aragon, who by his pragmatics of 1466
and 1484 granted the communes the right to sell their produce without regard to baronial restrictions and abolished enclosures. During
his reign the commune achieved again something of its pristine
stature.[1] In addition to favouring of the communes, the monarchy
also encouraged trade and commerce.[2] Its success did not extend to
the actual establishment of an industrial or commercial class, for
commerce remained for the greatest part in foreign hands. Charles of
Anjou sought to introduce the 'art of wool', and this art, as well as
the 'art of silk', was reintroduced by Ferrante the Old, who established their respective guilds and endowed them with privileges and
charters, on the model of the guilds under Louis XI of France. With
the administrative life of the communes, with the freer flow of trade
and the encouragement of industry, with minimal guarantees of
civil liberties against baronial encroachment, there began the preparation of the middle class, the class which was by degrees to displace
the feudal possessors and which in conjunction with the monarchy

[1] SRN, 78–9.   [2] SRN, 80–1.

was to express the national consciousness and the common good of the realm.

This preparation included another dimension upon which Croce in his ethico-political scale of values lays the greatest stress. This was the awakening of literature and the beginning of an intellectual tradition. The culture which had flourished under the Normans had for the most part died out or been continued elsewhere. Continuity of intellectual life was sustained principally in the area of law which was nourished in its turn by the activity of the courts and the magistracy. Mediaeval scholasticism, which reached its highest expression in the works of a Neapolitan, St. Thomas Aquinas, was not of its nature such as to foster a national consciousness. But the court of King Robert saw the first stirrings of humanism in the south, where Petrarch had both admirers and imitators. It was in the reign of Ferrante that a truly indigenous literature arose, flowering in Sannazaro, in Pontano and Gravina, and finding its publicists in Caraffa-Caracciolo and Galateo.[1] There was about this humanism the mark of a genuine intellectual ferment, pregnant with political and social values and it was from the movement and tradition here begun that Bruno, Campanella and Vico were later to emerge. The seat of this new culture was the city of Naples. The city was itself in a sense a creation of the monarchy. Under Ferrante of Aragon the future seemed heavy with promise, despite the darkness of the present moment; under the aegis of the monarchy the realm seemed to have set its feet on the path toward national consciousness and authentic historical existence.

Yet at this juncture, the realm was to be confronted by a crisis in which its basic and ultimately fatal weakness was starkly revealed, and from which it could find salvation only by the surrender of its autonomous state, the first of a series of such acts, by which it hopes to find its life by losing it. This crisis was precipitated most ostensibly by the conspiracy of Lacedonia. This spectacle of the conspiring barons exploded in an instant the image which had begun to form in the mind of Europe of a strong and robust realm and revealed the profound source of its weakness. As always, when the real weakness of the apparently strong stands suddenly revealed, adversaries arose on every hand. France, invoking ancient pretensions, was the first to move. Her designs aroused in turn both the protective and the predatory instincts of Spain, and into her power the realm was constrained to pass, to become a territorial and administrative part

1 SRN, 81–2.

of the Spanish empire and thus to lose the autonomy of the first phase of its national existence. A second phase was thus opened, the phase of the Spanish regency.[1]

The Spanish vice-regency over the Neapolitan realm endured in all over two centuries, from 1503 to 1707, and must from the ethico-political point of view be considered a basic formative principle in the history of the city and the realm. From the very nature of the case, a vice-regency might scarcely be expected to have as its conscious purpose the fostering, in a subject area, of a national consciousness which might prepare it for autonomous historical existence. Nor did the Spanish vice-regency depart from the norm in such instances; it ruled Naples primarily in the interest of Spain and the empire. Within the wide political strategy of Spain, Naples was a source principally of imperial prestige and of political and military leverage, and was exploited to these ends. At the same time, however, as Croce notes, that principle which Vico called providence, Hegel the astuteness of reason and still others the heterogeneity of ends, was operative here, as everywhere in history. The Spanish policy, though directed to purposes of its own, contributed substantially to the preparation of a national consciousness within the realm. In pursuit of its own purposes, it was led to destroy and to remove some of the major impediments which in the past had frustrated that process, and to initiate movements which directly fostered the conditions under which a national consciousness might emerge.

Two problems confronted the Spanish power when it assumed dominance over the realm. It had, in the first place, to guarantee the territorial integrity of the realm.[2] This integrity had been threatened during the 'time of troubles' preceding the vice-regency, when, as a result of the conspiracy of Lacedonia, the inner weakness of the realm was laid bare and greedy eyes were turned upon it from many quarters of Europe. Spanish power succeeded in re-establishing it by a series of military and diplomatic victories which included the repulsion of the French forces by Gonzalo de Córdoba, the rapid campaign against Pope Paul IV and the Duke of Guise, and the defeat of the French efforts to disembark their forces on the shores of the bay of Naples. By the league of Cambrai, the Venetians were forced to restore the areas which they occupied along the coasts of Puglia, and the Turkish threat was repulsed at Tripoli, at Malta, and finally at Lepanto. The realm of Naples, for so long the theatre of wars of pretension and the victim of foreign invasions, entered upon

[1] SRN, 93.   [2] SRN, 95.

a period of security and peace which was to endure a century and a half.[1] In all of these enterprises, the purposes of Spain and the empire transcended the interests of Naples; at the same time, however, they secured for Naples two basic conditions for the formation of a national consciousness, an undoubted territorial configuration and a long period of peace.

The moral responsibility for the failure of Naples to achieve this national consciousness during its first period of autonomous life had been laid by Croce principally at the door of the barons.[2] The baronage constituted the second of the problems immediately confronting the Spanish rule, and, acceding to Machiavelli's dictum [3] it addressed itself directly to the reduction of the political potentiality of the barons. The baronial forces, at the inception of the Spanish rule, were divided into two factions, that adhering to the house of Aragon, the last kings of Naples, and that aligning itself, in the name of an ancient fidelity to the Angevines, with the French pretensions. Spain dealt with each in turn, and astutely. The first it absorbed, by the strategy of the marriage of the Aragon pretender, Ferrante, Duke of Calabria, to the widow of Ferdinand the Catholic; the second, after the defeat of the French forces, was gradually dissipated and absorbed, the chief barons one by one coming to terms with the Spanish power, which enlisted their services in administration and in war.[4] The last effort of the barons to effect their traditional policy of conspiracy and rebellion took place during the campaign against the French under Lautrec, during the years 1527–8; aligning themselves with the French forces, some of the Neapolitan barons participated in the siege of Naples. With the end of the war, however, the vengeance visited upon them was swift and decisive. More than one suffered death and confiscation; their lands were redistributed among the Spanish and Italian captains of Charles V. After that, baronial rebellion was sporadic, individualistic, without political effect, and invariably repressed with decision. The dominant figure of this last phase of the baronial prepotence was that of the Sanseverini, dukes of Salerno, whose story Croce had narrated at length in another place.[5]

The Spanish effort against the baronage was not limited, however, to the extinction of its political power; it envisaged its social transformation, its reduction to the status of subjects and to an equal level with all other social classes. With the destruction of the political

[1] SRN, 95–6.   [2] SRN, 61 sqq., and *supra*.   [3] SRN, 59.
[4] SRN, 96–7.   [5] SLN, ch. I.

potential the military power of the barons was absorbed into that of
Spain, as under the policy of the viceroy Monterrey the barons were
forced to carry a proportionate part of the general burden of the
Spanish military enterprises. The vice-regal order compelling the
barons to live in the city cut them off effectively from those 'castelli'
which had been the eagles' nests of their independence, the seats from
which they could exercise a tyrannical local jurisdiction, immune
from appeal to a higher power. Their pretensions to ancient rights of
sanctuary and jurisdiction were systematically disabused, especially
under the viceroy Toledo. Deprived of these outlets and stays, constrained to a limited urban existence, the barons whom Machiavelli
had stigmatized as impervious to all culture, now began to exhibit
another division of their forces. A portion of them surrendered to a
life of dissolute luxury, becoming transformed from savage tyrants
and warriors into that type of the 'buon signore' which Croce had
discussed elsewhere [1] and which was of such importance in the social
psychology of the realm. Another, and more important section,
utilizing the same conditions of leisure, wealth and urban restriction
began to draw close to the emerging elements of the 'ceto medio', to
which, presently, it was to contribute the most energetic, aggressive
and enlightened leadership. And as it was in this 'ceto medio' that,
in Croce's view, the national consciousness was to reach its highest
expression in the realm, the policy of Spain again is seen to have
effected results which were beyond its intention, providing for that
'ceto medio' its greatest resource of leadership.[2]

The transformation of the baronage was but one dimension of
the social transformation of the realm effected under Spanish rule.
In its campaign against the barons, part of the Spanish strategy was
to seek aid and leverage in other elements of the population, and to
strengthen these. To this end, it fostered the 'middle classes', the professional and legal groups, merchants and manufacturers to a degree
beyond anything experienced before.[3] Ultimately this was to prove
of the greatest importance for the formation of a national consciousness, although the rising middle class tended in the first instance to
nullify its own effectiveness by seeking to identify itself with the
nobility through the purchase of fiefs and the assumption of titles, at
times to a point of extravagance and vanity. This process had been
rendered easier for them by the very concessions concerning transfer
and inheritance of properties and titles which the barons had wrung
from the monarchs, and this tendency constituted a transitional

[1] Cf. *supra*. [2] SRN, 99 sqq., 109 sqq., 117 sqq. [3] SRN, 118.

phase in the psychological history of its own character, as it sought to give meaning and stability to its new position by appropriating once-potent symbols.[1] A further impediment to the efficacy of the new middle class is to be found in the fact that the vice-regency while fostering its growth, provided it no real arena of political action and no real organs of political expression. These had gradually to be developed or conquered. The formation of the class itself was the substantial achievement and in happier circumstances it was quickly to show its power to generate its own effective organs. Nor was the tendency to associate itself with the discredited nobility an unmitigated vanity; this amalgamation was to impart a particular character to the 'ceto medio' in the kingdom, and above all was to prevent it from becoming that wholly economic group, with its corresponding set of ideas and motivations, that the middle class actually became in other countries. This combination of the middle class and the nobility, as has already been suggested, was in time to prove the most powerful organ of national consciousness and of enlightened social and political action which the realm was to develop.[2]

At the same time, however, the vice-regency tended to seek leverage in another element of the population which was to prove less amenable to any process of incivilment and was to constitute throughout the subsequent history of the realm an explosive principle. This was the 'proletarian' population, especially that extreme 'basso popolo' whose formation, we have seen,[3] had been one aspect of the growth of the city of Naples. This element of the 'lazzari' was to play an important role at every juncture in that history, but at no time was it to show itself capable of becoming an organ of national consciousness. For the purposes of the vice-regency, this section of the population, in both its urban and its rural branches, served as a foil against which to project the baronial pretensions it was determined to destroy. A taste of the volatile and explosive character of this dimension of the population, and of the uses to which it could be put by determined minorities, was offered by the revolution of Masaniello.[4] It cannot be said, however, that the vice-regency profited from this tragi-comic experience, for it continued to favour the populace as against the nobles, despite the fact that in this juncture the nobility had demonstrated its growing good sense by taking the side of the vice-regency and of Spain. The situation was aggravated by the failure of the vice-regency, in this instance as in the instance of the 'ceto medio', to provide expressive organs, a theatre of action and

[1] SRN, 120.　　[2] Ibid.　　[3] Cf. *supra*; SRN, 121 sqq.　　[4] SRN, 130-1.

direction to the forces it evoked. While using the populace for its own purposes, it made no concerted effort to relieve the social and political conditions in which the populace found itself, nor to educate it to any political consciousness beyond that of mob action. But this near-sightedness of the Spanish policy was not a flaw; it was simply that policy itself; educated beyond that point, the populace could no longer have been the instrument which that policy needed. Even in view of this obvious limitation, the social transformations which took place under the regency, considered from the ethico-political point of view and under the specific aspect of the formation of a national consciousness able to sustain an autonomous historical exist-ence, were beneficial without qualification. However much might be desired, what was accomplished was of indisputable value.[1]

The great failure under the vice-regency (and it was not the failure of the vice-regency, but of the Neapolitan people, for the vice-regency fulfilled its own idea adequately) was the failure to develop political and social criticism, the kind of criticism which is the indispensable condition of growth in national consciousness and which is the seminal moment of ethico-political life. In this respect the Neapolitans showed themselves still under the thrall of the myths of their national greatness. The necessary criticism was thus replaced by a vapid optimism, as Croce writes.[2] Reading the best of the his-torians of the time, Summonte for example (Pietro Summonte, 1453–1526), one receives the impression that Naples was the most beautiful realm in Europe, that it was an Eldorado, rich in every fruit of the earth and every delight of nature, inhabited by the clever-est and happiest of peoples, enjoying the government of sovereigns of superhuman power through ministers endowed with prudence equally exalted, surrounded by a nobility exhibiting every generous virtue. These same writers, apparently without awareness of the contradiction, intersperse these arcadian descriptions with a litany of sorrows and horrors, of acts of tyranny and brigandage, of con-spiracies and rebellions. So long as this state of mind persisted, Croce notes,[3] any movement of national life or of social reform must remain in the realm of mere velleity; for the effective sign, he writes, of solicitude for the common good is not complacency and optimism, but trepidation and pessimism; an active, not a passive pessimism, to be sure, a criticism both concrete and mordant, but criticism and pessimism none the less.[4] Such criticism, however, is not partheno-genetic; it needs cross fertilization with the thought and the experience

[1] SRN, 122 sqq.   [2] SRN, 147.   [3] SRN, 148.   [4] Ibid.

of the world beyond the narrow limits of time and place. Even in this respect the presence of the vice-regency was beneficial. The long peace which it ensured at home made it possible for the Neapolitan 'ceto medio' gradually to establish a network of contacts and relations with the world beyond the confines of the realm, the learned world, the cultural world and the world of affairs, and thus gradually to formulate the criteria by which life at home might be measured. That movement of cultural and intellectual renovation at Naples which the Abbate Galiani was to call a 'renaissance', and which had as its flower the work of such men as Vico and Giannone, transpired under the aegis of the vice-regency, and it is in this movement that Croce discovers the spiritual springs of modern Italy, as when he writes that the origins of the Risorgimento are not to be found in 1848, 1820, 1799, but in 1670.

Such criticism was not, Croce notes, entirely absent, even then; it was merely in the minority, repressed and unheeded. Proof of this he discovers in the writings of Antonio Serra.[1] Almost alone among the writers of his time, he exhibits that labour of spirit out of which historical renovations are born. While in prison for political reasons he composed and published his essay on economics, with special reference to the Realm of Naples, which is his chief merit. Whatever the status of the work as an essay in economics, Croce finds that, as a piece of political criticism, it is the most trenchant and realistic to be encountered in the entire literature of the period. Serra systematically sets about the dissipation of the illusions which held even such gifted minds as Summonte in thrall. To the illusion of the natural wealth of the realm, he opposes the fact of a Naples poor in *situs*, which could not attract trade to its shores, poor in industries, poorer in the natural talent and industriousness of its inhabitants, poor finally in the form of government under which it lived, which did not and could not have the good of that realm principally and directly at heart. Serra's criticism was read correctly by his enemies; for they saw in it a call, however veiled, to a new life of national independence. Nor can his criticism be said to have been without effect, despite its immediate sterility; its efficaciousness lay simply in the fact of its existence, which was conclusive proof that the springs of political criticism were not entirely choked in the realm.

There transpires, as a consequence, in Croce's view, a subtle shift in the centre of the life of the realm during this period, a shift most important for the future, when the realm would again embark upon

[1] SRN, 148 sqq.

a course of independent life. While the vice-regency remains the ostensible centre of the life of the realm, its real centre is to be found rather in the cultural process by which a class of persons capable of this necessary criticism and correlative action was gradually forming. The initiation of this process can even be fixed with a certain accuracy, for the return of Tommaso Cornelio to Naples, bringing with him both his rich experience in the schools of the north and a wealth of books, including the works of philosophers and scientists, who in other parts of Italy and beyond the Alps were transforming European culture is the symbol of this new era generally accepted by all its historians.[1]

The character of this cultural renaissance has been described and analysed both by Croce and others, and fixed most clearly perhaps by Nicolini in his historical commentary to the *New Science* of Giambattista Vico.[2] In the present context it is necessary to note only its political efficacy. This lay precisely in the critical spirit which it engendered. Inevitably, this criticism, no matter what its original point of departure, whether in the subtleties of Cartesian mathematics and physics or in the anti-Cartesianism of Vico, converged upon a single issue, the ethico-political. The proof of this is to be seen above all in the work which, with the *New Science* of Vico, must be looked upon as the finest fruit of this cultural movement, the *Civil History* of Pietro Giannone,[3] a work in which Fonseca-Pimentel recognizes the first voice of the cult of liberty.[4]

With this cultural renaissance and with the formulation of the ethico-political criticism with which it was pregnant the era of the vice-regency was over, not perhaps in fact, but certainly in idea. For the fruit of that civil criticism was inevitably the desire for political and national independence. It was, consequently, the remote but effective preparation for the restitution of the Realm.[5] The manner in which this restitution was to take place was necessarily obscure; the events which accompanied and conditioned it may have the appearance of extreme contingency, which Croce notes when he remarks that the realm was restored principally through the determination of one woman Elisabetta Farnese to see her son upon a throne.[6] In fact, however, the possibility of this new phase of life lay within the Neapolitan people, or rather in the spiritual disposition of

---

[1] SRN, 155 sqq., cf. F. Nicolini, *La Giovinezza di G. B. Vico*, Bari, 1932.
[2] F. Nicolini, *Commento Storico alla Seconda Scienza Nuova*, Roma, 1950–2.
[3] *Storia Civile del Regno di Napoli*, 1723.   [4] RN'99 *sub nomine*.
[5] SRN, 157 sqq.   [6] SRN, 181.

that portion of the people in which the power of ethico-political criticism had been reborn.

In a certain sense, the actual restitution of the independence of the Kingdom of Naples, under a prince of the Spanish house of Bourbon, was a contingent and subsidiary event. It was brought about directly by agencies other than those which were taking shape within the realm during the long peace of the regency. And it cannot be taken to be the actual rebirth of the kingdom. This had already taken place, as Fonseca-Pimentel was to write, when the growing power of self-criticism had reached effective expression in the work of Giannone and other writers of like stature giving evidence, as she phrased it, that a 'new nation had been born'. The quality of the new sovereign, however, was of crucial importance; and it was the great good fortune of Naples, that this quality proved to be remarkably open and liberal, and ready to co-operate with the aspirations of that 'new nation'. Thus was born that union between the monarchy and the 'ceto medio', which, as Croce had discerned in his earlier studies on the Neapolitan revolution, had been the strength and the hope of the restored independence. In this happy conjunction, the true motive principle was of course the 'ceto medio'; here it was that the critical faculty and the will to progress and reform resided. The role of the monarchy was not initiative but co-operative and the limits under which it operated were clearly marked, above all by its radical conviction of its own absolute character.

The strength of the 'ceto medio' of the 'new nation' lay above all in the critical faculty which it had developed and in the ethico-political will which this faculty in turn had generated. Under another aspect, however, a main source of its actual strength lay in its social composition.[1] While it might appear, on the surface, a minority, the 'ceto medio' in virtue of its social composition was truly representative of the nation. In the process of its formation many of the older lines of demarcation had been obliterated and with them the older tensions. It represented, in the first place, the amalgamation of the emergent intellectual class with that section of the nobility which, as a result of urbanization under the regency, had turned its leisure toward study and public service. With this basic amalgam there associated itself a large portion of the clergy, especially that portion which was able to make the careful distinction between the legitimate spiritual authority of the Church, which in the most Catholic realm of Naples was never seriously disputed, and

[1] SRN, 176.

the political and feudal pretensions which tended to mask themselves under that authority. The only portion of the nation excluded from the composition of the 'ceto medio' was the 'people'. This was not an explicit but a purely circumstantial and historical exclusion; it stemmed from the historical incapacity of the populace to rise to the level of the apprehension of the common good; an incapacity which could be remedied, as the leaders of this new national life realized, only by a long and difficult programme of education. However ardently this political education of the people, with a view to their eventual participation in the national life, might be desired it could be undertaken only by a nation which was already well established in its independent life and had, therefore, to wait on the accomplishment of more urgent tasks. Meanwhile there was consolation in the reflection that this whole effort toward the re-establishment of the kingdom and the reform of its institutions was actually, if obliquely, the initial phase of such an educational programme and that the people must eventually be the beneficiaries, if not the agents, of that reconstituted national life. For this reason, the 'ceto medio' could be certain of representing the nation and from this certainty draw the confidence needed for its work. In no sense could it be thought of as a class in the separatist and particularist sense of that term. It was the working organ of the nation.[1]

The monarchy, it was suggested before, had as an intrinsic limit to its mode of co-operation with the 'ceto medio' the sense of its own transcendence. Nor was it any part of the programme of the directive class to challenge this conviction. The reforms envisaged had not, as Croce indicated, in the first instance included even independence. Still less did they embrace constitutional reform, the restoration of ancient parliaments and procedures. The 'ceto medio' was content with absolute monarchy, so long as its co-operation and benevolence could be assured, for such monarchy promised the stability needed for the work of reform, while premature attempts at constitutional change must simply add a further element of tension to a situation already difficult.[2]

It was a mark of the political sagacity of the 'ceto medio' and of its sense of history that it envisaged immediately those reforms which would, on the one hand, strengthen the autonomy of the realm with respect to other powers and, on the other, contribute to its inner homogeneity and cohesion. Ecclesiastical reform became one of its first objectives. In this undertaking, so delicate and potentially

[1] SRN, 192 sqq.   [2] SRN, 180 sqq.

explosive, it displayed its political wisdom most clearly. Its pro-gramme was untainted by any of those elements of 'Josephism', as it was later to be called in another context, that is, by the temptation to mask laicist usurpation under the name of ecclesiastical reform. On the contrary, its whole programme was based on a delicate discern-ment of the diversity of the two powers and the unalterably lay character of the modern state. It anticipated, or foreshadowed, that delicate dualism which was to inspire Cavour in the Risorgimento. The ideal envisaged was a true pluralism, in which the state and the church stood vis-à-vis, with spheres of activity authentically dis-cerned and distinguished, yet able to co-operate because of a sense of the more basic unity of the nation in which both moved and worked. Even more urgent were its demands for revisions of feudal law, an immemorial spring of the internecine strife in the kingdom, burdened with numerous glaring anachronisms. In this area the criticism of the 'ceto medio' produced a masterpiece of legislative writing, relevant not only to the problems of the realm, but to the jurisprudence of the whole of Europe and even to the philosophy of law, the *Science of Legislation* of Gaetano Filangieri, a work which, in Napoleon's view, lifted the writer to the highest ranks of juris-prudentialists and which exercised a clearly discernible influence on the *Code Napoleon*.[1] Closely connected with the demands for reforms of feudal law were those for juridical improvement; the system of the courts which had been developed along with feudal law offered little of that regularity, and few of those guarantees of justice which an enlightened jurisprudence envisaged. Agricultural, military, educational reforms pressed close after in the mind of the 'ceto medio'. Viewed singly or together, these reforms were limited; equally limited was the procedure by which they were to be secured, the long and difficult one of presentation to the royal will, which alone could execute them. Proposals and method had one advantage however; they were realistic and attainable. And they converged on a great central good, the greater articulation and coherence of the internal structure of the nation, resting upon the realistic appraisal of its resources, both human and natural, as well as of the problems with which it was confronted.[2]

So closely associated with this strengthening of the inner life of the realm as to become almost inseparable was that other desire to increase the prestige of Naples in the international arena. This pro-gramme was happily initiated by the repulse of Austrian arms in

[1] *La Scienza della Legislazione*, 1780. [2] SRN, 183 sqq.

1744; though carried out with the help of Spain this was a Neapolitan effort.[1] It was followed up by a vigorous diplomatic effort, which was materially aided by the quality of its agents, drawn mostly from the ranks of the enlightened nobility which the king was able to send abroad. Its international stature was further increased when it freed itself from the last vestiges of Spanish tutelage and under Acton and other ministers undertook a more liberal policy orientated toward England and Austria.[2] Within the Italian peninsula, the new kingdom could move easily as among peers, with only the growing prestige of the kings of Sardinia to raise a cloud on its horizon.[3] At this juncture, so far as any project for the unification of the peninsula could be entertained, it might well have been concluded that the natural centre of such an effort must be Naples; but such ideas were still far in the future.

The atmosphere of the realm, consequently, in the last half of the eighteenth century was one of optimism. And it seemed a justifiable optimism on the testimony both of those who knew the state of the nation from within, and of those who viewed it from without. From within there is the testimony of Galiani and Cuoco, neither of whom was swayed by any congenital sentiment. From without, there is the testimony of the many travellers and visitors who recorded their impressions of the realm in books and articles. The impression was almost unrelievedly happy and promising. Not that evils and poverty did not exist; they did. But there existed in their midst the will to overcome them, and the creative effort to replace them by conditions more commensurate with the dignity of human life. In a word, the atmosphere was one in which it was clear that the national will and heart had been awakened. It was a moral triumph, the moral effort of a nation to create itself out of its own meagre resources in a form which must command the respect of others and satisfy its own critical intelligence. Beside this fact, the recounting of evils is secondary; for they are but the matter upon which that ethico-political will works and in the conquest of which its efficaciousness is realized.

It was upon this scene of justified optimism, at a moment when, for the first time in its history, the realm of Naples felt the groundswell of an authentic national consciousness rising within it, that the revolution of 1799 broke. The internal structure of this event, the contradictions with which it was laden, the illusions of which it saw the formation and the dissipation, and its impact upon the growing

---

[1] SRN, 201.   [2] SRN, 193.   [3] SRN, 201.

national consciousness of the realm, have all been studied by Croce, and formed, as a matter of fact, as we have already suggested, the point of departure for his wider interest in the history of the realm. In the steps of Cuoco, and also in the service of his belief that history is the history of reason, Croce endeavours to find the inner necessity of this event, its psychological and historical inevitability, so to say. The passage in which this attempt is made will scarcely recommend itself as one of the most brilliant in his narrative. His conclusion is that as a matter of fact no other path offered itself to the intellectual classes of Naples, when confronted by the French Revolution, but to become, as they did, 'jacobins'. For they recognized in the ideas which inspired the revolution, the ideas which they themselves had come to embrace, carried now to their 'logical' extremes. Why it was necessary at this moment, to embrace these ideas in this extreme form, when there was at work in the Neapolitan consciousness critical forces which were capable of warning of the results and of the intrinsic dangers of such extremism, Croce does not make clear, not even as relatively clear as Cuoco, who himself had lived through that ambiguity and had recognized it for what it was, simply a spiritual orgy.[1]

What Croce does make clear, however, is the manner in which this revolutionary experience altered the course and the direction of Neapolitan history, or more precisely, the direction it was presumptively taking under the aegis of monarchical and liberal co-operation. This course was now determined or marked out by the character which each of the elements of Neapolitan society had revealed in itself under the strain of that revolutionary experience. And in this sense the revolution may be said to have worked a real service in the history of Naples, for it served to dissipate an illusory calm, to lay bare the basic antagonisms, and to make it morally necessary that the future be worked out in such a way that these particular antagonisms would be eliminated. From that experience, as had been seen, only the middle class, the 'ceto medio', emerged triumphant. But its triumph did not consist in the realization of those projects in whose name it had worked the revolution. Its triumph meant that it alone of all the elements of Neapolitan society emerged from that experience with the moral force to redeem itself, to criticize its own action, and to direct its ethico-political will to the prosecution of its basic purpose under altered conditions. The monarchy, on the other hand, stood revealed, as the consequence of

[1] SRN, 212 sqq.

that experience, in its essential character: as essentially unable to exercise that historical self-criticism, and hence as unable to fulfil the promise it had offered; by this same token, that promise itself stood revealed as spurious and unauthentic. Again, it is a quality of the ethico-political will which is revealed. There was no will in the Neapolitan monarchy able to lift it above its own dynastic interests.[1] For this reason, the course which opened into the future was clear. It could only consist in the conflict *à outrance* between these elements which before had appeared to co-operate so effectively. And because the effective ethico-political will was clearly with the 'ceto medio' it was also clear that the elimination of the monarchy was inevitable, simply because it had eliminated itself morally from history by its reaction to the revolution. But it must be made clear here that by monarchy is intended not the monarchical principle, but the particular monarchy which ruled in Naples. The subsequent history consequently is a record of this conflict; but more importantly still, it is a record of the attempt on the part of the 'ceto medio' to find the answer to the very difficult question of whether it had within itself the moral and historical will to give to the Neapolitan realm that autonomous historical existence toward which it aspired. And in this struggle the 'ceto medio' found itself confronted by a monarchy not only in alliance with the populace but itself become plebeian.

The real terms of this coming conflict, and the course which it must inevitably take, were temporarily clouded and veiled by the interlude of the Napoleonic occupation and the Murat monarchy. In this period, the erstwhile jacobins among the Neapolitans lent their support to the Murat monarchy because of the elements of enlightenment which it exhibited.[2] But the real interest of this period lay not here in this political action, but elsewhere in the education which the 'ceto medio' was undergoing. This was an education in exile. Driven for the most part from the realm, its members were brought into contact with a whole world of new ideas, of new facts and of new possibilities. It was at this time that the double path of their political and historical education revealed itself. In the first place, it was during this life in exile that that self-criticism matured, which enabled them to free themselves from the incubus of jacobinism and to formulate that position of moderate liberalism which so much more truly expressed their sense both of ideals and of history and which Croce has so richly documented in his studies of such figures as the

[1] SRN, 244 sqq.   [2] SRN, 228 sqq.

family of the Poerio.[1] In the second place, these exiles were brought effectively into contact with the great new idea which had then for the first time taken effective form and will, the idea of the unification of Italy and its total liberation from all foreign rule.[2] And it was this second dimension of their political education which opened up before the chastened 'ceto medio' of Naples the path which really lay before them, a path which could not under one aspect but be dolorous while under another it was necessarily a 'royal road' in Vico's phrase, since it led directly to the historical goal for which they laboured. This was the path which led by way of the dissolution of the autonomy of the Neapolitan realm to its reincarnation as a part of the new national Italy. Between the revolution and that goal, however, lay the difficult path of continued revolution.

The first of these efforts was the revolution of 1820.[3] To understand its character, Croce believes, it is necessary to trace its background in the period of Napoleonic rule, to which Naples had acceded, but always on a tentative basis. The great value of the Napoleonic decade was its introduction of constitutional ideas into the realm; and with these, the many concrete social, economic and judiciary reforms which it had effected.[4] The return of the Bourbons at the end of that decade, consequently, was an occasion of the greatest trepidation. The Bourbon programme envisaged an immediate curtailment of all projects for reform, as well as the indictment of the constitutional principle itself. The revolution of 1820 was therefore, in its immediate form, constitutional, that is to say, it was the effort to exact from the restored Bourbon monarchy the constitutional guarantees. And, on the whole, this revolution promised success, for distasteful as this proposal was to the monarchy, it was entirely without an internal basis for resistance to these demands. The real cause, the only true cause in Croce's words,[5] however, of its failure, was the intervention of Austria, which rallied to the support of the monarchy, and while cautioning it to prudence and moderation, counselled it against the concessions it was about to make and offered it the great leverage of its armed support against these demands. At the same time, however, Croce suggests that there was another and a deeper reason for its failure. It did not demand enough; its aims were too limited, its vision too circumscribed. The reason for this lay in the fact that it was an old man's revolution.[6] It lacked new blood almost entirely and was the work rather of the superstites of

[1] Cf. UFP passim.   [2] SRN, 229.   [3] SRN, 235 sqq.
[4] SRN, 230.   [5] SRN, 235.   [6] SRN, 237, 229.

the revolution of 1799, who had profited to a degree by their political education and the Neapolitanic experience. These men were not closed to the wave of the future; that is, to the idea of an Italy united and free; on the contrary, it was they who provided the matrix for the formation of that idea. But they lacked the effective will to attempt it. And yet, once envisaged, that was the only logical goal of any political effort. For this reason, consequently, the revolution of 1820 can be said to have failed for more reasons than one. While the intervention of Austria was perhaps the immediate agency of its frustration, the deeper source was this spiritual and ethico-political limitation. And this second was a fault which could not be remedied merely by wishing it; there was necessary the formation of a new cultural ambient, of ideas and of will, which could effectively support this ideal. And even while this revolution of 1820 was running its ineffectual course, Croce indicates, that ambient was in process of formation, throughout Italy, and in Naples itself.

The key to this cultural renovation was the eclipse of illuminism and the rise of the romantic spirit in Italy and in the Neapolitan realm.[1] This cultural renovation was the work, as might have been suspected, not of those superstites who had undertaken the revolution of 1820, but of the generation which succeeded them, their own sons and grandsons. These had accompanied their fathers into exile, whether into other parts of Italy or into foreign lands, and there had shared their education. But this education, in the case of the younger men, went a step beyond that of their fathers. While the latter submitted for the most part simply to a modification of their earlier illuministic conditioning, the former, the young men, attached themselves rather to the new ideas which were everywhere on the rise in Europe and these were the ideas of romanticism.

The most radical, the seminal idea of romanticism, in Croce's view, and that which opposes it most clearly to illuminism, is its view of history, and this was an idea of German provenance. It came to Naples by way of France and of Lombardy. It was supported by a new idea of philosophy, opposed to the earlier sensism, and found expression in the new romantic literature of every land which it touched. In Naples it is indissolubly linked with such names as Cuoco and Galuppi, Troya and Tosti.[2] The force of the romantic ideas was universal, cutting across lines of demarcation which illuminism had set up, so that it found expression in a Catholic liberalism, a fact of the greatest importance since it was thus to bring into the whole

[1] SRN, 238 sqq.   [2] SRN, 229.

effort of Italian nationalism the religious unity of the people. Its effect above all was to be felt in the political sphere, for it was through the ideas of romanticism that Italy was enabled to pass beyond the political conceptions which had hitherto limited and defined her political will—those of a reformism under the aegis of an illuminist and benevolent monarchy, or of a cosmopolitan republicanism— and rise to the national idea. And in Naples this new idea was to find expression in a work which for its historical effect was to rival the history of Giannone, the *Storia del Reame di Napoli* of Pietro Colletta. With the birth of the national idea, the future was born and the destiny of Naples and of the whole of Italy clearly indicated.

Within the confines of Naples, the force of this idea defined itself anew with reference to the restored Bourbon monarchy. The final decision by which that monarchy eliminated itself from history was its rejection of the national idea. It was conceivable, within the whole picture, and when the particular character of the Neapolitan monarchy was for the moment held in abeyance, that the leadership in the national movement might fall to the kings of Naples. This idea had its ultimate root in the rivalry which had appeared in the eighteenth century between Naples and Sardinia; that rivalry was conceivably pregnant with a contest for the leadership of an Italian movement should such a movement ever emerge.[1] More immediately, however, its supposition would have been, on the one hand, the power of the Bourbon monarch to envisage such a future for itself and, on the other, a close unity between itself and that element of its own people in which alone the effective will for such an enterprise might reside, the 'ceto medio', now revitalized by its romantic re-education. But both of these suppositions were lacking. Any illusions of the first score were quickly dissipated by the utterances of Ferdinand II; his ideal was the ideal of the two Sicilies, independent of the rest of Italy and content with her historical boundaries; self-contained without external or internal ambitions; it was a rejection of history. And his relations with the 'ceto medio' had if anything worsened precisely because the whole consciousness and will of that class had now become concentrated on the national idea, in which the sole future of Naples was seen to lie. For this reason it might be said with absolute truth that the rejection of the idea of nationality, or simply the inability to grasp it, added to the historical traits which it had displayed at the crises of its power, was the real reason for the downfall of the Bourbon dynasty in Naples. It was an internal decay,

[1] SRN, 245.

an atrophy of the ethico-political will. The external circumstances of its fall were, consequently, really a matter of indifference.[1]

The revolution of 1848 struck the realm and the monarchy with great force. Yet it did not actually bring about the expulsion in fact of the monarchy. There was something which had first to die before that fact could be accomplished. This was the idea of the realm of Naples. Men and dynasties die easily; the aura of immortality about them is faint and their hold upon life tenuous at best. Ideas, by contrast, die only with reluctance and in an agony painful to contemplate, and the idea of the realm of Naples was a secular idea; it had behind it a life of five centuries and more. Yet it too had to die before the idea of the Italian nation, and in it, Naples, could live. Nor was it eliminated by the national idea, so long as it was even faintly conceivable that the agency of the national idea might be the realm; for then the Italian nation would be but the higher reincarnation of that realm, and its idea would not have perished but would have been apotheosized. The historic event of the revolution of 1848 was the death of the idea of the realm of Naples.[2]

The scene of its passing, naturally, was the political consciousness of the class which alone in its history had shown any effective will to the idea, the political consciousness of the 'ceto medio'. It is for this reason that Croce writes that in that revolution the intellectual class which had been the only real political class of southern Italy, performed its last political act.[3] Because it was not possible that Naples should place itself at the head of the national movement, that class bound Naples to the chariot of the national idea. Because the idea of the ancient autonomous realm had now become an obstacle, they did not permit themselves to be swayed by memories or moved by particularistic interests. They sacrificed, without remorse, the realm of Naples, the oldest and largest realm of Italy, to the new Italy. To expect that the cry of treason would not be lifted against them would be to expect too much. But by whom could that cry be raised? Only by those who sought to bind Naples to her tragic past and to close a future of promise to her. The cry must ring hollow. But not, for that, empty of its tragic resonance. For who, even while assisting at its demise, could forbear to weep at the passing of that noble idea and aspiration? A nation destined not to be born, that must Naples be before the whole gaze of subsequent history, and this was a judgment which could be passed only by the Neapolitans themselves.

[1] SRN, 247.   [2] SRN, 249 sqq.   [3] SRN, 251.

Here Croce's favourite aphorism, that history is not idyll but tragedy, had overwhelming confirmation and illustration.

To this act effected by the 'ceto medio' in the context of the revolution of 1848 the ¦subsequent events must stand by contrast as anticlimax. The actual fall of the monarchy in 1860, the actual process of unification, the long conflicts and the pains of actual incorporation into the life of the new nation; these were already transacted ideally within that great decision. With that decision, consequently, the history of the realm of Naples which Croce had set out to write is fittingly and necessarily concluded.

IV

ETHOS AND POLIS: THE ETHICO-POLITICAL CONCEPT OF HISTORY

WITH the narration of the 'dolorous history' of Naples Croce achieves his full stature as an historian; a stature which will be enhanced by his subsequent achievements, but never altered in its fundamental lineaments. The function of this matter, in which he felt himself so deeply committed, was to compel him, by the concrete exigencies it deployed before him, to traverse the stages by which that stature was gained. These stages are readily discerned. They are three: the idyllic, the naturalistic, and the ethico-political. But of these, only two, the first and the third, are positive. At the second, the naturalistic, Croce never rested. It was for him at all times a negative dialectical step, the examination and rejection of which enabled him to grasp more clearly the ethico-political concept to which he attained. This dialectical process was executed, not in a theoretical vacuum, but in answer to the exigencies of the matter with which he dealt. The narration of that history, consequently, and the attainment of the ethico-political conception of history constitute a single achievement.

The idyllic phase, as has been noted, is a phase associated with his youth. It is the phase which might be correlated, with the essay, 'History Subsumed under the General Concept of Art'.[1] In the one and the other, the practical and the theoretical moment, history ends in contemplation. He is delivered from both illusions, the theoretical and the practical, by the same consideration, namely, that contemplation can never penetrate to the reality of its supposed object. If history be subsumed under the concept of art, then it too must forgo that distinction between the real and the unreal which art is willing enough to forgo. And idyllic history engaged in the imaginative re-evocation of the past must remain innocent of the reality of that past. But the fallacy of subsuming history under that general concept, Croce comes quickly to realize, lies precisely here. For history cannot

[1] Cf. PS.

81

forgo that distinction; it is inexorably orientated toward the discernment of the real, the historically real. That subsumption must be fallacious, and idyllic history, though the beauty and the delight of the images it evokes can never be denied, and may without doubt form a legitimate dimension of aesthetic activity, cannot pass as history. Croce's idyllic re-evocation of the Neapolitan past constitutes thus a world of images, which had to be forgone, despite the delight it elicited, in the name of the necessity which the historical vocation imposes of reaching to the reality of history and of narrating it in the terms which express and convey its reality.

The naturalistic conception of history would seem to offer the readiest alternative to the idyllic, since here the reality of history would seem to be grasped in its most irreducible terms. It is the history of Naples which renders it impossible, however, for Croce to succumb to this idea. For the naturalistic posture had become almost immemorial in the narration of the history of Naples, and it had given rise to the basic illusions and delusions from which that history had suffered and which had made it incomprehensible. The postulates of naturalistic history had appeared with respect to the history of Naples in the series of 'conventional lies' upon which the narration of that history had been predicated. The greatest of these, which demanded the criticism of decades and centuries to dissipate, was that myth of the inexhaustible richness and fertility of the Neapolitan soil, which so beguiled its inhabitants that it led them to its neglect and corrupted their own spirit, while it made of that land the object of the cupidity of all beyond its borders. And Croce notes the curious fact that even the sovereigns of that land were bemused by this myth, such as Frederick II and Charles of Anjou, who writes of the land mellifluously, 'ex dispositione divinae gratiae rerum usualium ubertate fecunda naturaliter affluit'. The practical disasters to which this illusion led might be narrated in abundance. But it is rather the historiographic fallacy which, in this context, impresses itself upon Croce's mind. This fallacy is based, not upon that myth directly, but upon its final dissipation. From this dissipation, the false illation is then made, Croce notes, to the position that the whole history of that land, which is not really history, but a tale of anarchy and poverty, can be explained by reference to the natural poverty which stood revealed when that myth of its richness was dissipated. Because the land, it is argued, upon which that history transpired, rather than developed, was arid, sterile, unproductive, infested with malaria, immedicably poor, the history of that nation ended inevitably in disaster. This naturalistic reasoning, when in need of further support or corroboration, simply adduced further naturalistic elements.

Such an illation seems to Croce without foundation and disastrous for the authentic history of that land. To every naturalistic explanation adduced, he notes, an alternate and contradictory can be adduced with equal force. If it be asserted that the condition of the land in the south has been rendered worse by deforestation, this is but to say that at one time there were forests, and that those forests may be restored, as they are being restored; if malaria plagues the land, it is possible to deliver the land from malaria by remedial procedures as has been done elsewhere more than once; or, if the element of race be adduced, the counter-assertion is possible, that this same race, immemorially composite, in antiquity showed itself one of the strongest, as in its conflict with Rome, and that its inhabitants preserved, against the dominant Romanity, the character of the Italic. The races which in the course of time were to mix with the indigenous element were not inferior but among the most ingenious and daring that history has known, Greeks and Lombards and Normans and, in lesser number, French and Spanish. It may be shown, moreover, that to speak of race homogeneously in a land inhabited by such different strains as the Calabrian and the Abruzzian is to reduce the term to nonsense. But this opposition of naturalist fact to fact is otiose; it does not touch the real problem, which is, whether history can be narrated in these terms at all. That the natural environment of history can only be a neutral theatre, open to the exploitation of men; that the history which transpires in that arena will depend upon the type of men by which it is inhabited; that it is a spiritual and not a natural or material thing, and develops with reference, indeed, to the natural environment, but under no determinate compulsion from those natural factors—this is Croce's thesis. The naturalistic incubus which has rested upon the historiography of the realm since that first dissipation of the myth of its fabled richness, radically distorted historical vision.[1]

The basic error stands out in bold relief. A substitution has been made of a pseudo-history of nature for human history, the history of men and their spiritual and civil action. No escape from this false conclusion and this erroneous historiography is possible save by way of the recognition that history is not a 'natural', but a 'moral phenomenon',[2] and that it is to be explained, not by a single cause or

[1] SRN, 268 sqq.   [2] SRN, 272.

by a multiplicity of causes of a natural order, but only by internal reasons, by a spiritual, free activity which throws itself upon obstacles and overcomes them or is itself thrown back by them. Climate, richness of the land, ethnic dispositions and all other natural elements, if considered as conditions or material instruments of that spiritual activity, will always be of central interest for history. Taken in themselves, without reference to the historical centre of that spiritual activity, they are inert, incapable of leading to any conclusion. Each of these natural factors is neutral and may become, on occasion, a source of weakness or of strength, as the same climate, in Hegel's example, supported with indifference the works of the Greeks and the indolence of the Turks. True history can only be the record of that spiritual activity, great or modest, triumphant or defeated. It is the only history, the only human history.[1]

To recognize that true history is the history of spirit (not the history of spirit in any transcendental sense, which might lead to the extravagances of the 'philosophy of history' or the construction of a mythological history over and above the concrete history of man), the spiritual activity of men, that is to say, their moral activity in community, is to recognize the basic principle of ethico-political history. The fundamental character of that history is political; that is to say, its true subject is the 'polis', the human community and the spiritual effort by which the community is evoked and sustained. The 'polis', in its narrow sense, is sometimes interpreted as the state; but this is clearly, in Croce's view, an illegitimate constriction. The 'polis' which the spirit evokes and sustains in history is the whole human community in all its unity and complexity. That the state is a necessary dimension of that 'polis', is not to be denied; but that the rich life of the 'polis' can be constricted within the life of the state is untenable. Rather the 'polis' is co-extensive with the whole complex and unpredictable structure of relations which men can sustain with other men and will find expression in the whole range of institutions, arts, science, etc., which the spiritual creativity of man can generate.[2]

The existential evocation of the 'polis', or the human community, is itself a moral and ethical effort. Here, too, the terms 'ethical' and 'moral' must be preserved from the constrictions repeatedly imposed upon them. For what is, in Croce's sense, the ethical

[1] SRN, 273.
[2] Cf. the article of Nino Cortese cited *infra* and that of Federico Chabod cited *infra*.

effort of man? It is the effort to realize existentially and concretely the whole idea of his humanity; to give historical existence to the spirit that is in him in its totality and not in any of its unilateral aspects. For this reason, the direct and immediate object of the ethical effort is human community itself, under some concrete form; for without this community the humanity of the individual must remain perpetually absent, must inevitably atrophy and shrink away into barbarism. The ultimate effort or object of ethical effort, however, is not the mere form of community, but the rich content of community, that is, the whole wealth of relations which man can sustain to man and in which the fullness of humanity is achieved. Ethico-political effort is precisely this effort of the spirit of man to achieve ideal and existential plenitude in the structures of community through sustained historical effort. To compose ethico-political history is to compose the record of this spiritual effort. It is not, however, to compose only the triumphal hymn of the human spirit. It is to record its existential path, inevitably a pattern of achievement and failure, in both of which, however, it is always spirit which is agent and always spirit, consequently, to which history addresses itself.

In this sense alone is it possible to narrate the history of Naples, and in that history, the history of man himself. In this case it is a dolorous history, for the ethico-political effort of the realm of Naples was an historical failure. It could find its life as a 'polis' only by losing it in a higher unity and community. This is, nevertheless, its authentic record written in the only terms which are meaningful. Thus it is in the matrix of the matter of Naples that Croce achieves the ethico-political view of history, a position which realizes in the context of history the most ancient and classical tradition of political humanism.

PART TWO

THE ANATOMY OF DECADENCE: THE BAROQUE AGE IN ITALY

INTRODUCTION

THE second of the basic themes about which the historical writings of Benedetto Croce naturally group themselves is the baroque age in Italy. In many ways, the writings composed about this theme are the richest of his historical compositions. They are materially rich, for Croce has sought out with the greatest care, and the passion of the born bibliophile, the obscurest documents of the intellectual, the poetic and literary, and the moral life of the period, drawing again into the circle of historical reflection authors whose very names have been half-lost to memory. These works he has subjected to searching reading, at once critical and sympathetic, with the thought of fixing both their constitutive qualities and their place in the vast mosaic of that fertile and colourful age. Voices of song are heard again in these pages which for centuries have been silent; subtle debates, like the great contest about the 'ragione di stato' stir again, re-evoking intellectual struggles whose very terms have become dim. They are rich also in spiritual insight and discernment. Rarely has the mood (the unspoken mood, one is tempted to say, though it breathes in every form of expression) of a period been so faithfully, yet critically, captured and made to live again as in these pages, and within the period, the qualitative distinction of mind from mind, sentiment from sentiment, insight from insight presented with clarity and subtlety, so that no value is lost, or even diminished. They are, finally, rich in judgment. There is here no idyllic re-evocation of a past to which the imagination turns for aesthetic dilation. The whole presentation is firmly controlled by the overarching insight into the relation and significance of every mode of expression, indeed of every concrete expression, in the total economy of the age. The controlling insight is therefore ethical, in the sense in which that term has already been defined by Croce. And this insight is fulfilled in ethical judgment on this age. Such wealth of matter, of discernment and of judgment might be thought to imply a natural sympathy; but this is not the case. If anything, that age, as the period of

89

Italy's greatest spiritual and political debility and decadence, inspired him with spiritual nausea. This spiritual alienation evokes, however, his sense of justice, its most effective counter-agent; and it is justice, in the last analysis, that he seeks to render to the baroque age.

The compositions on the theme of the baroque do not mark a departure from, but constitute a logical, an almost inevitable, continuation of the Neapolitan theme. This continuity is discernible at all of the levels at which the wealth of the baroque histories has been distinguished. In its rich matter, the history of the baroque era extends and penetrates more deeply interests already opened in the history of Naples. A single example may illustrate this fact. The interest in the Spanish influence in Naples asserts itself early in Croce's study of Neapolitan history; the reminders of that influence surrounded him, even in the Naples of the Risorgimento. Inevitably this interest carried him beyond the limits of Naples, for the Spanish influence held in thrall the whole of Italy; and the work, *La Spagna nella vita italiana durante la Rinascenza*, though but a fragment of a vaster work projected but never completed, is the testament of this extension. At the same time, this work, as Croce recognizes expressly, is an introduction, a preparation for the history of the baroque age.[1] For even though he is led eventually to deny the popular dogma that 'spagnuolismo', that is to say, precisely this influence of Spain, is either the 'cause' or the 'essence' of the baroque,[2] discerning in the baroque rather a failure of the ethical will of the Italian people, nevertheless, the continuity between the phenomena of the baroque age and the Spanish presence in Italy is incontrovertible. And the same fact may be corroborated by another instance. Early in his career Croce had composed the study on the mask of Pulcinella;[3] in this study he opens one of the richest veins of inquiry he was ever to touch, dialectal literature. The full fruit of this inquiry is realized, however, only in the study of the baroque age, for in this latter context he is enabled to make his important distinction between spontaneous and reflective dialectal literature and to discover in the latter one of the positive elements of that negative and decadent period.[4]

This continuity between the history of Naples and that of the baroque age in Italy is discernible also at the theoretical level, the

[1] FPS, 1177 sqq.
[2] FPS, 912; cf. SEB, 34, SVI, 100 sqq., SLI'600, 189 sqq.
[3] *Arch.*, SPN, XXIII (1898), 605–68; 702–42.
[4] UCVI, I, 223–36; SEB, 161 sqq.; SPL, 344–64.

level, that is to say, of Croce's conception of history and its procedure. His basic insight as an historian, it has been suggested, was gained in the matter of Naples; there historical idyllism was overcome and the vision of history as moral drama, the ethico-political conception of history first glimpsed and formulated. It is this insight and this conception which are extended and deepened in the matter of the baroque age. In the context of the history of Naples, his effort had been to seize the spiritual, ethical reality of that history; that is to say, the intellectual, spiritual and moral will of the Neapolitan people to establish a nation and to achieve historical existence. In this history, the political dimension had appeared in prominent relief, for it was historical existence as a *polis* which was at stake in the experience of Naples. It was made clear, however, that this historical existence as a *polis* could never be the achievement of a political mind or will in any narrow statist sense of the term, political. The state could only be the achievement of a more profound and universal will, the ethical will; and the state, in its concreteness, could never encompass this will.[1]

Ethico-political history is rather, in principle, the history of the whole spiritual and ethical life of a people, in all its modes of expression, of which the political in the statistic sense is a central but limited expression. It was logically necessary, consequently, that the ethical dimension of this complex ethico-political conception of history be thrown into greater relief. And the occasion for this fresh direction of emphasis was provided by the matter of the baroque age. Not, to be sure, that there was any programmatic extension of Croce's part, any effort, that is to say, to exploit a wider matter for the purpose of a theoretical development. The movement was at all points spontaneous and unforced. It lay in the character of the matter of the baroque age, as this appeared as the extension and penetration of certain themes of the history of Naples, to evoke at the same time this extension and penetration of the ethico-political conception of history.

The most profound continuity between these histories is, however, neither material nor theoretical, but existential. Croce was

[1] It is for this reason that an excellent critic and historian, Nino Cortese, notes that ethico-political history, even in this restricted sense, can never be merely the history of the state, but must be also the history of the 'anti-state', that is to say, the ethical will as standing over against, as incommensurate with the state which it creates, and which it may have to destroy in order to fulfil its larger ideals; and this refers both to any concrete, historical state and to the state in its idea. Cf. *Rivista Storica Italiana*, 1925-6, pp. 229 sqq.

persuaded, as has been noted, that history cannot be written without commitment and the quality of his own commitment in the history of Naples was readily discerned. There he had traced the process by which the realm of Naples had achieved historical existence by renouncing its dreams of autonomy and seeking identity with the larger unity of the new Italy created by the Risorgimento. Croce wrote as a Neapolitan who willed that historical strategy, not only as an expedient, but as a good in itself. In the history of the baroque age he is writing, for the first time perhaps, as an Italian of the new Italy. The widest purpose of his history is to discover the roots and origins of that new Italy, not merely, again, in the narrow sense of the new Italian state which had been called into being by the Risorgimento, but in the wider sense of the new Italian ethical will, which itself had made the Risorgimento possible, and which had found its expression in a rich cultural and spiritual life which had included but had not been exhausted by the Risorgimento. This new Italy, he perceived, was not born full blown; it was a laborious creation of the Italian ethical will and must, therefore, have historical origins. And where else must these be found but in that very period when Italy presented to the world the aspect of decadence, of exhaustion of the ethical will, that is in the age of the baroque? This is the reason that he writes[1] that the origins of the new Italy are to be discerned not in 1848, nor 1820 nor 1799, but in 1670. In this way the history of the baroque era appears as the linear continuation and development of the history of Naples on the existential level of Croce's own historical commitments.

[1] SEB, 51.

I

THE BAROQUE

WHAT then is the 'baroque' in its historical reality? This, in the largest view, is the problem which the history of the baroque age in Italy sets out to solve. Before this larger purpose may be achieved, however, it is necessary, in Croce's view, to realize a more restricted goal. It is necessary to fix the object of this inquiry, not in its historical character, to be sure (for that can only emerge from historical inquiry, which does not presuppose, but creates its object), but in a limited form, in its simple existentiality, its givenness, as it first provokes historical reflection. Historical inquiry is concerned always with a problem; but the problems of history are not posited in a void. At the basis of every historical problem there is always a given, or presented, element by which the problem is evoked and it is with specific reference to this element that the problem is formulated. In the process of historical inquiry itself the givenness of this element is resolved, is taken up and transformed into historicity; its apparent givenness, consequently, is simply the limit of its historicity. Still it is from this limit that historical inquiry begins, and the case of the baroque age in Italy is no exception. Croce undertakes, consequently, as the first step in historical inquiry, to determine this element of the given; and this effort proceeds at three levels, that of the word, of the concept, and of what, for want of a better term, may be called the 'essence' of the baroque.

Both as term and as concept, he notes, 'baroque' bears from the beginning a note of disapprobation.[1] It is born of a critical effort of the Italian and the European consciousness, directed against an element of its own experience and history which, by means of this term and concept, it reprobates and which, by the self-critical act expressed in them, it seeks to transcend, or does in fact transcend.

As a term, its origins exhibit certain curious features. There can be little doubt, Croce believes, that the word is an adaptation and

[1] SEB, 20.

transformation of one of those terms artificially compacted by late mediaeval logicians by which the modes and the figures of the syllogism were committed to memory. There was a time when the repertory of these verbal artifacts, further compacted into verses of dubious metrical structure, was known to every school-boy: 'Barbara, celarent, darii, ferio, baralipton.' 'Baroco' appears in that repertory as the designation of the fourth mode of the second figure.[1] These terms, needless to say, were compounded with serious scientific and pedagogic intent. The circumstance which endowed this particular term, 'baroco', with reprobative intent was that weariness with the disputations of the schools so prevalent in the seventeenth century. The characteristic of the school logic which provoked ridicule was precisely its preoccupation with pedantic and vacuous argumentations. The form of the syllogism designated 'baroco', rare and recondite and without apparent scientific or rhetorical relevance, took on the status of a symbol of all such arguments, for they were called, *en bloc*, 'arguments in baroco'.[2] Evidences of this appellation are discovered by Croce as early as the middle of the sixteenth century, as in the *Rime Burlesche* of Giovanfrancesco Ferrari (1508–71) where one reads, 'e con qualche argomento in baricoco/far restare il messere un bel castrone'; and in the *Viaggio in Colonia* of Antonio Abbondanti, which dates from the early seventeenth century, where it is stated of one character that 'egli in baroco un argomento fino formò'.[3]

The transition or extension of this term in its reprobative association from this original context to the wider area of art was accomplished by a spontaneous movement of the same sentiment although, as he discovers, such an extension does not appear to have been achieved until the middle of the eighteenth century and then in France earlier than in Italy.[4] When the term does appear in this extended form, it is directed against the art of the seventeenth century. And the affinity between the quality in that art which suggested the term and the quality of argumentation which first occasioned its reprobative employment is not difficult to discern. So he discovers in the *Encyclopédie*, this entry: '*Baroque*, adjectif en architecture, est une nuance de bizarre . . . Il en est . . . le raffinement . . . l'abus . . . le superlatif' and this definition of the *Encyclopédie* is repeated almost 'verbatim' by Francesco Milizia (1725–98) in his *Dizionario delle belle arti del disegno*.[5]

[1] SEB, 21; cf. K. Prantl, *Geschichte der Logik*, 1855, *sub voce*.   [2] SEB, 21.
[3] SEB, 21–2.   [4] SEB, 22.   [5] SEB, 23 and n.

More important, though of course, in its formation, entirely immanent to the history of the term, is the concept of the 'baroque'. It is a concept of criticism and specifically of the criticism of art. It was excogitated to indicate the bad taste, aesthetically, which characterized so much of the architecture, the painting and the sculpture of the seventeenth century, of the age in which Guarini and Borromino worked. A further extension of the concept to literary forms, both in prose and in poetry, was inevitable, nor was music or, for that matter, the whole range of human sentiment, thought and action ultimately exempted.[1] At the same time, the historical localization of the phenomena of the 'baroque' was emphasized by the emergence of its synonym 'seicentismo', the 'seventeenth century malady'.[2]

Since the concept of the 'baroque' has reference to aesthetic bad taste, to a mode, therefore, of artistic ugliness, it cannot, in Croce's view, designate anything artistic, cannot, that is to say, be in any manner approximated to the concept of art in its positive character. It must, on the contrary, indicate something directly opposed to art. For the artistically ugly is not a form of art, or a form of the beautiful, nor is it the mere absence of beauty, or of art.[3] It designates something positive which masks as art and seeks to substitute for it. And since art is a form of knowing, the positive principle which accounts for the artistically ugly must be of an opposite character, that is, a practical principle. As such, it must exhibit and obey in its expression and development a law quite diverse from the law of art and of the beautiful, for these must develop always according to a law of poetic truth.[4] The practical root of the artistically ugly, however, provides too wide a context for the specification of the concept of the 'baroque'. In the first place, the forms of the practical are infinite and, in the second, they are positive in their own right. They can give rise to the concept of the artistically ugly, consequently, not in their own character, but only as they violate this character by assuming the spurious aspect of art and of the beautiful. It is necessary, therefore, to specify the manner of this intrusion and substitution of the practical into and for the beautiful, for the motive of the beautiful and of poetic truth, which characterizes the works of the baroque.

This would be a difficult if not an impossible task, Croce recognizes, from a purely critical and historical point of view, since

[1] SEB, 257 sqq.
[2] SEB, 40; cf. 'Seicentismo e Spagnuolismo', SLI'600, 189 sqq.
[3] Cf. Est., X, pp. 83 sqq., Estetica in nuce, passim. [4] SEB, 24.

these modes in their turn are innumerable. Fortunately, however, the critic and the historian of the baroque are excused from this effort by the documents of the period. For the poets of the 'baroque' through their 'prince', Marino, have revealed that practical motive as it intruded itself into the realm of art and poetry by making it the programmatic axiom of their school. Marino, defining the 'end' or 'purpose' of poetry and of the poet declares it to be the awakening of 'wonder' or 'amazement', the inducement of 'stupefaction'. He fortifies this statement by its converse that anyone who cannot succeed in this purpose cannot hope to succeed as a poet.[1] Nor was the perversity of this programme—the substitution of a limited practical end for the pure quest of poetic truth—lost on Marino's contemporaries. Villani, for example, notes its effects when he writes that little wonder should be occasioned by the fact that verse born of so practical and intrinsically unpoetic a principle should have no power to stir the passions and the sentiments. Frigidity, impotence to awaken poetic sentiments, the eventual mark of all baroque art, is but the alternative sign of that substitution of the practical, masking as sentiment, for the true poetic motive in which the artistically ugly consists.[2]

Evidence of this perversion presses on every hand. The testimony of Villani has been noted. On his own account, Croce adduces the sonnets and prose compositions of Ludovico Leporeo, whose name lent itself to a whole class of compositions of this quality, called 'leporeambi'; this writer, in pursuit of that purpose of 'wonder', introduces an intricate and senseless system of internal rhyme both in prose and in verse. Every word, very nearly, was made to flower into a rhyming mate, until the whole became a tintinnabulation in which the ear lost its way. Of these auricular and sonic extravagances this single line, quoted by Croce from Leporeo's eulogy of the contemporary architect Borromini (the collaborator of Bernini, Francesco Borromini, 1599–1667), may stand as the type: 'tutti edificij costrutti a beneficij de' Regi dagli artefici de' Pontifici egregi'.[3] Historians of architecture, of painting and of sculpture add their testimony. Cicognara (Leopoldo Cicognara, 1767–1834) in his history of sculpture depicts in great detail the exaggerations and virtuosities which distort the works of this time, concluding his account with the sweeping judgment that no 'sculptor of the seventeenth century expresses

---

[1] SEB, 25; cf. De Sanctis, *Storia della Letteratura Italiana*, Bari, 1949, II, pp. 181 sqq.

[2] SEB, 27.　　　　　　　　　　　　　　　　　　[3] SEB, 26.

genuine (artistic) sentiment' such as is so richly and widely expressed in the works of the fourteenth and fifteenth centuries.[1] Much later Burckhardt in his turn speaks of the 'falsely dramatic life' which at this time was intruded into both sculpture and painting for shallow ends of wonder and surprise, so that the profundity of sentiment and the extravagance appear to him to be, in these works, in inverse proportion.[2]

Such examples and authorities might be multiplied without end; but no purpose would be served. Croce is concerned rather to note the extreme and violent alternatives into which the baroque artists fall precisely because there is absent from their work a central, dominant and authentic poetic principle. They pass, he notes, by sudden and violent transitions from the most subtle intellectualism to the crassest realism and verism in representation. It is impossible for them, seemingly, to attain to the true poetic image which is at once sensibility and idea. Instead, they exhaust themselves in antitheses between empty concepts, or in the reproduction of the signs of things in their mere external and material character, as though to compensate by sheer plastic power and skill, expended in the service of a shocking realism, the vacuum within. Even in the area of the comic these extreme alternations and contrasts appear. True laughter is a mark of a serious spirit; but the comedy of the period seeks to surpass these limits and to provoke a laughter which is beyond the comic and succeeds only in inducing a mood, which, in its distaste for this extreme, falls little short of melancholy.[3]

The history and the criticism of art, Croce notes, falls ready victim to the 'generalizing fallacy'. This fallacy consists in the abstraction of the salient qualities of a number of concrete works and their combination into an ideal 'type' or 'model'. This 'type' or 'model' is then given a substantive and a substitutive value so that in discussion it replaces reference to the works from which it was extracted. Thus released from its existential reference, the ideal type is free to wander through history and to attach itself with greater or less verisimilitude to other periods and other works than those which constituted its original reference.[4] In such procedure, he notes, there is both convenience and disadvantage. The convenience lies in the facility with which vast bodies of historical material can, through these types, be ordered and related; the disadvantage and the danger to truth are readily apparent, for all too easily the type or model wandering thus freely through history loses its original force and

[1] SEB, 26-7.   [2] SEB, 27.   [3] SEB, 28-9.   [4] SEB, 30.

gives rise, by way of superficial and loosely analogical predication, to serious confusions. The history and criticism of the 'baroque' have not been free of this fallacy. The attempts to transform the term and the concept 'baroque' into a 'free denominative' or an 'eternal type' have been frequent enough. Thus it has seemed possible to some to speak of 'seicentismo nel quattrocento' or of the 'barocism of the poets of the Latin decadence' or even, of the 'fathers of the Church'.[1] The fact is overlooked that the baroque consists in an attitude of soul and not in any exterior qualities or combination of qualities which may be abstracted and combined from works of the period. Those qualities, taken in themselves and in the combinations in which they may be determined in concrete situations, may become something quite diverse from and even opposed to the 'baroque'.[2] It is necessary, he concludes, that the term and the concept 'baroque' retain their original historical reference; to the works, that is to say, which originally provoked their formation and the formation of the vocabulary in which they have been elaborated. The 'baroque', consequently, has a definite reference in history; it signifies that artistic perversion, dominated by a practical motive of wonder and amazement, which is to be observed in Europe and in Italy more than anywhere else between the last decades of the sixteenth and the end of the seventeenth centuries.[3]

His account of the 'baroque' would be incomplete, Croce feels, if he were not to note the truly positive traits which it displays. These are all, from the point of view of art, minor, but none the less positive. They consist, in his view, above all in a stylistic dexterity, a rhetorical *afflatus*, and a refinement and diffusion of the methods of the arts and their techniques. All of these positive characteristics are, it is to be noted, practical, and flow from the practical motive of the baroque. Technique is the practical dimension of art, the practical vesture, the *organon* which the theoretical activity must assume for its existential concretion.[4] These achievements, though of the practical rather than of the theoretical and genuinely artistic order, were of genuine service to European culture. Europe was in need, Croce points out, of such practical instruction relative to the arts in order to free its artistic life from technical limitations inherited from earlier centuries.[5] He discerns, however, a still more significant service which the 'baroque' experience rendered to European culture. Just as, he writes, in the life of the individual there are evil tendencies

---

[1] SEB, 24. [2] SEB, 32. [3] SEB, 33.
[4] Cf. *Est.*, XV, pp. 122 sqq.; *Poesia, passim.* [5] SEB, 39.

which are to be exorcized only by being actualized, so it is with the lives of peoples, nations and entire cultures; indeed, with the life of mankind. The baroque experience effected such a 'catharsis' in western European culture. Its exaggerations, its 'conceitism', its worship of 'argutezza', its distortions and its fundamental perversity, once lived through, were then repudiated by the spirit of western culture as something intimate to itself, and it was purged and stronger for the trial.[1]

Croce has opposed, it was noted, the transformation of the baroque into a false universal by the generalizing fallacy. There was another type of universalization, however, which he did not oppose but, on the contrary, effected in his historical studies of the period. The historical reference of the term, he had noted, had been primarily artistic. The essence of baroque had been discovered to reside, however, in a disposition of soul or spirit which only incidentally could be limited to artistic expression. Art is not an isolated activity of the human spirit; it is related vitally and integrally to all of the activities of the spirit. A disposition of the spirit which finds a distinctive mode of artistic expression may be expected to find similar expression in all of the other forms of its activities. His own history, consequently, while it is silent on the figurative and plastic arts of the baroque, to which the term and the concept had in the first instance been referred, addresses the areas of thought, of the moral life and of the literary arts, especially poetry. This extension of the area of the baroque is justified in principle only by that unity of the spirit which Croce has signalized. He is, as it were, completing an unfinished portrait, which had depicted only certain features; because every portrait is a mirror of the soul, it needs be extended to the whole countenance.

This extension establishes a vital relation between the history of the baroque and the ethico-political conception of history. Even more accurately, it might be said that this extension is justified logically only in the name of the ethico-political conception, and constitutes an organic development of it. For ethico-political history, as has already been indicated, even when, as in the case of the history of Naples, the problem of historical existence as a political entity is in the foreground, does not address itself to the political in any restricted sense of that term, and least of all in a statist sense. The 'polis' which it envisages is the total community of mankind, of humanity, of

[1] SEB, 39–40; compare with Croce's view the interesting position of René Wellek: 'The Concept of Baroque in Literary Scholarship' in *Journal of Aesthetics and Art Criticism*, V (1946), 77–108.

which the state is indeed an integral part, but not the whole. So true is this, that in some instances ethico-political history must find its centre in ethical forces which are outside the state, or against it, in the anti-state. The informing principle of the human community is the ethical will; and the ethical, as Croce conceives it, is essentially the dynamism toward an integral expression and realization of life which informs the central effort of the human spirit. The expressive forms of the ethical will, consequently, must be co-extensive with the modes of expression open to the human spirit. If the essence of the baroque resides, as Croce has suggested, in the 'animo barocco', it cannot logically be expected to characterize only certain modes of expression, certain cultural forms.

This extension is not without its effect upon the notion of the baroque itself. As a matter of fact, it alters it profoundly. It transforms it from a limited concept to a concept relevant to the human spirit in its integrity, in its ethical character. If this is true, however, is it still possible to retain the idea of the baroque as first suggested? This consisted precisely, it has been noted, in a certain perversion in the human spirit, whereby certain modes of its life were intruded into and substituted for other modes. More precisely still, in the case of art, as has been seen, there was a substitution of practical for theoretical and poetical motives. What is the correlative of this perversion or confusion, when the baroque is transformed into an ethical concept having reference to the unity and the integrity of the human spirit? It can only be a perversion in which the totality and the integrity of the spirit itself is involved. But the only manner in which this integrity can become the subject of such transvaluation and substitution is to stand in opposition, in alienation, to itself. At the level of the ethical will, consequently, as will be seen more clearly presently, the baroque can only be the negativity of the ethical will itself, its absence, or its relative depression. And this is precisely the value which Croce will finally assign to the notion of the baroque, thus evincing anew its continuity with the ethico-political conception of history.

II

POSITIVITY AND NEGATIVITY
IN HISTORY

CROCE's attempt to fix the term and the concept of the baroque in their original reference and significance as the point of departure for the establishment of the baroque in its historical reality had one clear result. The term and the concept were established as radically negative and reprobative. They had arisen in the cultural life of Europe in a moment of self-criticism in which a part of its own historical creation had been evaluated and reprobated. Their concrete reference was to a 'corpus' of objects: works of architecture, of sculpture, of painting, literature, poetry and music; and this reference was spontaneously and inevitably extended to embrace the whole range of the works of the human spirit, philosophy, politics, the moral life, until it became clear that the true and ultimate reference was to the human spirit itself in a specific disposition, the 'animo barocco', of which Croce speaks. Yet this reference is not complete, because it exhibits a spurious positiveness due to the concreteness of those objects. The full significance of term and concept becomes clear only when their reprobative dimension is noted. This character has two aspects: the subjective, as it may be called, the European spirit as enunciating this judgment of reprobation on those works, and the objective, the quality in those objects toward which that reprobation is directed. It is immediately clear, however, that this distinction is one of convenience alone, for it is the same spirit which pronounces that reprobative judgment and suffers it. Hence the radically negative sense of both the term and the concept baroque.

This radical negativity of the term and the concept gives rise directly to the problem of the baroque. This problem may be stated in the form of two questions: how and why write the history of a negation? History, Croce has written a score of times or more, is positive and only of the positive. A negative history, the history of a negation, is simply not history.[1] A history of a negation, of a period

[1] Cf. TSS, 75: '. . . la storia deve spiegare e non condannare; essa pronuncierà soltanto giudizi positivi . . . Un fatto che sembri meramente cattivo, un'epoca che

of decadence, would seem to have neither rationale nor method and to be, quite simply, outside the realm of history which is rationally, and not merely passionally or imaginatively, conducted. Croce, in his reply to these questions which constitute the problem of the baroque (in the *History of the Baroque Age*, that is to say, for this entire history is his answer) is wholly consistent with this theoretical statement. There is no rationale nor method for a negative history, *in se*. Such a history can be composed only obliquely, for the sake of the positive element which it conceals. The anatomy of decadence is a delicate surgery by which life is released from the burden of death which encumbers it. And this fact in turn dictates the method of such a history. It can never have the negation in itself for its object. It must be a delicate technique for revealing the positive elements which that negative wrapping conceals. Before this reply can be amplified theoretically or effected in practice, it is necessary, he believes, to dissipate a false conception of the positive character of history which has arisen precisely with respect to the problem of the baroque.

Persuaded, like Croce, that history can only be positive, some recent historians and critics have sought to meet the problem of the baroque by denying that radical negativity of the term and of the concept and conferring upon them a primary significance which is positive. But this attempt must necessarily fail, Croce believes, because it violates the basic reference of the baroque historically; this, as he has shown, is indubitably negative. It must fail also because the positive character thus assigned the baroque is spurious and not the authentic positivity of history. For these reasons, he writes, his own history is a conscious reaction against these efforts, and is directed, in its initial stages at least, toward the vindication of that original and basic negative character of the baroque.[1]

Croce distinguishes three modes in which this spurious transformation of the baroque from its negative to a positive signification is attempted. The first assigns to the baroque a positive artistic-ideal content; the second, an artistic-historical content; the third, finally, reflecting a larger appreciation of the term, discerns in it an ethical or a 'spiritual' content. In each instance, the effort is identical. The original negative and reprobative value of the term and concept is replaced by a positive, or seemingly positive, content which by the very fact that it is positive cannot be reprobative.

sembri di mera decadenza, non può essere altro che un fatto non istorico . . .' Cf. FPS, 528, 679, 884, 931–2, 969.

[1] SEB, 491.

In the first of these cases the 'baroque' is identified as one of the basic and irreducible categories or 'styles' of art, and the concrete works of the period are treated as its collective epiphany. The presupposition of this attempt to render the baroque a true subject of history by assigning it a positive value is, of course, a specific theory of 'style'. 'Style' is conceived, in this theory, as a fixed and transcendent form or type, not without resemblances to the Platonic idea, save that style is multiple, so that the unity of art can be divided among an uncertain number. These multiple styles, into which the unity of art may be divided, are irreducible to each other. And the specific style stands to its concrete members in a relation not unlike that of the Platonic model in which the individuals were said to participate. By asserting that the term and the concept baroque designate one such 'style', whose constitutive notes are but the synthesis of the characteristics of the works of the period, the historian and critic transfer their immediate reference from those concrete works to the ideal form thus constituted. The works themselves are then considered, as we have suggested, as the collective epiphany of that ideal or model or style. It is to this point, naturally, that Croce's criticism of this spuriously positive interpretation of the baroque is directed. His own reflections on the nature of art, and especially his basic intuition into the unity of art, had rendered unacceptable this notion of a 'heaven' of ideal artistic types or styles on the model of the heaven of the Platonic ideas, which historiographically becomes a repertory of categories for the judgment of art. He discerns here the same logic that he has discerned in the theory of 'genre'. Abstract and general formulae are transmuted into ideal entities; and a fictitious history of these entities is then composed, displacing the true history of art itself, that is, of the concrete works of art which historically exist.[1] In the case of the baroque this effort appears to Croce all the more reprehensible in that it lacks a serious motive. It is comprehensible how the power and the purity of the artistic sentiment of certain ages might tempt the historian or the philosopher to lift the specific properties of that art to an ideal status. In the case of the baroque, however, any such motive is lacking. Not only are its works, as he has pointed out, lacking the element of aesthetic sentiment, but they are consciously informed by a non-artistic principle, a thaumaturgic principle itself of a trivial quality. The only possible justification for this effort which he can conceive (and it is a weak one) is the laudable desire to save

[1] FPS, 209–11, 256–7, 410, 690, 1090; *Est.*, 197–8, 236–7, 308–9, 327–8, 334–5, 372–3; *Poesia*, 174 sqq.

the occasional works of genuine artistic sentiment from summary and prejudicial condemnation by historical association. This justification is weak because the strategy to which recourse is had is as pernicious as the initial fact of the negativity of the baroque. There are available, as he will presently make clear, other means of recognizing the occasional genuine works of art which flowered inevitably during the baroque as in every period of history.

The transformation of the baroque from negative to positive by assigning to it an artistic-historical content rests, in the first place, upon the recognition of the baroque as a distinct period in the history of European art and culture to which temporal limits can be assigned and, in the second place, on the recognition of the practical motive which in the works of the period has, as Croce has already noted, displaced, and disguised itself as, the true motive of art. There exists, consequently, between his own analysis and this effort a certain correlation which he does not fail to recognize. This correlation is broken immediately, however, by the fact that the attempt is made, by the critics and historians of this persuasion, to assign a positive artistic value to this practical motive. Croce recognizes that such a transmutation of a practical into a theoretical motive may take place whenever art is made a function of a practical element in a culture (as, to cite a more recent example, of economic production and its ideological superstructures); but it must always be a specious transformation, and even more than specious, perverse, for it distorts beforehand and obscures any genuine ray of aesthetic intuition which may shine out. Art and beauty are functions only of themselves. Art is capable, through sentiment and image, of transforming the practical motive by taking it up into its own vision. Conversely, it is possible for the practical will to draw into its own patterns certain values of art. But these possible relations are based on the distinction, not on the confusion, of the two motives of the life of the spirit. In the case of the baroque, all this is made doubly manifest by the quality of the practical motive involved; for it is essentially trivial, directed not, for example, to exalted didactic or moralistic ends, but to vain and transitive ends of thaumaturgy. The inner contradictions of this programme for the positive transformation of the baroque are not entirely lost even on those historians and critics who have expended their best efforts to realize it. Croce cites Cysarz,[1] who is forced, by the clarity of his artistic insight, to recognize that all the works of the period which exhibit any genuine character of art transcend

[1] SEB, 494-5; S. Cysarz, *Deutsche Barockdictung*, Leipzig, 1924.

the practical motive in which he pretends to discover their artistic principle. In another context, this same critic is forced into the strange position of maintaining that while the baroque exhibits a positive motive of art it is of necessity a mediocre art, inspiring no superior creations. Croce is inexorable in drawing the absurd inferences of such assertions. The great spirits of the period, if such there were, cannot, by definition, belong to its history; a conclusion which violates common sense, which admonishes that these great spirits are rather the only true subjects of history in this as in any other period.

The third and final effort at the positive transformation of the baroque is that which would assign it a positive 'spiritual', and not merely artistic, content. The similarity between this attempt and the others which Croce has identified is quite clear. It has, moreover, one characteristic upon which he must look with favour; it recognizes that the limitation of the term and concept of the baroque to the areas of art is accidental, that logically they must be extended to the whole life of the human spirit in history. It is possible and even necessary, according to this view, to speak of a 'baroque era' in the same sense as one must speak of the Christian era, of the Middle Ages, of the Renaissance. The ages in the spiritual history of mankind are marked, Croce notes, by the human ideals which they advance and cultivate. What then, he demands, are the ideals whose formulation and cultivation would justify the inclusion of the 'baroque' among the spiritual epochs of humanity? It is just these ideals, in his view, which even the most sympathetic examination of its works fail to reveal. When such positive marks are discernible they prove on closer examination to be persistent elements of earlier periods, the Renaissance, or the Middle Ages; or anticipations of ideals which are struggling to be born but whose statement and cultivation belong to a later age. It is in these anticipations of ideal motives, as will presently appear, that Croce will himself find the principle of the history of the baroque; but these anticipations cannot be made to substitute for the actual quality of the age.[1]

None of these efforts, consequently, may be recognized as successful. On the contrary, they corroborate the original and reprobative significance of the term and concept 'baroque' by indicating three fallacious modes of its positive transformation. For this reason Croce is confirmed in his original conviction that the history of the baroque must take the negative and reprobative value of the term

[1] SEB, 495.

and concept as its point of departure. At the same time, however, he recognizes what is valid in these attempts. Even more, he had himself formulated this valid element in purely logical and formal terms. It is the principle that history is always positive. These efforts had revealed themselves as spurious forms of the positive transformation of the baroque. Yet the positive principle of that history had, on Croce's own recognizance, to be articulated. What then is Croce's conception of the positivity of history, and what is its application in the matter of the baroque era?

For the response to this question one must turn to the ethico-political conception of history as this conception had been formulated in the matter of the history of Naples. The positivity of history is defined by Croce in terms of the ethical activity of spirit, and this in turn becomes the basis for the concept of negativity and decadence and reveals the methodological principle of its history. The ethical activity of the human spirit, it has already been noted, consists for Croce in its effort toward inward qualitative plenitude. This notion of qualitative plenitude is based on the distinction he has elaborated of the moments of spiritual activity. Unlike the idea of the plenitude of the spirit, of the idea, which Hegel had developed and which Croce had rejected,[1] this plenitude does not deploy itself through a phenomenology which is temporally extended, so that the moments of spirit are thought to succeed one another and through an inward dialectic of opposition, to transcend each other. Such a phenomenology, as Croce notes, must lead to a conception of the plenitude of spirit which is a fullness without distinction and is hence itself a void. By his doctrine of distinction,[2] Croce had found it possible to conceive this qualitative plenitude as completely immanent, and existentially realized in every moment of history. This is the object of the ethical will of the human spirit; its qualitative plenitude in every moment of historical existence. In this effort spirit is seeking only its own being which is a perpetual becoming, the realization of its full ideality in every moment of time. Under this aspect, the spirit may be denominated as ethical will; but ontologically, the ethical will is simply spirit as it seeks this qualitative plenitude. Nor is it conceivable that spirit should will anything but this plenitude; for no other object is possible to it. This notion of qualitative plenitude is in turn concretely the basis for the notion of culture, and of the culture of an era; for the diverse elements of culture are but the distinct moments of spirit taken in their abstract qualitative distinction, while

[1] SH, I, 89 sqq.; TSS, IV, 53 sqq.   [2] Cf. FPS, 48 sqq.

culture is itself the unitary effort of spirit toward its qualitative wholeness. This ethical will, as we have called it, is the ontological principle of the positivity of history. It must be noted, however, that from Croce's conception of spirit, this positivity is not something attained, or realized in certain moments of history. It is the ethical will itself in its continuously operative or actual character. And thus the positivity of history cannot be conceived as a material value; for the ethical will is never commensurate with its concrete historical achievement, but transcends it.[1]

The dynamism of history, the ethical will, is subject to an inner economy or rhythm of its own. It describes in its temporal course a continual periodic line of which the moments measure the inner fluctuations of intensity of the ethical will itself. This makes it possible for Croce to define a negative moment of history, a moment of decadence, in and through the concept of the positivity of history. A moment of decadence, a negative moment of history, can only be a moment of inner relaxation of the ethical will, a fluctuation of its intensity. Such a relaxation, or fluctuation, can, of course, be only relative; were it absolute, it would spell the extinction of spirit. Such a fluctuation, again, cannot be caused; it is a fluctuation of a vital principle obeying an inward rhythm; for this reason Croce rejects any account of the 'decadence' of the baroque era in causal terms, just as he had earlier rejected any similar account of the historical failure of the Neapolitan realm.[2] Such fluctuations in the intensity of the ethical will of man in history may only be qualitatively narrated; they cannot be causally explained. And such he conceives the decadence of the baroque era to have been; a relative failure of the ethical will in European and especially in Italian culture. It is for this reason that he finds himself in substantial accord with those historians of the period of the Risorgimento who had stigmatized that earlier period as an age of moral decay, and specifically, of a patriotic failure. In this form, Croce believes, they were identifying the ethical will in a moment of its inward debility.[3] What is important from the point of view of history and of historiography, however, is not the mere fact of such fluctuations, but their relative character. For the converse, and the presupposition, of this relative character is, as Croce has already suggested, the continued activity of the ethical will, its basic positivity. It is the ineradicable positivity of spirit which is central and which becomes the object of the historian's concern and

[1] Cf. SE'900, 257: 'la libertà neppur essa è un *ergon*, ma una *energeia*.'
[2] SEB, 34; SRN, 259.   [3] SEB, 41 sqq.

which suggests the method he must follow in this most difficult type of historical narrative.

Croce is now in a position to offer a reply to the two questions which constitute the problem of the baroque: how is it possible to write the history of a negative period, a period of decadence, and why is it desirable? His answer has at least the merit of unambiguity. A negative history is neither desirable nor possible. The object of historiography is always positive because history itself is always positive; the historiographic motive is always presence and never absence of spirit to itself, and negativity is absence. Of the forms of absence there can be no history. The history of a negative period is undertaken only for the sake of the positive element which underlies and is the supposition of that negative or decadent character. The history of a negative period, consequently, does not differ at all in its essential character from positive history, the history, that is to say, of a highly creative, ethically active and integrated period. The fact that this positive element may be scant, that it may lie buried beneath masses of alien matter, that the intricacies of the historical consciousness may disguise and distort it, does not alter the basic motive of history. Nor does it alter the method; for the method of negative history is identical with that of positive, namely, to fix the traits of the positive achievement of spirit, however minimal it may be. It is the procedure which is immensely complicated. It is necessary, as has been noted before, to effect the transformation of all of the 'negative' elements into their positive character, thus setting them in proper relation to the entire history of the age. In the case of the baroque, for example, the task of detecting and qualifying the authentic notes of poetry vocal during those decades is immensely complicated by the task of unmasking all the spurious poetic creation and of revealing it for the trivial thaumaturgy that it is. History remains what it is, in purpose and in method, wholly positive.

The positive elements which form, as it were, the limits of the negativity of a period (the gleam of true poetry, for instance, which flashes out through the tenebrous thaumaturgy), do not have their full value, for Croce, simply in themselves. He reads them in another sense, prognostically, as the signs of a future struggling to be born. The human spirit is never merely defensive in its activity, never seeks merely to preserve that which it has achieved. At the very nadir of its negative moments it is actively preparing its own resurgence. Thus in the few strains of true poetry which make themselves heard in that 'silence of great poetry' which was the baroque era, Croce detects the rising notes of Arcadia and even of the great voice of romanticism which will renew Italian poetry in Foscolo, in Manzoni, in Leopardi. Or again in the occasional flashes of political wisdom, in the dim stirrings of national sentiment, he senses the first movement of the rising tide which will reach full crest in the Risorgimento.

All this is succinctly reviewed by Croce in his reply to Luigi Salvatorelli's criticism of the *Storia della Età Barocca in Italia*. This work, Salvatorelli had protested, was not a history of the seventeenth century but an adumbration of the eighteenth, for Croce had singled out the better elements, that is, the elements which were to develop into the positive motives of the culture of the succeeding century, neglecting the seventeenth century 'as it was', that is in its negative and decadent character. Materially, this criticism is unfounded, for Croce, in this and allied works, had surveyed that material with the greatest patience and care. He does not, however, defend himself on this ground. His defence is a restatement of his whole theory of decadence and of the role and method of its history. 'Since the "better elements" open always on the future, in the history of any period emphasis is necessarily accorded to them; born of the vigour of the will it is they which will live and develop in following periods.'[1]

[1] NSLI'600, ix.

III

THE COUNTER REFORMATION

THE anatomy of decadence is thus revealed by Croce in its true light. It is a delicate art, a delicate surgery whose purpose is to separate the living from the dead, and to release the living into historical consciousness. This is the art he undertakes to practise upon the matter of the baroque era, or perhaps it were more accurate to say, on the body of Italian culture in the seventeenth century. For it is the spirit of that culture which he is seeking to release from the encasement of that decay. In a wider sense, it is the spirit of the new Italy, the Italy which realized its historical existence in the Risorgimento, whose origins he is seeking. It is intimately consonant with the conception of history as moral drama, that these origins must be sought precisely in that era of general cultural decadence, for no more forceful demonstration could be forthcoming that the creation of the new Italy was a work of the ethical will of the Italian people.

This delicate art Croce applies first of all to the Counter Reformation. The logic of this beginning is apparent. The Counter Reformation and baroque are for most purposes synonyms. The Counter Reformation is the baroque age itself in its most inclusive aspect and in its most coherent and programmatic articulation. In subjecting this movement to the first touch of the critical scalpel Croce displays a surgeon's intuitive sense of the crucial point where life and death meet. And it is his purpose, in this movement, as in the whole of the baroque, to separate the living from the dead, the positive from the negative element, and to discover the diminished but still vigorous activity of the ethical will in the Italian people.

Croce's widest indictment of the Counter Reformation is that it is a negative movement. But this indictment, before it can become the object either of proof or of disproof demands specification. And its true significance for Croce becomes apparent only slowly as he develops the theme of this chapter of the *Storia della Età Barocca*. For there transpires here the identical transformation which he had pointed out in his general remarks on the negative in history. The negative, it was seen, has the positive in history as its presupposition; even more, every element in history which may from one point of view or another be denominated negatively, in its own character is actually positive. To characterize the Counter Reformation negatively, consequently, involves two distinct steps; it involves first of all the revelation of the positive presupposition with reference to which its negativity is defined, and in the second place, its positive characterization in its own right. As the poetry of the baroque age was seen tentatively to be a practical thaumaturgy masking as poetry, so from Croce's point of view the Counter Reformation is a movement of one quality masking as another.

The specific quality of the Counter Reformation, its specific negativity, is defined obliquely by Croce, by means of the contrast which he sets up between this movement and the Renaissance and the Reformation. These earlier movements, he believes, have a common trait: they express universal and ideal exigencies of the human spirit, to which in turn they minister by the positive ideals they embody. The radical exigency involved is the seeming necessity of the human person, the human soul, to orientate itself definitively toward one or the other of the poles which attract its life: toward the transcendent reality of a life in God or toward the immediate and palpable life of this world. Seeming necessity, Croce believes, because the true mark of the modern spirit is that it has reconciled these alternatives, has seen that they cannot be dichotomized, that the soul must of necessity embrace both, in a living union, though in the actual process of history it describes an errant path from one pole to the other and has perhaps never grasped clearly the principle of their unity. But in the movements of Reformation and Renaissance, these poles were effectively dichotomized, effectively enough to impart to their times its specific spiritual configuration. But the dichotomy, from the point of view of the contrast between these movements and the Counter Reformation, is of less importance than the trait they possess in common. They were both wholly ideal movements of the human spirit, for the apparent dilemma in which they were involved was divided between poles equally ideal and ultimate. For this reason, although these movements are historical movements, they are at the same time, he believes, more than historical; they are eternal, for the dilemma which they propose is one which is lived through in every age and indeed by every person to the degree to which spiritual discernment is attained. And the fact that the dilemma is radically illusory does not dim the ideality involved; for it is necessary that the problem appear in this false form, that is as a dilemma which is not a dilemma, an alternative which is not an alternative, before its adequate solution, which consists precisely in the denial of this alternative, can be conceived.[1] These movements are bound to time and place only contingently, as it were; in their essence they are movements of the human soul itself.

This conception of the Renaissance and of the Reformation is the positive presupposition, in Croce's analysis, of the negative characterization of the Counter Reformation. For it is by contrast to these movements, conceived in this manner, that he discovers the quality of the Counter Reformation. The Reformation and the Renaissance advanced two opposed but equally ideal attitudes. The Counter Reformation, by contrast, is wholly a practical movement. The three movements, consequently, cannot be placed upon the same plane.[2] The practical character of the Counter Reformation lies in the fact that it has no ideal, eternal, profoundly human and hence divine point of reference; a point of reference which transcends history even as it manifests itself in history. Its point of reference is wholly in time, in the order of concrete fact; it is a limited strategy of the human will directed toward a specific fact or value of history. It was a movement, in a word, for the defence and rehabilitation of a single institution, the Catholic Church. Not that Croce is concerned in any manner to diminish by a jot the value of the Catholic Church as an historical institution; on the contrary, he has himself brilliantly essayed its vindication and for that matter he is convinced that from this point of view the Counter Reformation, limited and negative though it must be accounted, was an unqualified success, for it saved and to a degree rehabilitated that institution and in the process demonstrated its intrinsic power and value.[3] The Counter Reformation was a negative moment, not because the institution which it defended was inferior in idea or power, but simply because it was an institution. For no institution, in Croce's view, can equal or be commensurate with an eternal and ideal moment of the life of the human spirit. The human spirit creates all institutions as historical transitory embodiments, specific concretions of its eternal values; but it is incommensurate with any of those institutions, or with all of them. An historical and spiritual movement, consequently, such as he conceives the Counter Reformation to be, which is directed toward the

[1] SEB, 6-10. [2] SEB, 10.
[3] SEB, 13 sqq., of 'Perchè non possiamo non dirci cristiani' in DVF, I, 11 sqq.

salvation of any such institution, however great, must be accounted negative with respect to the ideality of spirit itself; for its gaze and its will are turned toward the immediate, the historical, the concrete. The negativity which he ascribes to the Counter Reformation is thus clearly a relative negativity, the negativity of every practical moment which is not orientated toward an absolute and eternal value, which does not, that is to say, attain to a genuine ethical status.

The negative character appears under another aspect when the Counter Reformation is considered, not in contrast to other movements, but in its own internal economy. The mark of its negative character, to Croce's mind, is its non-creativity. Creativity is the mark of all genuine ideal movements of the human spirit. The Counter Reformation has as its central spiritual mark, not this power of creation, but another virtue, astuteness, which is essentially a practical virtue. It consists in the power to employ all available agencies to the end of one's own intention, and to select and organize these agencies; but it falls short of the power to create that one supreme and commensurate agency which would be the incorporation of that movement itself. With this virtue the Counter Reformation shows itself supremely endowed. But every such manifestation is at the same time evidence of its negativity. Thus it was able to borrow and turn to its own end, not only the wealth of its own past, but the very attributes of its adversaries; it took with supreme discernment all that it needed or could use from whatever source, from humanism, classical culture, from the political thinkers of the Renaissance the 'reason of state' and the arts of prudence; from the same source the ideal of the practical life as opposed to the contemplative ideal of an earlier Christianity. From the Reformation it drew the necessary hints as to the reforms which were necessary for the ecclesiastical body. Of all of these elements it could construct its own instrument of policy, but this instrument, like that policy itself, was not a creation but an adaptation.[1]

That astuteness is a sterile virtue is amply demonstrated, to Croce's eyes, by the Counter Reformation and forms yet another proof of its negative character. This intellectual and moral aridity is especially striking when it is placed against the foil of the luxuriant creativity of the Renaissance. No great book, he believes, of that small number which reveal man to himself ever more profoundly has sprung from the inspiration of the Counter Reformation; nor any great work of art, for the art of the seventeenth century, he

[1] SEB, 16.

holds, when it is not thaumaturgy, governed by a practical end, runs to mere sensuality. The movement was able to enlist in its service some of the greatest minds as well as the most elevated spirits of the time; but it placed upon these in turn its own mark, for great spirits though they were, they display a lack of moral inventiveness, the power of creating new and progressive forms of the spiritual life which is the ultimate mark of spiritual greatness. And the secret of this sterility is not far to seek. Due to its practical and political character, the Counter Reformation, though it was able to enlist powerful ideal forces in its cause, could not permit them genuine freedom to develop according to their own intrinsic character. It could not do so, because, being ideal, they could not fail immediately to outstrip and even to turn against its more restricted and practical motive. Thus the movement rendered sterile even the spiritual and ideal forces which it was able to draw to its side.

All of this cumulative and, to his view, overwhelming evidence of the negative character of the Counter Reformation does not impede Croce from perceiving that that movement had still an historical office, and consequently, a positive character as well. Most immediately, that positive character lay in the success of its practical aim. Its aim, he has pointed out, was to defend the Catholic Church as an institution. Though negative with respect to the ideal character he assigns to the Renaissance and the Reformation, the Counter Reformation is positive in its address to this limited, contingent aim, and this positivity is realized in the fact that it did defend that institution against the forces which seemed to threaten it. These inimical forces were limited to the forces of the Reformation; for it is not possible to oppose the Renaissance and the Catholic Church, or any movement in defence of the Catholic Church, in the same manner that one must oppose that institution to the Reformation. The Catholic Church and the Renaissance had from the first been allied; the Renaissance was a movement within the framework of the Catholic culture of which the Church was the informing principle. It is a myth, Croce agrees, to try to apparentate the Renaissance and the Reformation historically, and he is not unsympathetic to Nietzsche's view that the Reformation impeded the historical development of the Renaissance by forcing the Church into the pattern of the Counter Reformation.

The Counter Reformation did not oppose the Reformation, it should be noted, under the ideal aspect which he has ascribed to this latter movement. It opposed the Reformation in its historical concrete form; and Croce finds it impossible not to recognize the discrepancy between this historical form of the Reformation and the ideal character he has assigned to it. For, in his own words, 'the Reformation was not at that time the principle of subjectivism nor the establishment of free thought and of religious tolerance, nor liberation from dogmas and from papal power; rather, it opposed one theology to another, and one papacy to another'.[1] On this plane, he remarks (the only plane, incidentally on which the two movements can really be compared or contrasted, as we shall note more fully against Croce's analysis), the Reformation proved no match for the Counter Reform. What motives could there be, in such a confrontation, which could induce the Catholic Church to confess herself inferior to the Reformation? The Roman theology was less insipid than that of the Reformation; it involved difficulties, but none greater, or even so great, as that of Protestant doctrines; the historiography of such writers as Baronius (Cesare Card. Baronio, 1538–1608) shows itself more learned and no less critical than that of the centurions of Magdeburg; the logic of its controversialists, such as Bellarmin (Roberto Card. Bellarmino, 1542–1621) was more cogent than that of their adversaries; its Latin was in general purer than the Latinity of the reformers, while its culture was larger by far and more versatile; finally the men whom the Church and the Counter Reformation could draw to their cause were in no way of lesser stature or fewer in number than the reformist champions. Under a certain aspect, it was a facile victory and foreordained.[2]

In a wider area of positive effectiveness, Croce states that the Counter Reformation saved the principle and the fact of national unity, so potent in the later history of Europe and of the world. For in the most serious of its strategical errors, perhaps, the Reformation had let itself be drawn into political strife. On theological grounds it had introduced strife between the citizens and the subjects of cities and nations and kindled the flames of civil war in its most terrible, that is to say religious, guise. But the Counter Reformation appeared as a saving principle, exercising this office in Spain, in France, in Italy and throughout the extensive domains of the house of Austria. Croce notes that Italy has especial reason to recognize the positive work of the Counter Reformation. It may readily be imagined, he reflects, how immensely the work of Italian unification, so difficult in any case, would have been complicated had the element of religious difference, for example a Protestant north and a Catholic

[1] SEB, 12.   [2] SEB, 12–13.

south, been introduced into the already numerous motives of separatism in the peninsula. In addition, he recognizes that the Catholic Church exercised a salutary ethical and moral discipline over the peoples whose fidelity she had retained, an achievement which can be measured accurately only when contrasted with the disorders and the moral impoverishment which the Reformation had induced and to which so unprejudiced a witness as Giordano Bruno testifies. Further still, the Counter Reformation had shown itself the preserver of a great part of the culture of the Renaissance toward which the Reformation had shown itself hostile, the love of letters inherited from the humanists and the cultivation of the figurative and architectonic arts. Finally, directly drawing the sting of the Reformation, the Church had brought about extensive reformation within her own body, clarifying her teaching, improving her discipline, and even, through missionary activity, extending her domain.

By this enumeration, Croce might seem to have tipped the balance heavily in favour of the positive dimension of the Counter Reformation. His own view would not, however, support such a conclusion. For the positivity of the Counter Reformation is wholly at the level of its intrinsic practical character. It is, however, pre-cisely this practical character which establishes the negativity of the movement when measured by the criterion of creative ideality and ethical will. Positive and negative elements still remain, therefore, incommensurate in the Counter Reformation; the one, the positive, is never able to overcome the intrinsic limitation of the movement, because it remains qualitatively negative with respect to the pre-supposition against which it is measured.

There can be little temptation to deny the profundity and bril-liance of this analysis; at the same time, however, it is impossible to suppress certain doubts which arise and which have their origin in the very course of his narrative. The first of these concerns, of course, his characterization of the Counter Reformation simply as the defence of a single institution. This characterization appears too limited when one contemplates the extent of the efficiency he assigns to it, the character of the institution in question. The fact is that the Counter Reformation can be called a defence of the Catholic Church when the Catholic Church is considered not as a single isolated insti-tution but as the representative of a whole historical complex of institutions, values and attitudes. To admit this is to change radically the characterization of the Counter Reformation. Although it had its focus in the Catholic Church, its reference is that whole cultural tradition of which the Church through her historical agency in the formation of that tradition has become representative. If this rectification be pressed, the contrast between Reformation and Counter Reformation in terms of ideal and practical becomes much less cogent if not entirely untenable.

The resolution of this question depends on the clarification of another obscurity in Croce's exposition. This is the apparent anti-historicism of his stigmatization of the Counter Reformation as practical and non-ideal. He called that movement practical and political because its forces were directed to the conservation of a particular institution and not toward the invention of new forms of the ethical life. This would appear as a rejection of that conservatism toward which any theory, such as Croce's own, which takes history seriously, would seem to incline. Why is a movement non-ideal simply because it is directed toward the preservation of institutions or of a representative institution, if this institution represents the achieved ideality of history which, according to his own theory,[1] represents the existential basis of all further ideality in history. There would seem to be here a *non-sequitur* which, if not exposed and corrected, might prove disastrous for his whole historiographical enterprise. The basic insight is that the human spirit is incommensurate with its own historical phenomenology; and this cannot be denied. The conclusion is then drawn, quite illogically, however, that orientation toward that phenomenology cannot be in its turn ideal but only practical. The conclusion should, on the contrary, be that the conservation of its past is a basic ideal value for the human spirit, and hence can inform a conservative as well as a progressive movement.

Finally, there would appear to be a serious flaw in Croce's conception of the Reformation, as he establishes a contrast between this movement and the Counter Reformation. On the one hand, he characterizes the former movement as ideal. When, however, it becomes necessary to carry this contrast into particulars he is compelled to recognize that the historical actuality of the Reformation does not correspond to the ideality he has assigned to it. And he recognizes further that the Reformation to our own day shows no signs of actualizing that ideality.[2] It is difficult, if not impossible, consequently, not to conclude that the ideality which Croce discovers in the Reformation is an ideality of pure attribution and not

[1] Cf. SPA, 19 sqq., 30 sqq., 32 sqq., 42 sqq., *passim*.   [2] SEB, 12.

an historical characteristic. The contrast with the Counter Reformation in these terms, consequently, loses much of its force. Croce here attempts to find in the Reformation the antecedents of his own liberalism; but his success in this effort is dubious. Nor, if it had been successful, would the quality of that liberalism be enhanced by this genealogy. His historiographic insight here has become clouded by certain theoretical and programmatic preoccupations. His own description of the Reformation in this same work remains closer to the truth.[1]

[1] SEB, 11 sqq.

IV

THE SILENCE OF GREAT POETRY

WHILE the earliest reference of the term and concept of the 'baroque', as Croce has noted, was to the architectonic and figurative arts, it is in poetry and literature that the 'animo barocco' found its clearest, most self-conscious and even programmatic expression. It was the poet Marino (Giambattista Marino, 1569–1625) who had distilled the baroque ideal (if so it may be called) into an epigram and erected this in turn into an absolute criterion of taste and of artistic achievement when he wrote that the object of art must be to induce wonder and that one who had not this power could never merit the title poet.[1] The real significance of his utterance lay in the fact that it laid bare, in the words of its greatest representative, the basic malady of the baroque soul, its substitution of a practical and trivial thaumaturgy for the ideal of poetic truth. Because of the degree to which they are marked by their self-consciousness of their own inner quality (though it is not a critical self-consciousness), poetry and literature assume a central if not indeed the central place in Croce's anatomy of the baroque age. Here it is that he sees that baroque soul reflected in all its grotesque, distorted and bizarre lineaments; but it is here, also, that he discerns, in rare gleams of authentic poetry, the positive life of the spirit.

Before that vast symphony of dissonance, which is the poetry of the baroque age, arose there had descended on Italian culture a vast silence, 'the silence of great poetry'. Great poetry had been, as it were, the native tongue of Italy. Since first she had found voice in Dante, when amid the waning cosmopolitanism of the middle ages the sentiment of nationalism had first begun to stir, she had not lacked great poetic souls who in great works of fundamentally poetic motivation had made vocal the positive life which surged within her. But now those voices were silent. The last of them had been raised in the *Gerusalemme Liberata* of Torquato Tasso, a work which though

---

[1] *Adone*: 'È del poeta il fin la mera viglia/chi non sa far stupir, vada alla striglia.' Cf. F. DeSanctis, *Storia della letteratura italiana*, Bari, 1949, II, 210.

it is allied to the new age, the baroque age, by certain of its secondary aspects and by certain of its weaknesses and failings is still in the great tradition. Later criticism, stressing these secondary aspects and emphasizing these weaknesses and failings, had obscured its native grandeur: neo-classicism, as in Boileau, which saw in its author a mere 'lavorante in orpello', a tinsel weaver, and romanticism, tinged with mediaevalism, which had seen in him a false and artificial repetitor of the great epics of the Crusades. But Tasso had appeared in a truer light to his contemporaries and to the sentiment of the people; to them he had spoken from the heart to the heart; his poem, with its lively, vibrant and exciting rhythm, poured forth from a soul that was moved and hence possessed the power in turn to move. It seemed born of a dream of glory and of love, of power and of pleasure, of severe and noble joy and of delicate melancholy. It was at once sublime and tender, virile and feminine; its inspiration not epic but pathetic. And throughout it was pervaded by a religious tonality, the quality of a religion which was wholly devotion, faithfulness, loyal service, the religion of a knight of God toward his Lord. Its moral elevation is sincere; the struggle which it depicts—between pleasure and glory, duty and inclination—is a real struggle, and not the false combats which will be fought in the frigid lines of Marino. Beside its excellences, the baroque elements which intrude and which seem to make it a harbinger of the false age to follow, count for little; they are more than redeemed by the overwhelming poetic truth of Tasso's vision. Still the *Gerusalemme* is a swan song; the swan song of great poetry, which would not lift its voice again for a century. When it had died away there reigned only the great silence.

Contemporaneously with Tasso, another voice had been raised, but one whose true note, unlike that of Tasso, went undiscerned by his own times. This was the voice of Tommaso Campanella (1568–1639). His too, to Croce's mind, was the voice of great poetry, though in a vein greatly diverse from that of the singer of the *Gerusalemme*. Campanella's was the note of true sacred poetry; its antecedents must be sought in Jacopone da Todi, in the visionary portions of the *Commedia* and in the prophets of the Old Testament. Campanella was both man of action and philosopher; but he was poet before all else, and the poetic afflatus is diffused through his thought and his activity. This very diffusion had, however, a weakening effect upon the poetic strain itself; it tended to remain in potency, so to say, and not to be condensed into pure moments of expression. But when such condensation does take place, the purity of the distillate cannot be questioned.[1]

Campanella, it was noted, passed unknown as a poet in his own time; this lack of recognition was symbolic, for he was not of his own age. Tasso, by contrast, was known to, and tended even to dominate, his period and the age which followed; but that dominion was not poetically fruitful. Since poetry is not generated by poetry, but only by the direct movement of sentiment, that dominion tended rather to foster an imitative strain, to which the new age was strongly inclined. For it was an unpoetic age, and its unpoetic character was due, not to any accidental circumstance, such as a failure to rise to its models, but to a basic cause, the failure of the affective life itself. The special character of this age, Croce states, is the absence of vivid religious, political or ethical ideals. There was not lacking either conservative or formative power, nor poetic ability; it was the life of the affections which ran dry; and while the affective life is not poetry, it is the first condition of poetry. The purest voice of the age would by general consent be recognized as that of Metastasio; by the same recognizance, however, the temptation to call Metastasio's poetry great is easily resisted. His was a clear but tenuous vein of gracious, even coquettish tenderness. Breaking forth, as it does, amid the pompous machinery of his dramas, it is infinitely refreshing. If the epithet great should be applied in any sense to him, he might be called the great poet of the superficial,[2] if such a characterization is not itself a denial of greatness. In Arcadia the baroque age achieved its greatest act of poetic self-purification and in a certain sense transcended itself; so that from another point of view[3] it constitutes a turning point in artistic history; but the ideals of Arcadia were not themselves poetic, and much less in the vein of great poetry. Correctness, restraint, discipline, these are the qualities of a critical reaction, rather than of a poetic renaissance.[4] To detect an echo of great poetry, paradoxical as it may seem, one must turn to prose. The great poetry in this age spoke out in a philosopher, who in many ways is the successor of Campanella, in the creator of the *Scienza Nuova*, Giambattista Vico (1668-1744). The animating principle of great philosophical exploration is poetic in the profoundest sense of the term, and his deepest insights flash out in images and break into rhythms now harsh, now solemn, but always of true poetic strength. In Vico, Croce also detects the precursor of the romantic revival in

[1] SEB, 240-2.   [2] SEB, 243.   [3] LI'700, 1 sqq.
[4] SEB, 243; LI'700, loc. cit.

poetry, the forerunner of Alfieri, of Foscolo, of Leopardi and Manzoni, in whom the paradox of a poetry in prose is resolved, and great
poetry finds unmistakable voice again.[1]

It is a characteristic of the baroque age which Croce will note
many times, that it was wholly unaware of the malady which
afflicted it.[2] In the present context, it showed itself unaware of the
silence which enveloped it, that silence of great poetry which culturally is so ominous. And it was fortified in this insensibility (if not
seduced into it), by its own theoretical preconceptions. So long as
poetry was confused with rhymed eloquence and with versification,
so long must the silence of great poetry have gone unadverted and
the age continued rapt in a haze of tinsel melody, taking the false for
the true, rejecting the true, when it appeared, with reasoned error.

If then, the baroque age was an age of the silence of great poetry,
it was, at the same time, an age which was completely persuaded of
its own greatness, in poetry, as in all else. This is the very soul of the
age, the reality of its 'decadence', this intransigent illusion in which
it wrapped itself. Reading the poetry (the pseudo-poetry, as Croce
says, adverting to the basic substitution of practical for theoretic
motive) against the background of the great poetic heritage of preceding periods or in contrast with the rich poetic expression of subsequent eras, the reader finds it is difficult to suppress a smile, to believe that it could be expressed and offered, *seriously*, as poetry. But
the versifiers of this age were inspired by a profound conviction—a
terrible conviction, is Croce's phrase—of the seriousness of their
intent and of the stature of their expression. It is this precisely which
makes of their poetry a simulation, a pseudo-poetry. And in evidence
of this seriousness, since the poetry itself cannot be its document,
there may be adduced the readiness with which they compared their
work, and themselves, most favourably to the ancients, and the
moderns as well. Marino, the same Marino who gave the age its
supreme criterion of taste and expression in a couplet, is the equal
of Virgil, of Homer, and of Dante; by contrast to him, the great
Tasso is but the dawn which precedes the sun of noon. An image of
collective madness spontaneously suggests itself and Alfieri (Vittorio
Alfieri, 1749–1803) could not help exclaiming, 'The seventeenth
century was taken with delirium.'[3]

[1] SEB, 244.
[2] For a characteristic passage cf. Fausto Nicolini, *Benedetto Croce: Vita Intellettuale*, Napoli, 1944, 90.
[3] SEB, 245–6: 'Il seicento delirava.'

Again and again the name of Marino has suggested itself in the discussion of this age. By a vast synecdoche, Croce takes first Marino, and then by extension of the figure, one poem of Marino, as the epitome of the baroque soul in poetry. In the man, and in that poem, all of the vices of the age are distilled, so that they can be studied in their purity, so to say, unalloyed by any element of a saner vision. The *Adone*, Settembrini (Luigi Settembrini, 1813–76) had written, is a unique work, the like of which neither ancient nor modern poetry can boast. In what does this uniqueness consist, Croce demands; in this alone he finds that, pompous and fabricated though it is, it is made quite literally of nothing; filled with a world of things, it is innocent of any poetry or authentic sentiment. It has been called the poem of voluptuousness. But of this he finds no trace; nor any trace, for that matter, of those qualities which are sometimes mistakenly identified with voluptuousness, sensuality and luxury. What he does find, is an intimate and constitutive frigidity, and a plenum of irrelevances which only momentarily conceals the void within.

What he discovers in Marino and in the *Adone* above all is the apotheosis of the fatal trinity of the baroque spirit, conceptualism, or conceit, ingenuity and musicality, qualities which derive most clearly from the basic substitution of the practical for the poetic and which in turn give rise to a host of attributes which fortify the unpoetic character of the composition. The notion of conceptualism, or conceit, as Croce applies it to the *Adone*, to Marino and to the poetry of the baroque age in general and as it is thence properly transferred to the baroque spirit itself, is complex. It indicates, in the first place, the fatal substitution in the poem of the abstract element for the concrete immediacy of the image; or even more precisely, perhaps, the weaving of a pseudo-image out of these abstract elements. In this manner there occurs a complex transaction of counterfeits; for the only true coin of poetry is the image itself, whose metal is sentiment, which, in the process of image formation, is itself transformed. The mark of the poetic image is integrity and its wholeness, its immediateness, its entire particularity and concreteness and above all the warmth of the affection which flows through it. It can no more be a compound of abstract elements, than an acorn can be a compound of the abstractions of colour, or size or taste. It is like the acorn, all *this*, in its immediacy, its wholeness, its concreteness. But for Marino, as pseudo-image after pseudo-image of the *Adone* illustrates, the image is something altogether diverse. It is a mechanical fabrication whose elements are abstract particulars woven according to a pattern which has its principle not in a spontaneous movement of the affections, but in some device of the fancy. It is through this latter circumstance that the second characteristic of conceptualism, that signalized by the term conceit, finds entrance. For the image of true poetry is wholly spontaneous, which means that its concreteness and unity is established by an immediate principle of sentiment and insight generated by sentiment. The image springs full grown from the imagination moved by sentiment; it is not laboriously confected according to some artificial design. But in the *Adone* the latter is precisely what transpires. And from this circumstance derives the basic failing of the poet, as Croce sees it: Marino cannot create an image, which is to say, without further qualification, that he is no poet.

In place of the power to create the poetic image, Marino displays another, which is its counterfeit, and which Croce calls descriptivism. Whenever the reader expects, according to the logic of poetry itself, the image, he finds himself confronted instead with an elaborate fabrication, which is like nothing so much as a rich Brussels tapestry seen at too close range. The expected unity recedes and in its place there advance to meet the eye the multitude of delicate threads out of which the fabric is woven. Or with even less order, Marino offers again and again, in place of the concrete image, a litany of abstract traits which no principle unifies, which exhausts the eye, the ear and the mind, but leaves poetic hunger, that is the hunger for the true and concrete image of poetry, unsatisfied. This descriptivism is rich, so rich indeed, that in its mere quantitative character it cannot represent any synthesis of immediate experience. And the poet exhibits at this juncture that quality which is more frequently imputed to the scholar and the pedant and which is in the poet like the killing wind of the desert: bookishness. Literary imitation is the invariable companion of descriptivism, and we are confronted by that unnatural process of books breeding books, poems breeding upon poems, with no mediation of personality and sentiment.

The descriptivism he detects in this poem leads Croce to the consideration of the second member of that fatal trinity, ingenuity. For descriptivism has its root in ingenuity, of which it constitutes but one variety. The ingenuity which pervades the baroque spirit springs from its basic practical motive, the thaumaturgic. Seeking always to overwhelm with wonder and amazement, that spirit finds it difficult to discover fresh devices to this end. For this reason, it cultivates above all this power of ingenuity, which seeks out the ever new, the rare, the unexpected, the strange and arresting combination which will work the thaumaturgic effect. Ingenuity introduces us into the workshop of the magician, where all of the marvels of the flood-lit stage are seen to be ponderous contraptions put together by a clever, but shallow fancy. Ingenuity works in the soul itself, with thoughts, with sentiments; and here its poison is most lethal, for it tends through deceit to kill the soul itself. Descriptivism is a less virulent form of the same venom; it is ingenuity operative at the level of physical vision, seeking to combine physical details in the same striking and thaumaturgic fashion. But in itself it is the same activity. Sometimes this descriptivism has been mistaken for realism; how unfounded such an identity must be is easy to see. For a virile realism seeks in its own way and on its own presuppositions that same concreteness which is the mark of the poetic image. It would never rest content with the concatenation of abstract details according to some arbitrary and artificial principle which is the procedure of descriptivism.

Musicality has sometimes been thought the highest achievement of the poetry of the baroque and in itself a high poetic achievement. For, it has been said, here the intimate yearning of poetry is fulfilled, its yearning to be dissolved into its pure form, freed of all specific content. Such an identification, Croce remarks, reflects little perception of the character either of poetry or of music; it is to mistake the nature of music to conceive it as a poetic structure, emptied of all relevant content, rather than, as it really is, a mode of expression capable of its own concreteness. At the same time, it shows little perception of the quality of poetry to conceive of it as yearning toward the negation of that very concreteness of image and sentiment which is its most intimate principle and which in turn generates that music which is proper to poetry and which is not an artificial transplantation of music in its formal character. The musicality ascribed to the poetry of the baroque as an achievement is in reality another of its devices for concealing the void within itself. The musical flow of the verse creates a false sense of the presence of poetry. But when one resists the temptation to glide with the movement of the music of the verse, and attends to the essentials and the reality, that absence is at once revealed and the mind disabused.

All of these pejorative characteristics, and above all the supreme trinity of baroque pseudo-poetry, are comprehensible more clearly in their origin. This is, as Croce has noted again and again, the basic substitution which lies at the heart of baroque poetry and which is the source of all its failing. Once the poetic principle, that is poetic truth, is forsworn, the host of vices which may spring up is innumerable and unpredictable. The baroque generates those which he mentioned; but a thousand other might as easily have followed from the same basic failing. The phenomenology of error, in every order, is infinite; the centrality of truth alone is fixed and invariable. In this present instance, this truth is the truth of poetry which is nothing other than the candour of the spirit, the genuineness of its affections and its sentiment and the purity of the poetic impulse by which affection and sentiment are transformed and transfigured into the poetic image. A basic substitution, such as that of the thaumaturgic for the poetic motive, draws in its train a certain set of negative characteristics by a logic of its own, and these are the qualities which he has discerned in the *Adone*.

A characteristic of the poetry, or of the greater part of the poetry, of the age more indicative in Croce's eyes of decadence than any of the qualities enumerated is sensuality. This sensuousness of the baroque age is not the mere delight, that spontaneous immersion, in the life of the senses which is sometimes thought to be the primary quality of paganism; for this delight, this immersion, is, after all, as Croce indicates, a human thing, a minimal humanity which is still the basis of the life of the spirit.[1] Even more is it to be distinguished from the sentiment of love, the cult of love, with its moral elevation and its religious and cosmic afflatus as this was known in the poetry of the golden 'dugento' the thirteenth century, and as it continued intimate to Italian poetry even to the threshold of the baroque itself, to Tasso. Finally, it must be set over against that sensuousness which is the essence of poetry itself, by which the poetic intuition seeks its real existence in the concrete sensuous form, in which, through this intuition, the spirit is incarnated. If it were any of these, that poetry would be lifted to a plane of human realization which would purge it of all negative characteristics.

The sensuous quality of this poetry was, on the contrary, the very negation of all these. In a certain sense, it was not sensuality at all, but rather a frigid approach to the sensuous which is closer to obscenity. It was concerned not with the inner quality of love, but with its mere surfaces, that aspect under which, in the words of Chamfort, love is merely contact between two 'epidermi', with no inner effulgence either of the affections or of the imagination. Here was the quality neither of Petrarch, all aspiration, nor of Boccaccio,

[1] SEB, 305.

all spontaneous and festive enjoyment of the senses, but a quality which only the prince of the baroque poets, Marino himself, could aptly name, as he did, 'lascivious'. And the very fact that this chief of its practitioners could find the uniquely fitting name for it, demonstrates with new force the particularly perverse quality of this sensuality. It was a studied thing, which could contemplate both itself and its object from a psychic distance which is the measure of its perversity. A substitution takes place here analogous to and having great affinity with the basic substitution of the practical for the poetic motive. Finally, and the ultimate mark of its decadence, there is the seriousness with which the pursuit of the sensuous in the frigid and anatomic manner was carried on. The fact was, in Croce's view, that the baroque soul had no standard by which to measure this obscene pursuit and hence could neither transcend nor evaluate it; neither reason nor humour intervened to awaken it from this nightmare quest. And as typical of all of these characteristics he again selects a poem of Marino, the *Pastorella*, so grave and dignified in its well-turned octaves, which narrates all the ancient details of pastoral dalliance as though it were narrating the most sublime and moving of histories.[1]

Innumerable are the themes about which this sensuality, like a choking growth, entwines itself; all of the themes of the classic anthology, themes torn from Tasso and the other giants of earlier decades of Italian art, the great themes of the Renaissance. But one theme above all other seemed both to attract and to exhibit this aspect of the baroque soul in all its liquescent decadence. This was the theme of the Magdalene. The reason, retrospectively, is not difficult to discern. Here was a theme which under one icon satisfied all of the perverse urges of the baroque soul. What more appealing to that 'concettosità', that hunger to bring together all extremes, all violent contrasts, all pure contradictions and hold them in a thaumaturgic unity? In the Magdalene the most striking extremes and contrasts, religious conversion and sexual lasciviousness, could be united in one form, one person, one soul. What infinite variations could be played upon this theme! How, under the mask of the religious symbol, the sensual element could be toyed with, dilated, coloured with the subtle motive of intensifying the religious contrast. How, under the sensual image, the cool enumeration of sensuous detail, the religous and devotional element could be mocked, gently but with infinite irony; or when no shade of mockery or irony intruded, could it

[1] SEB, 306.

be brought down to a level where the sensuous soul could find in it the reflection of its own inner quality lifted to a plane of approbation beyond all cavil. This was the theme upon which poet after poet expended his effort, in a joyful rivalry, exhibiting all the extravagances of the baroque touch. Verbal extravagance, ingeniousness, conceit, descriptivism, musicality—each lent its peculiar embellishment.[1]

This, with the other favourite themes of the period, exhibits the ultimate characteristic of the baroque in its nudity: the unity of the intellectual and the sensuous in a purely extrinsic relation, which has aptly been called the wedding of the syllogism and the sensuous image. The sensuous details which the imagination evokes are organized and expounded with the frigid mechanism of an 'argomento in barocco'. The life of the senses is approached with the pedantic detachment of the scholastic logician, who handles the terms of his argument without reference to sense and meaning but according to the abstract rules of his syllogistic art. To syllogize about love, the sensual surfaces of love, in perfectly moulded octaves, not to move the emotions, but to tickle the jaded fancy and to astound the 'cognoscenti' with metrical, psychological and physiological virtuosity, this was the sensuality of baroque poetry.

To this point Croce has done little more than concatenate a litany of negations to characterize the baroque era in its poetic expression. By doing so he is, of course, violating his own canon, that to write the history of a negative period one must seek out the positive and creative elements which, however tenuous and weak, must still lie smouldering beneath the vast incumbrance of pseudo-poetic expression. There is, however, a rationale in his procedure; the negative characteristics must be delineated, he feels, as the foil against which the quest for the positive and creative elements must be conducted. And it is with genuine relief that he turns to this latter, more grateful undertaking.

The first positive element he discerns is the contemporary criticism of the baroque mannerisms and perversities. So long as the critical faculty is not entirely extinguished, the life of the spirit has not actually expired. Not a few critics of the period, he notes, penetrated to the fundamental vice of the baroque soul,[2] and they sought to bring home their critical barbs both by direct censure and by oblique satire of the extravagances, distortions and perversities of the

[1] LI'600; 'Sensualismo e Ingegnosità nella lirica del seicento', pp. 435 sqq.
[2] SEB, 268, 243.

age. As a matter of fact, however, criticism is not a definitive and autonomous activity. Effective criticism can only be measured by the quality of the expression it inspires, and not by any criterion intrinsic to itself. Criticism is a catalytic. And it is this fact which throws into relief the failure of the critical efforts of the baroque age in Italy. For while that criticism was strong enough to penetrate to the root-evil of the baroque mode, it lacked the strength or clarity to oppose to this pseudo-poetry a creative ideal of true poetry.

Instead, it recommended a course which, under certain aspects, is worse than the failings of the baroque spirit: an imitative return to the past. Weak, perverse, superficial as the pseudo-poetry of the baroque period was, he declares, it had discerned one thing, that the past is dead. The poetry, the art of the past is always beautiful in its own right; but it is past, and it cannot, therefore, be a guide or a model for the beauty which yet awaits creation by the human spirit. It is an illusion for the human spirit to seek models for its own creative activity in the past. The effort to do so breeds a host of vices, the very opposite of those exhibited by the art of the baroque, but vices still.

The basic ideal of such imitative art can only be correctness. Correctness expresses nothing specific, only the imitative relation itself. It cannot, clearly, be an inner quality of the artist's own crea-tion. Art can never be grafted from without; it must be nourished from within. Aridity is the inevitable consequence of imitation. Aridity, the antonym of creativity, and its synonyms, pedantry, frigidity, designate simply the absence of poetry.

The faint gleams of critical discernment in the period prove, consequently, a fatuous light. They lead Croce into the arid wastes of 'literary poetry', a desert of forms diverse but no less grotesque than the forms of pseudo-poetry which he has escaped. Here in these salt wastes he encounters the 'petrarchists', the 'casists', the 'portuans' and the other nomadic bands, huddled together beneath the banner of some hallowed name from the past, but sterile; their passion for correctness makes it impossible to utter a word not to be found in the pages of their master. There are the purists of sentiment, who constrict their affections within the artificial bonds of the sentiment of another soul, singing again of the cruelty of the lady who is the object of their sighs, bewailing her death, forming proposals of repentance and of a return from worldly to heavenly love, as though they had encountered Beatrice upon a bridge across the Arno or stood upon Campidoglio with the laurel on their heads as Laura smiled down from the countenance of the sun. Or the purists of form who build only doric columns when the doric soul is dead; in this case, compose heroic poems, when the heroic afflatus is still. As Croce writes, it was almost a matter of honour with these poets to compose an heroic epic, and they are to be numbered in the hundreds on every theme; but each is a temple without a god, a poem empty of poetry. This critical movement inspired Arcadia and of Arcadia it is possible to say many fine things, but not that it is poetry.[1]

The human spirit languishes but does not die; in moments of deepest depression it retreats to the simple affections, where it finds sustenance. So it is in the baroque age. In the midst of that vast body of extravagant, perverted, pretentious verse, the verse of men who had not only perverted the idea of poetry, but had turned perversion into a programme, he discovers the warmth of the simple affections now and again. In the poet Marino, who had given the baroque era its model and its formula in four lines of his *Adone*,[2] in whom the extravagances and the postures of that baroque 'style' had become a second nature, even in him, the positive flame of genuine, untrammelled, human affection was not altogether extinguished; rather it burned, deep within his soul, which after all was the soul of a man, orientated toward truth and sincerity of the affections and ultimately toward his God, waiting only the occasion strong enough to tear aside that false façade of affectation, of pose, of sensuality and sentimentality hopelessly intermingled, and to expose the heart in its simple humanity. This occasion was the death of his mother. Confronted with the soulless countenance of the woman who had born him and pierced with a sense of loss wholly immediate, personal and, for the instant, without consolation, he abandons style[3] and permits the affections of his heart to find direct expression. The result is a strophe unmatched in all the vast proliferation of a lifetime of versifying: fresh, faultless in its kind, wholly spontaneous. His heart, as it were, was taken by surprise.

Similarly, one and another of his followers are surprised by their own simple humanity, betrayed, by occasions of moving affection, into free utterances, springing from a poetic source which, laboriously, they had concealed and distorted by the mask of 'style'. Thus the poet Sempronia, revisiting the city of Bologna, is in turn visited by the memory of his student-days there, rough, laborious, boister-

---

[1] LI'700, 1 sqq.　　　　　　　　　　　　　　　　　[2] Cf. *supra.*
[3] For style, he writes, is powerless to express great sorrow—SEB, 324.

ous, but wholly spontaneous and sincere; rapt by remembered affections, he sings of those days with freshness and spontaneity. Della Valle, revisiting Cosenza, his native place, and Palma, returning to the place of his birth in remote Dauno, are surprised into verse of unpremeditated lyric purity. And the sensitive and cultivated Neapolitan, Torquato Accetto, upon whom the cumbersome armour of the baroque style must have weighed like an iron shroud, speaks in unguarded moments of his profound need of an interior and meditative life into which he might withdraw and which in turn might save him from the violence and the rudeness of the society in which he lived, and tells of the hours he stole from sleep to devote to 'silence, the pen and wise thought'.[1] In others, Croce notes, the force of habit, of 'second nature' is too strong; such moments of pure and spontaneous affection are betrayed; they are victimized by the versifying mechanism they have themselves fashioned. Thus Ciro di Pers, made sleepless in his bed by the solemn thought that in this very bed death might visit him, cannot give spontaneous expression to this primordial fear of the human spirit confronted by its inevitable end; he must transmute this thought into stilted and mortifying symbols, antitheses, alliterations and conceits. The case of di Pers, it must be confessed, is more the rule rather than the exception. The pure affection strong enough to break the iron hold of perverse style become a second self, remains a rarity.

The 'religious' poetry of the period was abundant; indeed, superabundant; and with the admission of a certain distinction it is possible to count much of it as sincere and without affectation. The necessary distinction is that between religion in its pure, severe and exalted character—such as it is to be discerned in the poetry of the Old Testament, in the rhythms of Francis of Assisi, of Jacopone da Todi or of the poet whom Croce has not hesitated to compare to these, Campanella—and devotion. The poetry of the baroque age was devotional rather than religious. It is necessary to appreciate, however, that devotion is not simply sentimentalized religion, but exhibits certain positive and primordial characteristics. Its fervour was genuine and its concern for the salvation of souls no whit the less authentic and capable of inspiring deeds absolutely heroic in the practical order. The quality of its expression, however, was very diverse, reflecting the qualitative difference of inspiring sentiment. The conquest of heaven was for it no longer the heroic 'impresa'

[1] SEB, 326–7; for all the men cited here cf. *Lirici marinisti*, ed. Croce, Bari, 1913, *passim*.

accompanied by inward torment which it had appeared to the religious sentiment of Campanella. It was the movement of the heart to God in a spontaneous efflux of possessive love. And such in turn was the tonality of the poetry it inspired. Much of this poetry, it is true, fell victim to the prevailing stylistic dogmas and exhibited them in their most extravagant forms. More sounded a true and gentle note, which cannot but be recognized for what it is, corresponding to and expressing an affection and a sentiment pure and without blemish in its kind. Croce cites as an example the *Puer Jesus* of del Ceva; and he recognizes that this devotional expression reaches its peak in Alphonse Ligouri who synthesized in a wonderful manner so many of the conflicting elements of his age.[1]

It is in the little things that the poetry of the baroque age was betrayed despite itself into simple affective lyricism. Its constitutive malady embraced an infatuation with the grandiose; but its humanity could not be closed to the appeal and charm of the simple and spontaneous, to the vision of a young girl confiding to a companion the strange yet delicious torments of first love, or the awe of a simple country girl visiting for the first time the fabled streets of a provincial town, or the simple sentiment which accompanied a basket of fruit and flowers to a sick friend, and the admiration inspired by a seamstress delicately embroidering a design of birds and flowers on a filmy bit of lace. When vignettes such as these flashed upon the inward and unguarded eye, they inevitably evoked a lyric response. And in such moments pure poetry persisted, vindicating poetic truth amid the vast fabrication of that age.

Yet it was not here, either in the inexhaustible surprise of simple things taking the spirit unaware, or in the literature of religious devotion, with its sincere though saccharine approach to religious experience and truth, that the truly liberating force was to be found. It resided, rather, in two other elements of the culture of the time. These were the comic or humorous strain, immemorial in the literary and poetic tradition of Italy, and the novel phenomenon of the artistic transformation of the dialectal literatures. These were, in root, diverse. The one was born of the depths of the human spirit, in which the demon of laughter is frequently enough the demon of truth and sincerity. The other was born of a need of the time to find new material upon which to deploy its marvellous poetic and literary technique. Nevertheless, they frequently intermingled, for the spirit of laughter, the rich earthy humour of the human soul is most fre-

[1] SEB, 330; cf. NSL'600, 134-53.

quently to be heard in the songs and the tales of the people, for whom laughter and irony and satire are many times the only weapon against fate and despair.

Croce had noted before that one of the salient characteristics of the baroque soul was its lack of humour, its lack above all of the power to laugh at itself. It took even its most extravagant enterprises with the greatest seriousness, shamelessly comparing its grotesque constructions with the venerable masterpieces of the western and Italian traditions. Its inability to laugh at itself was perhaps the clearest indication of the depth of the baroque malady. Conversely, the surest signs that the seeds of humanity, that human sanity and spiritual health had not been extinguished entirely, were to be discerned precisely in the re-awakened power to achieve aesthetic distance from itself and to become the object of its own discerning humour, satire, and irony. This was the first sign of the liberation of the Italian soul from the baroque malady. It was a feeble movement indeed, like the first smile, or the first lighting of the eyes of a man who had journeyed to the confines of death, but now returns. In the Italian tradition and the Italian soul, this sign was especially significant; for during all its history, the Italian spirit had given this one sign of its essential soundness and humanity, that it was able to take human life at once seriously and lightly and itself most seriously and most lightly of all. Other nations had frequently mistaken this capacity for cynicism; but closer scrutiny reveals it to be genuine humanism, the only possible mood for a being, like man, who skirts the edge of the abyss while labouring to reach heaven. He is like a mountain climber, who must at all costs, while scaling the most precarious heights, remain relaxed. It is his own inner tension which will hurl him into the depths.

Not that the baroque soul was able to arrest itself in mid-course, as it were, and turn upon itself and its own extravagances, absurdities and contradictions the streams of a pure and potent satire. This could hardly be expected in the nature of the case and did not, as a matter of fact, occur. On the contrary, the satire, the irony, the jocularity which the baroque soul was able to direct against itself arose from within, from the inevitable relaxation of a cord which is drawn too tight, in Croce's words.[1] The humorous, the satirical, appear time and again as the only sane step beyond the extravagance into which the age had pushed so headstrongly. From the sublime, and especially

[1] SEB, 296: 'simile alle corde troppo tirate . . . di tanto in tanto per non spezzarsi si rilassano.'

the speciously sublime, to the ridiculous, it has been said a thousand times, is an easy step; and a thousand times, the baroque spirit, in order to save itself from delirium, takes this step. In this Marino again leads the way, as when, comparing his Rosa to the rose, he compounds the image to create the antithesis of enthroning her as the sun of earth and the sun in turn as rose of the heavens, and breaks beneath the weight of his own extravagance. Or again, in the conversations reported by Stigliani (Tommaso Stigliani, 1573–1651), Marino, hard put to it to defend some of his compositions, finds ridicule, self-ridicule, the only escape. The cult of woman, and the extravagances to which the celebration of feminine beauty so readily led, again and again presented this occasion to humour, to satire and to laughter; as in the case of Narducci,[1] who was confronted with the impossible task of converting the fact that his mistress was greying fast into a theme of adulation and praise. Almost anything he could say must prove eventually ridiculous, above all since he had, obviously, to avoid as the plague any reference to old age; and nothing more ludicrous than his image of the 'shafts of ivory amid the waves of gold' could be conceived.

As might well be expected, the sense of the ludicrous as it became more self-conscious and as it turned upon the weakness of the baroque manner with greater deliberativeness, sought instruments apt for its purpose. The readiest of these proved to be the dialectal literature, which, by a process to be noted presently, had ceased to be naïve and spontaneous and had become ingenious or 'dell'arte'. The facility with which it became possible to mimic, to carry to even greater extravagance the bizarre, grotesque and absurd mannerisms, and all the highly polished mechanism and techniques of the baroque style, can be appreciated only by one versed in the subtleties of those dialects, which are, of course, not localizations of a central linguistic form but indigenous linguistic phenomena, possessing resources at once inexhaustible and unpredictable. The Neapolitan dialect, one of the oldest, richest and most characteristic of all Italy, proved especially resourceful in this enterprise. It was, to begin with, possessed of a vein of humour, of irony and satire which ran deep, deeper perhaps than in any other regional form; its technical development, moreover, was immense, and as Basile was presently to demonstrate, by no means limited in its power of expression to elementary forms of thought and sentiment but capable of developing and exploiting the most complex and sophisticated. The irony of

[1] Cf. *Lirici marinisti* ed. cit.

all this was rendered the more poignant by the fact that Naples was the home of marinism and its special temple.

The master of this dialectal satirization of the baroque proved to be one Sgruttendio.[1] He created an entire 'canzoniere' which was for the greatest part a parody of the 'canzonieri amorosi' or love-cycles of the period. All of the technical virtuosities of the baroque style were employed with the greatest of skill; the sonnets of the cycle and the sections of free verse are turned as well as anything in Marino. Through all, however, runs one constant strain: the extravaganza woven upon extravaganza engendering and compounding mirth and ludicrousness. Do the poets exhaust themselves in praising the hair of their beloved? Sgruttendio outdoes them, analysing, describing, embellishing to a degree they never dreamed of, and with a resource of localisms whose associations render the whole process hilarious. Or is it her breast that the poet exalts? His own matchless metaphors, redolent of the earthy source of the dialect itself, put all other images and metaphors, hyperboles and synecdoches to shame for glowing tribute and extravagant claim, while revealing the basic imbecility of the whole process. Others join him in the same chorus, Panchiatichi (Lorenzo Panchiatichi, 1635–76), Cortese (Giulio Cesare Cortese, c. 1575), and the great Basile himself. It is a type of humour and satire, Croce remarks, which would scarcely move our own sense of mirth; but in context, its intrinsic value as well as its cultural effect can be appreciated. Its emergence marked the approaching end of the baroque era, the approaching extinction of the baroque spirit itself. Its sense of humour has more than once in history proven the salvation of the human spirit. The fact that the baroque era was able to laugh at itself even in this sly and oblique way, proved again that the spirit lived—the spirit of sanity, of measure, of sincerity, of poetic truth. A people, a culture, which laughs, above all which laughs at itself, is far from perishing though grievous maladies afflict it.[2]

The fresh growth of the dialectal literatures during the baroque era was occasioned in the first instance by the artistic vices of the age. Under the compulsion of thaumaturgic ideal artists explored every possible avenue and exploited every possible source of the astonishing, the novel, the amazing, the extravagant. In this pursuit they were led inevitably to the dialectal literatures which ministered to several

[1] Filippo Sgruttendio, a 'nom de plume' ascribed by critics and historians to various persons. Cf. Antonio Belloni, *Il Seicento*, Milano, 1947, 328.

[2] SEB, 295 sq.

purposes at once. They were, in the first place, rich in fresh and artistically unworked material; they were wealthy in situations, in personages, and in gnomic wisdom; and finally the language itself had, from a cultivated point of view, an exotic, piquant and slightly ludicrous flavour. The contrast which these literatures and the life they portrayed offered to the life and manners of cultured circles was a source of that sense of superiority which always supports an over-refined culture in its own self-esteem. It was thus that the 'commedia dell'arte' came to be so heavily laced with the dialectal element and developed its stereotypes of the regional characters such as the Neapolitan.[1]

In stirring the sleeping giant of dialectal literatures, however, the delicate and rapier talents of the baroque were probing deeper than they knew. A power lay hidden in those literatures great enough to confound their trivial motives, to lay hold upon the minds and the imaginations of the very poets who toyed with them. Thus it came about that the dialectal literatures took a course, in the baroque era, independent and diverse from the first purpose which they were made to serve. There grew up in this era a new art, which Croce calls variously 'letteratura dialettale riflessa' or 'dell'arte', which has a history of its own and which proves one of the most unequivocal manifestations of the positive life of the spirit in that era.

What was the achievement of this dialectal literature 'dell'arte' that gives it, in Croce's view, a unique and supremely important place in the positive achievement of the baroque era? This question can be answered with directness and simplicity. That literature achieves a synthesis between the technical mastery of the baroque spirit and the rich, immediate content of the regional, dialectal liter-atures, which redeemed at once the vacuous facility of the one and the native rudeness of the other, and created a new art form at once accomplished in style, technique and manner and pulsatingly human, rich-blooded, 'spiritoso' in matter, with the power to move the sentiments directly and impetuously. In this synthesis the mal-direction of the baroque spirit is corrected. No longer does it exhaust itself in the fatuous pursuit of a thaumaturgic end alien to poetry; it seeks anew the end of poetry itself which is simply poetic truth and reality. At the same time, a vast wealth of poetic experience, which heretofore had lain imprisoned within the limited achievements of regional talents, was made artistically available to the cultured Italian mind. Croce goes so far as to say, in his analysis of this achievement,

[1] Cf. ASPN, XXIII (1898), 'Il Personaggio del Napoletano, etc.', pp. 702 sqq.

that this new literature contributed an effective element to the national consciousness only then beginning to awaken.

The most striking feature of this dialectal literature 'dell'arte' is its complete freedom from any taint of primitivism. The high level of technical achievement in the arts was, Croce has already pointed out, a positive element in the baroque picture, and it was in virtue of this achievement that Italy was to become the schoolmaster in the arts to the whole of Europe. It is characteristic of the dialectal literature 'dell'arte' that it does not abandon this achievement, that it is not seduced by the typically primitivistic confusion that art of strong and direct sentiment must be rude in its manner, naïve or sentimental. No hoax of the Ossian type could be perpetrated upon the Italian spirit as a whole. The difference lay in this, that the vast technical accomplishment which before had been expended in the vain pursuit of a thaumaturgic and extra-poetic end, now found a genuinely poetic service, and in the process lost all of its glittering 'virtuoso' quality, losing itself, as technique in genuine artistic service must, in the unity of the work of art.

Nothing can exhibit the height of this achievement or its inner quality so well as the experience of the chief practitioner of the new art, Giambattista Basile (1575?-1632). Croce notes in an especial manner, not only the vast *Pentamerone* which was to prove his enduring monument, but the less ambitious, more tenuous and virgilian *Muse Napoletane*. Basile, he remarks, had first approached the dialectal material in the jocose manner of the age. It was to be a new field for the exercise of the 'aulic' mastery of poetic techniques which he had demonstrated a thousand times in all accepted forms: encomia, verses of love, dialogues of wit, pastorals. The verbal exoticness of the dialects first attracted his baroque soul. Gradually, however, his poetic talent expanded in the new medium, especially in the dialect which was, after all, his own, the Neapolitan. He discovered that it imposed no literary obligations upon him, as did the 'lingua aulica', it solicited his poetic insight with no suggestions of its own, but permitted him to express and to pour forth what lay concealed in his heart. In this manner, he was led to fashion his 'eclogues', short and gracious dialogues in verse, to each of which he assigned as title the name of one of the muses and which together he called the *Muse Napolitane*. In their substance these 'eclogues' are vivacious pictures of the customs of the people, sketched with a sure artistic hand guided by a frank and sincere moral sentiment. Two youths, playing at dice, pass from words to blows, to arms; their strife is

interrupted by an old man who admonishes them, with the persuasive accents of age, that peace is a beautiful thing. A young man,
caught in the toils of an unhealthy infatuation for an older, experienced woman, confesses his bewilderment, the alternating waves of
irresistible attraction and inexplicable revulsion which cross his soul;
his friend gently remonstrates, pointing out the fallacy, the danger
and the sadness of such a passion, but without success, for only
experience can cure this malady. There follows a vivid picture of a
low place in the city, a haunt of thieves, of counterfeiters and of
blackguards; the scene is enlivened by a tussle between drunken
young women marked by a dionysiacal exchange of profanities; and
in immediate contrast, a domestic scene: the preparation for the
wedding of the young daughter of a good family, who beneath the
chaste but covetous glances of the bridegroom and the worshipping
care of her parents adorns herself for the ceremony. What is of
importance in all this is not the matter itself, though this too marks
a vast step toward poetic simplicity, truth and humanity when compared with the artificial and contrived scenes of pastoral bliss, heroic
splendour or amorous dalliance or sycophantic adulation with which
the aulic literature abounded; it is, rather, the triumph of poetic
truth over thaumaturgic falseness, the re-entrance of a marvellous
artistic technique into the service of poetic truth. Banished are all
conceits, antitheses, verbal 'bizzarie'; simplicity, the simplicity of an
art become unself-conscious because wholly absorbed in the contemplation of its poetic object, is the basic note. Even the moral
sentiment is imperceptibly absorbed into the artistic unity of the
whole. The dialect, in this process, loses its rudeness, its provincial-
ism, its limitations; it becomes a universal tongue speaking universal
sentiments, because it too is in the service of an art that is all humanity and to which, consequently, all limitations and barriers are
foreign.[1]

The spirit of Basile was formed in the composition of the *Muse
Napolitane*; it found its full expression and the dialectal literature
'dell'arte' its chief monument, in the *Cunto de li cunte* or *Pentamerone*,
as it is better known. This is a vast enterprise in which Basile essayed
the collection and the artistic refashioning of almost the entire wealth
of Neapolitan dialectal literature while drawing upon other sources
as well. Its remote model is the *Decameron* and according to its full
plan it was to comprise fifty tales distributed over five days. Though
drawing upon rude sources, it is a work, Croce notes, fashioned by

[1] SEB, 450–1. Cf. SLI'600, 3 sqq.

an expert, for the delectation of 'cognoscenti' in his own words, 'per uomini letterati ed esperti e navigati che sapevano intendere e gustare le cose complicate e ingegnose'.[1] With the same disposition he had displayed in the *Muse*, that is, a mood compacted of deep moral sentiment laced with gentle satire, closely controlled by a technical artistic mastery and conscious always of the slightness and humility of his material while smitten by its simple humanity, Basile narrates anew the traditional fables of the people. His personality, his artistic personality, so highly endowed both with the skill of his art and sincerity of artistic and moral sentiment, acts as the alchemic medium which transmutes this dross into the pure gold of art.

It cannot be said with any truth, in Croce's view, that Basile set himself this task with an overt purpose of satirizing the baroque spirit and its artistic errors and foibles. Basile was and remained a man of the baroque era as his works in the 'lingua aulica' attest, and he never consciously repudiated its ideal. It was a subtle chemistry which was at work here. Basile was overtaken by the matter of the fables, and this in turn worked a magic upon his own art. The result was something far more forceful and historically far more interesting than any direct satire might have been. It was the ironical dissolution of the baroque from within. Basile effected this transformation of the baroque from that ponderous, mechanical, artificial construction, to the simple, gay, festive, half-mocking, wholly delightful art of the *Cunto de li cunte*, unconsciously.[2] This unconscious, or unpremeditated character of his criticism and transformation of the baroque manner makes his work a pure document of the positive spirit at work at the very centre of the baroque soul beneath the vast accretion of its artificial purposes, its mannerisms and its decadent sentiment.

In Croce's view, the dialectal literature 'dell'arte' as it was practised by Basile, and by others, like Cortese, exercised a still more important historical function. It had been contended by some critics that the recurrence to the dialectal literature in the baroque age was a retrogression and militated against, or at least retarded, the formation of a genuine national consciousness which had to wait rather upon the awakening of the romantic spirit. This opinion, Croce believes, is erroneous. The dialectal literature 'dell'arte' was, on the contrary, a powerful factor precisely in the formation of the national

[1] SEB, 452.
[2] SEB, 457: 'egli riesce con ciò inconsapevolmente e artisticamente a un ironizzamento del barocco.'

consciousness, and deserves, therefore, a notable place in the formation of the spirit of the Italian nation. In order to make his position
clear, he establishes the distinction between spontaneous dialectal
literature and that 'dell'arte' with reference to the problem of
nationalism. In this context, he points out, the spontaneous dialectal
literatures cannot properly be called dialectal at all; since they pre-
sume no common point of reference, they are autonomous literatures. The dialectal literature 'dell'arte', by contrast, throws into
clear relief at least an embryonic national idea, for it sets these special
dialectal literatures in the perspective of a larger common consciousness with reference to which their particularity is established.
At the same time, by its activity, it was engaged in overcoming the
very particularity which it had established and in integrating all of
the immense wealth of these literatures through their artistic transformation by means of an art which, if not strictly national, was
surely not provincial and might, when viewed in its largest references, even be called cosmopolitan. The development of dialectal
literature in the 'seicento', he concludes, was not an anti-unitary
process, but the very opposite, a process of unification because it did
not contemplate the rejection or the substitution of a national literature, but rather took the national literature as a model to draw into
the circle of the national life voices which up to that time had been
unheard or heard only in restricted theatres.[1]

[1] UCVI, I, 222 sq.

V

THE PHILOSOPHY OF AN
UNPHILOSOPHIC AGE

THE verdict of history, Croce remarks, is that philosophy in Italy ends with the great figures of the Renaissance. This judgment, while exhibiting certain marks of truth, also bears every mark of being too summary. Its truth resides in the fact that the movement of thought initiated in the Italy of the Renaissance transferred itself elsewhere and flourished, but in Italy seemed to die. It is implausible, however, that a people like the Italians, with so rich a heritage of experience and culture, should forgo completely all philosophical criticism and meditation. Again, therefore, the problem of the baroque age is the same: to seek the quick in the moribund, the 'punti vivi' among the 'punti morti'.[1]

This quickness is not to be found, he observes, in the religious field, in that criticism of tradition and of dogmas upon which humanism in its last stages and under the stimulus of the Reformation had embarked. Criticism had given way to apologetics. At the same time it would be erroneous to consider this weakening of religious criticism in Italy as the effect of external pressures; such pressures, Croce remarks, never explain movements of thought.[2] It results rather from the spontaneous resolution of the dilemma of the two authorities, Bible and Church, or more accurately perhaps, the principle of free private interpretation and an historically continuous process of interpretation embodied in the Church, in favour of the latter. The new orthodoxy which followed upon the resolution of this dilemma is purely spontaneous. One looks in vain, consequently, for those movements of rebellion which repression must inevitably have produced and which romantic criticism conjures up. Those in whom this orthodoxy was not spontaneous left the country, sensing that they did not express the persuasion of their people.[3]

In the same way, systematic or academic philosophy, that

[1] SEB, 55.   [2] SEB, 56.
[3] SEB, 56-7; cf. UAFP, 187 sqq. 'Il Marchese di Vico, Galeazzo Caracciolo.'

141

philosophy which seeks to give a total conception of reality, also disappeared. The principle of the double truth whose intrinsic contradictoriness had been recognized much earlier, was now also recognized extrinsically, so to say, and the Church restored the scholastic philosophy to a central position; there arose in consequence a new cult of Aristotelianism, less profound than the similar current of the high middle ages, but no less spontaneous. While this movement showed signs of internal vigour, speculative and controversial, it did not move beyond the limits of prescribed domain and marks no advance in speculation. For this reason, it too must be counted among the 'punti morti', a framework which, while it kept alive by its mere presence the idea of a strong speculative tradition, did nothing to enrich that tradition. But formal or systematic philosophy, as the history of philosophy well recognizes, is really but a part, and a small part, of philosophical activity. Those closed systems, while they were able to minister to some spiritual needs, fall far short of satisfaction.[1] Outside of that systematic philosophy, sometimes in opposition to it, sometimes innocent of any sense of opposition, thought of philosophical significance was germinating. A feeble life, to be sure, for it was a period of decay, but nevertheless genuine.

This fresh germination is to be found in the area of the nascent mathematico-physical sciences of nature. It is true, he remarks, that the mathematico-physical sciences are not in themselves philosophical or speculative. They are empirical and logical constructions. Such constructions cannot stand, however, without a philosophical orientation and conception and hence have philosophical implications. The Church was correct in its intuition, and Galileo mistaken, when she maintained and he denied that those sciences had philosophical and theological import.[2] This independence is only another form of that double truth which had twice been rejected, and Galileo's position could not be maintained.

It is not this implicit philosophical orientation of natural sciences which contains the germs of fresh speculative activity. This germ lies rather in the reflective understanding with which Galileo, for example, approached his own method. The image of Galileo as protopositivist current at the apogée of positivism in Italy, Croce believes, was false. Galileo takes his place among philosophers not as a protopositivist, but as a methodologist; a fact which can be readily made clear from the manner in which he expounds and defends his positions, for his very physical discoveries at times take the form of

[1] SEB, 58–9.   [2] SEB, 61.

exemplifications and illustrations of a principle which generates and transcends those discoveries, the theory of the physico-mathematical method. The positive element to be discovered here is the germinative conception of philosophy as methodology rather than as system, which was to bear fruit in the future, after the conception of philosophy as system had shown its sterility or, rather, the limits of its truth.[1]

Galileo was not a solitary, an exception in the Italy of his time. As he had had predecessors and contemporaries, so he had disciples and followers, in his life time and in succeeding generations. Zeal for these studies in physico-mathematical science was to be found at every level of society, and it is well known what contributions were made by such academies as that of the 'Lincei' at Rome and that of the 'Cimento' in Florence and how patronage was showered upon the scientists in Rome, in Florence and in the Neapolitan provinces by those in power. Even the Jesuits, who might have been expected to show themselves the most zealous as they were certainly the most competent exponents of the official systematic philosophy, became expert in this field also, as indeed they did in every field of positive learning. What is finally important, however, is the effect which this type of criticism and meditation had upon the general spirit of the time. In Croce's opinion, it was this criticism which brought about the final decline of Aristotle's authority and effected a general reformation of culture; an effect, to be sure, not large enough to lift the age to speculative heights, but strong enough to constitute one element of an awakening self-criticism which would eventually lift Italy from the slough of decadence.

The basic rhythm of decadence and progress also informs the area which had furnished Croce his definition of these concepts, moral and political theory. Indeed, it may be said that here, more than in any other area, the basic strength and weaknesses of the period, the dead forms to which it clung and the promise it held for the future are most clearly distinguished.

The religious orthodoxy which characterized the Counter Reformation in Italy and which, Croce has already pointed out, was a spontaneous thing, expressing the will and decision of the Italian people, had one negative effect: it tended to turn ethical speculation away from the problems of the ultimate character and norms of morality. These clearly were fixed, on the one hand by the religious dogma which found expression in the moral theology of the Church,

[1] SEB, 62–3.

on the other in that philosophical system or galaxy of philosophical systems to which the Church lent the support and authority of her name, the 'second scholasticism' (the term is that of Carlo Giacon). Morality, as a consequence, tended to assume more and more, not a theoretical and speculative form, but a practical and legalistic form. The logical development of this practicalistic and legalistic tendency was a rich casuistic and preceptual growth, so rich indeed that it has become, to the popular mind, the mark of the age.[1]

It has been the custom of many historians to condemn this casuistic tendency out of hand. Croce is most reluctant to follow their example, alert as he is to the positive elements immanent not only in the period as a whole but in its every part and movement. This casuistic science in its positive aspects, of which Alphonse Ligouri has become the classic, exercised an immense effect on ethical science.[2] On the one hand, because it was fundamentally anti-ascetical, that is, did not tend to seek human perfection outside of the practices and pressures of daily life but within them, it brought and kept moral theory and principles in direct contact with life and its irrepressible needs. On the other, by its very gigantism it tended to induce a revolution against legalitarianism in morals, and to prepare the way for that distinction between utility and morality which modern ethical theory was to develop. Nevertheless, despite the positive influence which it exercised over ethical science, the casuistic procedure was ideally sterile: it did not advance upon but simply repeated principles which had become fixed. As a consequence, it presently becomes clear that it did not occupy the central place in the life of its time, that the real and active centre of thought lay elsewhere, just as in the field of philosophy it had been seen that the dominant or official systematic philosophy did not tend to foster the germ of future developments, which were to be found outside of it, sometimes in contrast and sometimes simply without relation to it.

The centre of originative and germinative life outside the orthodox morality and its casuistic development is to be found, Croce believes, in the need which then awakened for a distinct and independent political science.[3] In this connection he develops in greater detail the parallel between the situation in speculative philosophy and in the moral disciplines. It had seemed possible in speculative philosophy to disengage oneself from ultimate problems and so accede to the orthodox and traditional philosophy; in the end, however, the exigencies of the natural sciences proved this an illusion.

[1] SEB, 72 sqq.   [2] SEB, 72.   [3] SEB, 75.

Similarly in the moral sciences, it had seemed possible in a certain sense to disengage oneself from the theoretical problems of the soul; in the end, however, it proved impossible to restore the older doctrines of society, the state and politics. The new fact which confronted political speculation just as the new discoveries and methods of the natural sciences confronted the old theorists of the philosophy of nature, was the fact of the worldliness of contemporary politics.[1] The political principals of the time pursued policies formed on quite other than moral and religious grounds and were not loath even to turn morals and religion to their own mundane purposes. The papacy in its character as an elective monarchy and a temporal power, pursued a sagacious policy on identical principles. The need, the actual need, consequently, was a science which would penetrate the ideal character of this new order of facts, and place it in some relation, if possible, to the order of moral and religious truths. This problem was to become the most urgent of the time and to elicit its most solid speculative achievement.

The science of mundane politics had, as a matter of fact, already been established by the political writers of the Renaissance, above all by Machiavelli. It had even acquired a name which, like the fact itself, was accepted by all, 'Reason of State'.[2] In its complexity, the 'Reason of State' was both theory and practice, providing both norms and procedures. The baroque period had nothing to add to Machiavellianism in its pure form; it marks, in this respect, no advance upon the Renaissance. While the Renaissance produced the Machiavellian political science, it was, however, left to the thinkers of the baroque to grasp and to a certain extent to overcome its problemicity and unilaterality. In a word, the political science of the Renaissance became the problem and the point of departure for the political theory of the baroque era.

This problem was the attitude to be taken toward this new science which seemed to rise independently of religion and Christian morality, indifferent, and at times even hostile, to them. It was equally impossible to accept or reject it unequivocally; to accept it, in view of the structure of the Counter Reformation and, for that matter, of the Reformation itself; to reject it, because the political operations and procedures from which it arose were apparent to the eyes of all and clearly called for directive principles to guide its intrinsic force. Only one alternative offered itself, either to emasculate it, or to reconcile it to religion and Christian morality.[3] This was the problem

[1] SEB, 74.   [2] SEB, 75.   [3] SEB, 76.

of the 'ragion di stato' which was to preoccupy Italian thought for eighty years, and even to penetrate to the level of popular opinion.

An effort to reject the 'ragion di stato' appeared earliest; this effort was continuous during all that period and, it might be added, has been repeated since.[1] In this direct opposition to Machiavellianism, the leaders were the Jesuits. They sought a precedent in Campanella, who, in his own time, had opposed Machiavelli; his authority had, however, to be invoked with caution. Campanella had not been inclined to reject Machiavellianism entirely, but rather to recognize its one-sidedness, and thus to become, in Croce's view, a forerunner of the simultaneous rejection and development of Machiavelli's doctrine which Vico was to effect.[2] With Machiavelli, in this general rejection, were included other writers of like mind but lesser genius, Bodin (Jean Bodin, 1530–96), and Cardano (Gerolamo Cardano, 1501–76). This effort could only fail; it could not overcome, by the rejection of Machiavelli, the fact of Machiavellianism. This fact expressed an elementary need which could not be eluded.[3]

Before this inescapable fact another strategy was devised, worthy, Croce writes, of the times. This was the expedient of masking Machiavelli with the figures of the great Roman historian Tacitus and of his prince, Tiberius. In Tacitus, it was supposed, there was to be found the limpid mirror of contemporary politics. The name and figure of Tacitus took on such proportions that one author[4] writes that the *Annales* provided the key to a great treasure, the art of establishing and maintaining a tyranny.[5] The expedient of 'Tacitism' could not prove entirely opaque; indeed, to some contemporary writers it was easily transparent and served as point of departure for the second of the alternatives mentioned, namely, that of conciliating Machiavellianism with religion and Christian morality.[6] The right instinct of this programme cannot be denied; it failed, on the whole, because it did not recognize its own preconditions. Among these was a logical distinction of the elements to be united, and a clarification of the manner in which religion and morality resolved the contradictions engendered by political science. Instead, this unification was attempted on the basis of simple identification, or reduction, in which that fundamental distinction is lost in equivo-

[1] SEB, 77.   [2] SEB, 79.   [3] SEB, 80.
[4] Traiano Boccalini, 1556–1613, in *Commentari sopra Cornelio Tacito*, SEB, 84.
[5] On 'Tacitism' cf. Toffanin: *Machiavelli e il "tacitismo"*, 1921; but on Toffanin's work cf. Chabod in *Cinquant' anni di vita intellettuale italiana*, 1951, I, pp. 145 sqq.
[6] SEB, 86.

cation. The writers who took this path showed themselves little able to rise to the logical problems involved in it; nevertheless, they mark an advance in political theory. While Machiavelli had with great genius posited the new principle asserting the value of politics as politics, he had isolated the circle of political action and had failed to place it in relation to the moral conscience. As a result, political science, while it could not turn back beyond Machiavelli, could not take up a definitive stand on his propositions.[1] The moment of political action could not stand alone; it had to be placed in relation to all of the other moments of the life of spirit. This is the task the writers of this period actually addressed, and this address itself constitutes the positive and progressive dimension of their thought.

In facing this problem they again seemed to be confronted with a complex alternative: to attempt a simple identification of morals and politics, as the middle ages had done, to consider the political moment merely as something negative, or, finally, recognizing it as both positive and distinct, to establish its real relation to the moral moment.[2]

The first path was attempted by many; but its procedure was historically redundant: the mediaeval attempt to subsume politics under the virtue of prudence. If the 'reason of state' be prudence, and if the moral virtue of justice has need of prudence, the problem remains of determining the relation between prudence and moral wisdom. And if, on the other hand, the 'reason of state' is an exception to a rule, it must be determined whether this exception is made for moral reasons or for mere prudential and political reasons. The failure of the efforts of the second type was as complete; they could not resolve into pure negation the positive character and proper perfection of politics.

The thought of the baroque period entered resolutely on the third path with the writings of Zuccolo.[3] Zuccolo begins by securing the absolutely necessary premise, the distinctness and the positivity of the political moment. Reason of state, he writes, is simply 'a mode of acting conformable to the essence or the form of the state which men have proposed to establish or to conserve'.[4] It consists in nothing else but the apt means for ordering or conserving any constitution or republic, whatever its character. If this be good, the reason of state is good; if evil, the reason of state shares that character. Even in

[1] SEB, 89. [2] SEB, 90.
[3] Lodovico Zuccolo, 1568–1630, *Della ragione di stato*, 1621; SEB, 93 sqq.
[4] SEB, 93.

the service of an evil state, however, the 'ragione di stato' does not lose its efficacy or positivity; it then appears to him as prudence or astuteness, the shadow, not the substance, of justice which could, of course, be found only in an effective politics serving a good state. 'Reason of state' as a pure form of action, he recognizes, is very rare; man's economic, political and utilitarian actions are always performed in a moral context; there arises, consequently, the necessity of ordering the 'reason of state' to the idea of justice.[1]

Croce recognizes in this effort of Zuccolo a first step toward the solution of the problems to which the political thought of Machiavelli had given rise; a first step but a secure one, from which there could be no turning back. Pure politics or the 'reason of state' appear as the indifferent root of good and evil in the moral sense, possessing, at the same time, its proper perfection, astuteness or prudence. The debates concerning the 'ragione di stato' ceased about the middle of the sixteenth century, giving way to the rationalistic constructions of jusnaturalism, inaugurated by the *De jure belli* of Alberico Gentile (1552–1608). But the position which Zuccolo has established was implicit in these later constructions; they neither identified these orders of human actions by reduction of the moral to the political, nor made of the political the mere shadow of the moral.

The political historiography of the baroque continues the tradition of that of the Renaissance, developing its latent power and revealing its weakness.[2] Although the position of Italy in Europe was not such that she could wield a decisive influence in politics, she had by no means become a provincial state. Rome, for example, and Venice were still centres of power; the one, Rome, was in her 'imperial' period, as it has been called, while the other, though already entered upon the path of eventual decline, still held the reins of power and possessed vast political leverage. As a result, the tone of Italian historiography was anything but provincial; on the contrary, it was cosmopolitan, as even a glance at its bibliography reveals. Its concern is with movements in every country of Europe, with their internal affairs as well as with the relations between them. Even America was not omitted while the Church naturally pre-empted vast attention.[3]

A striking characteristic of this historiography, setting it in contrast to that of the Renaissance, is its anti-humanistic and anti-literary character.[4] The classic form of history, with its styled nar-

---

[1] *Della ragione di stato*, pp. 476 sqq.; SEB, 93 sqq.
[2] SEB, 99.   [3] SEB, 101.   [4] SEB, 106.

ration of battles and its adroitly interpolated orations replete with relevant and irrelevant reflections, gives way to a fresh attitude which Croce recognizes as a first stage in the transformation of history from literature to science. The ideal of these writers (the professed ideal, of course) is truth, and they defined this ideal in the norms which they set for the historian.[1]

Their concern was almost exclusively political, in the narrower sense of the term already encountered. Within this concern they demanded, first of all, authenticity; they held in scorn the historian who worked without first-hand experience in the material, that is in the intrigues and manipulations of governments, courts and armies, or who relied on anything less than personal observation and re-search into original sources.[2] This ideal of the science rises to the level of a clear-cut distinction between history and chronicle in such men as Brignole-Sale,[3] and to a narrow but authentic distinction between the relevance and irrelevance in the historiographic order. More impressive still was the positive aim they set themselves, heap-ing scorn on those who write history in the old literary manner, who content themselves with appearances without seeking to penetrate to the intrinsic reasons by which events are formed, and asserting the ideal to be the search of these reasons in their highest sources, the counsels of cabinets, the wills and intentions, the wisdom or un-wisdom of princes.[4]

Departure in fact from this ideal was to be expected; indeed, it might be considered inevitable in an anti-literary and anti-human-istic historiography which had not yet formulated adequate scientific laws. That anti-literary and anti-humanistic bias opened the door to many men of lesser mind and abilities who sought to minister to curiosity rather than to science, and this peril was increased by the fact that political historiography performed a social function which was later to be exercised by journalism.[5] Its contact with current events and the absence of controlling literary norms exposed this historiography in a special way to the pressures of interests and fostered venality. From this situation many writers of a more serious mind and purpose took refuge in the past, preferring to treat of remote events and forming for their own encouragement and con-solation an illusory image of the austere disinterestedness of ancient historical writers, an illusion which a contemporary did not fail to note, pointing out that ancient history was composed by men

[1] SEB, 108. [2] SEB, 109. [3] SEB, 113.
[4] SEB, 109–10. [5] SEB, 115.

equally subject to pressures and passion and liable to the same weaknesses.[1] The interests and venalities which swayed these men ought not to be exaggerated; they were no greater than in any other period. Their positive merits and the degree to which they contributed to our present conception of that age can be appreciated only from their treatment of specific problems. Sarpi (Paolo Sarpi, S. I., 1552–1623), for example, anatomizes with remarkable acumen the interests which were locked in struggle in the Council of Trent. Bisaccioni (Maiolino Bisaccioni, 1582–1663) does much the same for the political motives which wove themselves into the pattern of the religious wars harassing Europe, while Siri (Vittorio Siri, 16 ?–1685)[2] dissects with a surgeon's skill the illusions of the 'Grand Design'.

Concentration on the political dimension of public life was at once the strength and the weakness of this historiography. Theirs was the strength which always flows from fixed attention to a selected object; and their work possesses the fine clarity, but limited scope of a cameo. This concentration served to destroy many of the older mythical formations which had been the framework of historical interpretation for so long, those of the four kingdoms, for example, and of the two cities. At the same time, this concentration was its weakness. Concentrating on the part, it could not see history whole, that is as the work and creation of the whole man. Destroying those myths it could not replace them with positive concepts or interpretative principles nor even develop the germs of profound truth which those myths carried. For this reason, both the science of history and the ideal of civil history were still things of the future.

It is a part of the whole spirit which animates the baroque that even the interior life and the ethical path should be submitted to that process of externalization, formalization and exaggeration which permeated the artistic life of the period. This tendency expressed itself in a rich literature of which every period of decadence has given examples concerning the guidance of life according to its diversity of status and fortune and with the purpose of making of the very living of life a matter not of spontaneous and creative decision but of rule and precept. Our own age with its extroversion, to borrow a psychological term, its conviction that everything, from living a sane sex life to choosing a life mate or a profession, can be reduced to rule and precept, should be well able to understand this

[1] Sforza Pallavicino, Card., 1607–67 in *Vita di Alessandro* VII; SEB, 120.
[2] *Memorie recondite*; SEB, 127 sqq.

phenomenon. This vast body of literature Croce treats under the rubric of 'preceptistic', the literature of precepts. He is careful, however, to point out that, beneath this wilderness growth of rule and example, questions of basic import to the spiritual life in its individual and social dimensions are exercised with insight and acumen.[1]

In this literature, he remarks, the religious and the mundane themes run parallel, cross and sometimes mingle. The religious life shared that quality of extrusion, as it were, and gave rise to a rich ascetic and edifying literature. At the same time, however, the worldly life gave rise to its own documents instinct with its own quality and character; and it is symbolic of the age that the pragmatic character of the latter not infrequently penetrates the former, endowing the struggle for perfection with the same strategical and tactical structure as the effort for worldly advancement. As the pure type of this last, Croce naturally selects the 'Spiritual Exercises' of Ignatius Loyola (1491–1556) with their images of kingship and war and numerous rules for the 'particular examen' and the discernment of spirits.[2]

This literature is readily categorized according to the state of life of the persons to whom it was addressed. The richest category was that of the guidance and instruction of princes and rulers, not only of tyrannical, but of aristocratic and democratic constitutions. Through these works, composed in many instances by men of vast experience, there runs a vein of real, though mundane wisdom; some of them, like the work of Malvezzi (Cristoforo Malvezzi, 1547–97) became the bibles of rulers. The second category, addressed to a larger audience, was quantitatively superior, but of inferior quality. It comprises works addressed to persons in the most various walks or states of life, and is unified by the constant purpose of revealing the 'secret' of each, the principle of its success. This literature of precept took every form; the tract, eloquent in exhortation, the didactic poem, tragedy, romance. Most importantly, however, it expressed itself in the form of historiography; most importantly because here it gave rise to problems of real significance.[3]

The key to the relation between preceptistic and historiography was the opinion, certainly not new, but of which this age seemed especially persuaded, that the function of history is to teach and especially to teach by precept and example. This both explains its function and prescribes its goal. The purpose of the study of history

[1] SEB, 137.   [2] SEB, 137.   [3] SEB, 141.

as Mascardi (Agostino Mascardi, 1590–1640) wrote[1] is to learn
wisdom; while Tomasi[2] spoke of it as the 'experimental science of
man, the true tables of the law, the navigation chart of life'. The histories of the period are permeated with this purpose even when they
are motivated by those fresh ideals of history as science already
noted. Indeed, the conjunction of these two ideals in historiography
is less astonishing than might be expected since even in the developing natural sciences the relation between research and 'control' of
nature was stressed.

What is of importance in this whole matter, however, is not the
pervasive character of this persuasion, but that modicum of doubt
which troubled it. Whether the function of history is, indeed, to
teach; whether in fact history has that power; what, finally, the
intrinsic character of history must be; these are the questions the
doubters dared to raise. The form in which these questions are stated
is limited and by no means profound but they are stated. Again, the
solutions are for the most part tangential, directed not to the heart of
the issue, but to some peripheral aspect of the problem, in some
limited context. Thus Bisaccioni objects to the notion that the art of
politics can be learned from the readings of histories; this form of
instruction does not take into account the all-important fact that
accidents may occur, a factor which must be of paramount importance to everyone who actually engages in politics. He insists that
every divergence or difference in time has results which can be calcu-
lated only on a geometric ratio, which makes the divergence between the present and the past even greater than at first might seem
the case.[3] Malvezzi criticizes Machiavelli because he has preferred to
illustrate his material with maxims from ancient history, while
modern times are so different with respect alike to religion, customs,
and laws; finally, going to the heart of the matter, for having be-
lieved at all that the profit of history lies in using it as example.[4]
Doubt of a different quality was raised in the minds of men like
Paolo Sarpi; he remarks that this persuasion and the correlative belief
that the course of history depends on the counsels and decisions of
men, led men to forget that the event in history lies with God.[5] This
doubt, which rested upon a sincere religious basis in Sarpi, also
found more profane expression in the lines of satirists like the Abate
Lancellotti, who reduced all human prudence to the supreme art of
guessing. Despite the limited form in which the problems are stated

---

[1] *Dell'arte istorica*, 1674; SEB, 120, 141. [2] *Il principe studioso*; SEB, 141.
[3] SEB, 145–6; but cf. 141 *ad finem*. [4] SEB, 146. [5] SEB, 147.

and the tangential character of the answers, genuine insight is not rare. Thus Malvezzi writes that what really demands explanation in history is precisely that super-individual scope of individual action and decision which is its true dynamic principle.[1] The corollary of this character of history is the impossibility of transferring, whether by precept or example, that quality of human action and decision which imparts to it that transcendent value. This value he recognizes as something of a mystery and as nothing less than providential and divine, so that to him historical precepts seem to belittle the action of God and to raise that of secondary causes, i.e. of men, to an absurd height.

At the other extreme from those who sought to minimize the value of precepts on the grounds of the presence of an element 'je ne sais quoi' in human history stand those who dreamed of reducing the preceptistic itself to a rigorous science on the pattern of the natural sciences. Such efforts could be successful only to the degree to which it might be established that human decisions are subject to the same, and the same kind of, laws as physical motion, that their objects are homogeneous and therefore subject to a calculus. The extent to which this possibility is real was explored by some writers who in this effort approached a 'pure' economics: Scaruffi (Gasparo Scaruffi, 1519–84), Serra (Antonio Serra, 1550–1625) and others.[2] As this effort was to clarify itself, however, it became evident that a calculus is applicable only to the natural conditions of human action and not to human decision itself; between decision and the infinite variety of its conditions only empirical relations and rules can obtain and, finally, that not through mere contingency but because of the absolute diversity of the principles of nature and spirit, action resists preceptual formulation. Within these limited terms these writers confronted the very real and basic problem of the creative liberty of spirit which inevitably eludes capture in the nets of a formal logic.

Finally, Croce finds, this material taken simply as it stands is exceedingly rich in psychological and sociological observation.[3] Indeed, in some of the studies of the period, such as the *Piazza universale di tutte le professioni* of Bagnacavallo (Tommaso Bagnacavallo, *c.* 1585), so severely criticized by Gracian, he discovers the earliest of treatises on descriptive 'sociology'. It is the psychological penetration and finesse of those engaged in the cure of souls as well as of those concerned with the conditions of more worldly success which is most arresting. The mark of these writers is a subtlety and

[1] SEB, 148.   [2] SEB, 150.   [3] SEB, 151 sqq.

realism which no transformation of the protean human psyche can escape; a subtlety more profound than any which modern analytic procedures has achieved because inspired more by a perception of the basic spirituality of the human subject and hence less concerned, as later analysis has been, with abstract schematications and deterministic patterns.[1]

As the negative character of the baroque was established first in art, so it might be expected that in the area of the theory of art there should be some clear evidence of the dialectical movement between the negative and the positive, the perishing and the germinating elements. Croce finds that this is indeed the case. Although the baroque must be characterized as a negative era in the history of art, this is not meant to imply that it was a period of artistic inactivity. On the contrary, the productivity of the age was superabounding in architecture, in sculpture, in music, in poetry and literature. The arts were patronized by the Church with a lavish hand. This patronage biased the art toward sacred subjects which, as Croce points out, the spirit of the age immediately turned to its own purposes. They were patronized almost as lavishly by secular agencies, by kings, princes and viceroys, by the nobility and even by the rising 'middle' or urban classes. This abundance was no assurance of excellence, but it inevitably induced a rich literature in the theory of art and in artistic and literary criticism.[2]

The art theory of the period consisted in a reweaving of the basic themes of Renaissance criticism; nor were the mediaeval theories expressly rejected.[3] All the attitudes which are to be found in earlier periods recur in an eclectic pattern. The concept of art as allegory, for instance, still persisted, and with it ample disquisition as to the nature of true allegory. There persisted also the concept of art as moral and philosophical instruction, as an incitement to virtue, which the writers of the Renaissance had introduced into their elaborations of the Aristotelian poetic, borrowing it, in their turn, from later antiquity and from mediaeval sources. These theories were altered and their older sense superseded. Dante, for example, was accused of contenting himself with mere allegory, that is, with a mere extrinsic juxtaposition of symbol and symbolized, while other writers of epic vein were praised for achieving their complete fusion.

[1] Croce cites, as an example, the *Della dissimulazione onesta* of Torquato Accetto, SEB, 156; cf. *Politici e moralisti del seicento*, Bari, 1930, and NSLI 600, 82–91.

[2] SEB, 161–2.

[3] SEB, 162.

In the same manner the pedagogical concept of art underwent a sea-change, the stern notion of instruction giving way to the more amiable end of delight.[1]

The element of the Renaissance heritage which the baroque period seizes upon with greatest vigour, which it expanded and exaggerated and which in this very process of exaggeration it forces to yield new significance, was the notion of art as beautiful form, directed to the evocation of pleasure and delight. In extreme instances pleasure was interpreted simply as sensual. In more restrained and reflective statements, a qualified pleasure was intended, peculiar to art and not to be confused with anything above or below it. The fresh significance which the baroque gave to this doctrine, however, is the identification, still in these equivocal terms of pleasure and delight, of the end of art with art itself; the perception that art and poetry do not have an end or purpose beyond themselves, to which they must be subordinated and from which they must accept rules and norms. The notion of delight was lifted to the status of a symbol of the autonomy and independence of art, to the extent to which this symbolism could be expressed within conventional terms. The expression of this insight could not but be equivocal; development of the theoretical and critical concepts which could give it positive and unambiguous formulation lay in the future. Yet it was a new direction which could not be mistaken. Certain statements, as that of Guarini (G. B. Guarini, 1538–1612) in defence of his *Pastor fido*, do achieve perfect clarity, for Guarini speaks unequivocally enough for his purposes when he writes that the end of art is not to teach but to delight by the imitation of any object whatsoever, whether good or bad in itself.[2] The tendency to recognize, even in these limited terms, art's autonomy constitutes genuine progress, in the same sense, Croce writes, that an empirical scienticism is progressive with respect to a speculative philosophy become vacuous, or a workable utilitarianism with respect to an abstract and pretentious ethics.[3]

At the same time and in close relation with this conception of poetry as pleasure and delight in the beauty of art itself, another positive and (again relatively) progressive element makes its appearance. It is the idea, whose importance for the future development of aesthetic theory will be easily recognized, that the judgment of the work of art, the critical function belongs to a particular attitude of spirit, to a special 'faculty' which came to be characterized variously as 'taste', 'sense' or 'sentiment'. The relation of this concept to the

[1] SEB, 163.   [2] SEB, 163-4.   [3] SEB, 164.

notion that the end of art is intrinsic can readily be seen. Again it is Guarini who achieves a forceful statement, for he remarks that art cannot be judged with reference to any of the special ends which had variously been assigned it, but only to its own internal quality. An even clearer statement may be found in Zuccolo's (Lodovico Zuccolo, 1568–1630) treatment of the problem of Italian versification.[1] From the argument whether the meters of Italian and Latin verse are similar and whether the Italian ought to be called quantitative or accentual, he passes to the question of the faculty and the point of view from which judgment of the beauty of verse should be made. He asserts, unequivocally, that judgment belongs to a faculty *sui generis*, which is, in its positive character, a bit mysterious, but which, he is certain, can be identified neither with reason nor with mere sense. It is 'a certain higher power united at the same time with the ear and with the eye which make such a judgment'. 'The human mind', he writes, 'has well been able to recognize that a body, in order to be beautiful, requires one proportion rather than another; but as to why one proportion is beautiful, the other not, judgment is remanded entirely to that power united with the sentiment, which discourses without discursive reason.'[2] Reference to this power recurs again and again in the writers of the period, in Menzini, (Benedetto Menzini, 1646–1704) who celebrated in verse the power and singular mode of operation of 'good judgment', and Bellini (Lorenzo Bellini, 1643–1704), who wrote figuratively of 'le dita pensose'.

Correlative to both these movements and bound, in a certain measure, to a rudimentary insight into the unity of art was the decline of the rules established by the older poetics for the so-called 'genres' of poetry and art. These 'genres' had been intended as the universal models both for the production and for the judgment of art and had been endowed in extreme statements with a kind of 'natural', ontological status. It was now suggested that they possessed no such natural status or universal validity; that they could be understood only as examples of existing poetry which had been approved as beautiful. In much the same manner, Croce had noted, the political writers had criticized the value of political precepts, reducing them all to the historical dimension of political actuality, and pointing out that political decisions are made, not by rule but by 'discretion'. Boccalini (Traiano Boccalini, 1556–1613) places Torquato Tasso on

---

[1] *Discorso delle ragioni del numero del verso italiano* 1623; SEB, 165.
[2] SEB, 166.

the stage to protest to Apollo against critics who judged by rule and precept, and to assert that in the composition of his poem he had laboured long and arduously, inspired and guided only by the talent which nature had given him and the inspiration of Calliope; and he similarly depicts Aristotle as protesting that he had intended no such rigid precepts as the theorists had foisted on him, that he had intended only to help others by indicating the path which some poets had successfully followed. And Zuccolo,[1] presenting his new theory of Italian metre, expressly recognized that the rules he proposed offered no absolute criterion of judgment.

Together with these developments, there appeared as complement to the concept of 'taste', or the general doctrine that judgment of art pertained to a special power or attitude of the spirit, the concept of 'ingegno'. This concept contained the seed of what, in the following century, was to be called 'genius', that is the inventive faculty in general and, more specifically, the power of poetic invention. This power was distinguished from both 'judgment' and 'taste'. These terms were not new, but the emphasis given them was. Henceforth, they were never to be absent from the discussions of the philosophers of art; and only by means of the distinctions they enunciated was criticism finally to perceive that 'taste' is rooted in 'genius' and that genius, as Horace wrote, is a law to itself.[2]

There appeared also, at this time, the concepts of the 'personality' of the author or artist, and of 'style' which is the expression of that personality. The conclusion was reached that style could be neither elocution nor the 'characters' or 'genres' of expression; for the 'genres' are three, while styles are infinite in number, as numerous as the artists themselves; and within the same 'genre' there are to be found writers with very different styles. The parallel between 'style' in literature and 'manner' in art, itself an indication of a sense for the unity of art, is developed; and it is asserted that the only possible basis for style is the 'ingegno' of the individual artist. For this reason, Mascardi (Agostino Mascardi, 1590–1640) writes, it is meaningless to inquire in what style an artist composes; only one style is available to him, his own, dictated by his 'ingegno'; in all others he can achieve 'virtuoso' imitation.[3]

All of these ideas, Croce believes, can properly be called positive and progressive, both with respect to what they reject and with respect to what they adumbrate. At the same time, however, it is

---

[1] *Ragguagli di Parnaso*; SEB, 169.   [2] SEB, 172.
[3] SEB, 173.

characteristic of the baroque that even these insights should be infected with its particular virus and take on the forms of the malady of which they are in fact the antidote. Artistic spontaneity, liberty and individuality; these are the positive elements. Immediately, however, they are subjected to equivocations and oscillations of intent. There arises the equivocation between art as having its proper pleasure and pleasure as art; between the elevated phantasy and caprice; between the sensuous concreteness of art and sensuality or lasciviousness insinuated into the place of art; between individuality, the originality and the novelty which belongs to every true creation, and the quest of the new as a means of exciting and titillating spirits satiated with old and habitual pleasures. This false and unhealthy element frequently submerges the positive and true in the theoretical affirmations and the programmes of Marino and the 'marianists'.[1]

At the same time, and as a sign of the fundamental health which was finally to overcome these pathological movements, this extremism and equivocation itself aroused a critical movement which is evidenced in the controversy over the *Adone* of Marino. Contemporary critics heaped reprobation on its lasciviousness, its fundamental sterility of sentiment and ideas, its limited and sensuous associative vocabulary, its incapacity to move with genuine sentiment. It is a positive achievement of this criticism that it identifies the fundamental issue of aesthetics as the contrast between hedonism and expressionism. The perception of this problem, or rather of the aesthetic problem in this form, was a progressive step; but it lacked the philosophical instruments to make it effective.[2] As a consequence, the critics of the baroque period tended to restate their fresh insights in obsolete terms. Thus in opposition to the confusion of art with a fabric of pleasant images, one of these critics (Salvator Rosa, 1615–1673) fell back on the older didactic concept of art, and, in the very manner of the baroque, wove variations on this ancient theme. Or a retreat was made to the position of Aristotelean verisimilitude although this position with its ontological ambiguities had been substantially overcome; this verisimilitude tended to open the door anew to the concept of delight, for it seemed patent that the verisimilitude of the work of art could have no other end but pleasure. Finally, the concept of the theory of poetry and art as a system of particular laws was taken up again; while they saw that the 'rules' of art are formed by abstraction from poetry and art already existing, these critics did not see that the 'genres' of art and literature are

[1] SEB, 174.   [2] SEB, 178.

formed in the same way. As a consequence, potentially fruitful controversies, such as that over the *Pastor fido* of Guarini, were rendered sterile.[1]

Finally, Croce writes, the criticism of 'conceitism', or the 'baroque style', while just on specific points and in its practical conclusions did not achieve logical coherence. To achieve such coherence would have demanded the conquest of such entrenched distinctions as that between the 'proper' word and metaphor, between 'natural' and 'artificial' form, a conquest not to be realized before Vico.[2] The difficulty lay in the circumstance that this criticism accepted the logical premises of the theories it censured. By accepting the Aristotelean doctrine of metaphor and by admitting the legitimacy of adding ornament to form for the purpose of delight and wonder, it had admitted in principle the legitimacy of 'conceitism'. Two means of escape from this fallacious sensual and hedonistic conception offered themselves, only to pass unnoted and unexploited. The first appears in the writings of Sforza Pallavicino (Cardinal Sforza Pallavicino, 1607–67). In the treatise *Del bene*, following the classical scholastic analysis, Pallavicino distinguishes the three grades of knowledge, simple, or first, apprehension, judgment and discourse or ratiocination. Simple apprehension, he holds, is concerned with the simple appearances of the object, and ventures no distinction as of true or false, real or unreal; in it he discerns the springs of poetry, assigning it a value all its own, the value of the imagination and the joy which the imagination engenders. Beauty does not delight in so far as it is an affirmation, but simply in so far as it is seen or apprehended with vivid force. The single scope of poetry is to adorn the intellect with images; that is to say, sensuous, new, splendid and wonderful apprehensions; if this were not the case, poetry would be without justification, for it would have deception as its end, offering the false as true. He goes on to say that the verisimilitude which all theory places at the heart of the work of art is not a transaction of reality but the vivacity of the representation. Pallavicino, as a result of the limits of the philosophy which he followed, was not in a position to reap the fruits of this insight; his doctrine is immediately invaded by the prevalent hedonism. The first apprehension is denied the character of a form of knowledge, and is asserted instead to be the mere presentation of pleasing and exciting images; in the end it is subjected to the judgment.[3]

A second means of advancing the concept of poetry might have

[1] SEB, 178 sqq.   [2] SEB, 183.   [3] SEB, 185 sqq.

been found, Croce believes, in the complex parallel which existed, in the common doctrine of the schools, between dialectic and rhetoric and the correlative distinction between propositions which affirm and propositions which merely signify. A development of this distinction might have arrived at the further distinction between two modes of knowledge, the one purely expressive and the other judicial and ratiocinative, and of two correlative sciences, aesthetic and logic. As a matter of fact, tentative efforts were made along these lines; Tesauro (Emanuele Tesauro, 1591–1677), for example, attempts to construct an independent organon of rhetoric and poetic knowledge. Unfortunately, these efforts degenerated into two vain and fantastic sciences, that of simple, dialectical and that of ornate or 'conceitful' expression, of syllogistic demonstration and of the oratorical enthymene.[1]

Important and positive must be accounted as well the constant tendency of the 'literati' of the period to pass from the limited consideration of the specific arts to a comparison between them and thus to approach the concept of a general notion of art, a unitary notion which would become the subject of aesthetic. This effort was suggested by the wide culture of the 'literati' rather than by a fresh speculative insight. Thus Pallavicino interpreted the ancient Horatian dictum, 'ut pictura poesis', as affirming their common character, opposing both to realistic discernment, to the judgment and to discursive thought. Addressing the problem of versification, he places it in direct relation with the problems of music and of linear proportion.[2] Similarly, Mascardi, in advancing his theory of the individuality of style, leaned for support on painting as well as on literature and poetry.[3] Tesauro included in his considerations of 'conceit' or 'wit', not only the art of the word, but the figurative, the pictorial and the plastic arts.[4] These attempts, it must be noted, were made by the men of letters; the cultivators of the figurative arts remained for the most part on the level of preceptistic, a fact that is to be traced to their more limited culture.

The criticism of the arts and of poetry, since it depends directly on ideas, could only rise as high as the level of contemporary theory. Since theory, despite the efforts already noted, did not achieve a high conception of art, there is lacking in criticism any sustained discernment and recognition of great art and poetry. The criticism of poetry was for the most part sensualistic, intent on and content with sparkling superficialities, a fact which may be documented for example

[1] SEB, 188. [2] *Del bene; Trattato dello stilo e del dialogo*; SEB, 188–9.
[3] *Dell'arte istorica*; SEB, 172–3, 189–90. [4] *Cannocchiale aristotelica*; SEB, 190.

from Achillini's (Claudio Achillini, 1574-1640) treatment of the *Adone* of Marino. When it was not thus engaged in flattering superficial attainments, criticism tended to become pedantic, laboriously seeking to apply the machinery of the theory of the 'genres' to the protean actualities of art. Thus Beni (Paolo Beni, 1552-1625) tries to prove that the Goffredo of Tasso is a more noble and perfect figure of the warrior-chief than any to be found in Homer or Virgil because Tasso has better observed the unities, etc.[1] Sometimes, happily, good sense broke through both superficiality and pedantry. Fioretti (Benedetto Fioretti, 1579-1642), in his opinion of the *Pastor fido*, remarks that its suavity has clouded the judgments of most critics, preventing them from seeing its essential vacuity.[2] So, too, Stigliani[3] in his analysis of the *Adone* of Marino notes its manner of developing themes only externally, its impotence to move the heart. Such glimmerings of good sense are all too frequently lost in the uniform enveloping gloom of rhetorical *schemata* and poetic precepts. Nevertheless, the impression of this criticism upon Croce is, on the whole, positive. The work of criticism, within these limits, actually progressed. It is necessary to note, he remarks, that despite logical incoherencies the discernment of poetic values (and the lack of them) is present. One must be resigned, however, to seek such discernment in a vast jungle of prejudices, ineptitudes and distortions. Lack of historical culture is a chief cause; inability to understand the poetic achievement of the past inspired a self-satisfaction as vast as it was unfounded. Pejorative judgments of the art and poetry of the past mingled with the most extravagant and unwarranted praise of the present. This historical blindness and its correlative complacency arose not only from cultural deficiencies, but also from the lack of sound canons of historical interpretation. As a consequence, Homer aroused in this period nothing but ennui; he offended by the very barbaric rudeness in which Vico was to see his greatness. Dante, in great part, suffered a similar fate. There ensued a fallacious theory of poetic progress, based ultimately on a false theory of the poetic activity, denying value to the poetry of the past save as a step to the present. A similar lack of historical understanding is to be found in the theory and history of the arts, in which such vacuities as Giulio Mancini's theory of stylistic cycles could command audience.[4] Little was achieved in these areas but bibliographical erudition.

---

[1] *Comparatione di T. Tasso con Homero e Virgilio*, etc.; SEB, 195-6.
[2] *Proginnasmi poetici*; SEB, 197-8.   [3] *Dell'Occhiale*; SEB, 199.
[4] *Viaggio per Roma*; SEB, 207-8.

During the last decades of the seventeenth century, a new wind began to stir in Italy. It blew from France, from England and from Holland. The most important aspect of this new influence was its philosophical spirit, rationalist and cartesian. Its first effect was to dissipate the lingering vestiges of scholasticism and 'jesuitism'.[1] It stirred a reaction against the philology and the historical erudition of the preceding period, against its preoccupation with 'minutiae', its lack of method and direction. The motto of the hour, spoken by Muratori, was 'good taste', the perfect motto against a period of which bad taste was the dominant note. The reaction inspired by the new rationalism was directed against certain aspects of the culture of the recent past and not against the tradition of Italian culture itself. Neither was it an uncritical reaction; for it was not blind either to the positive elements of that tradition or to its own limitations. The attachment of this new spirit to the tradition of Italian culture was demonstrated by its effort to make fresh contact with the philological and historical culture of the Renaissance.[2]

Supreme evidence of the sanity of this reaction was the limits which it imposed upon the rationalism from which it drew its force. This rationalism was liable to excesses of its own. While elsewhere (as in the case of Descartes himself) rationalism discounted the study of the past, in Italy it had an opposite effect. Men who, like Muratori, were to a greater or lesser extent devotees of the new rationalism, were at the same time promoters of the new erudition. The supreme example, of course, is Vico.

From cartesianism Italy accepted its method, that is, the generic need of positing aesthetic problems in a more rational and speculative manner; but it did not accept the reduction of art to a kind of logical or intellectual labour or deny art to the extent to which it resisted such reduction.[3] A more speculative formulation of the problems of art on rationalistic principles was attempted by Gravina (Gianvincenzo Gravina, 1664–1718); he was among the first to conceive aesthetics as a branch of the general problem of knowledge.[4] Gravina's master, Calopreso (Gregorio Calopreso, 1650–1715), had recognized the necessity of the analysis of the passions, and at the same time, that this analysis was not the work of the poet. It could not be substituted for the poetic activity. This was to prove the sin of much poetry of

---

[1] Croce uses this term with great caution; for he holds that there was no distinctive 'jesuit' style. Cf. SEB, 34.

[2] SEB, 211–12.   [3] SEB, 217.

[4] *Discorso sul 'Endimione'*; SEB, 217; cf. *Problemi di Estetica*, 363 sqq.

the 'illumination'; analysis of the passions was substituted for that transmutation of passion in expression which is the work of poetry, and intellectual exercise for the poetic act. The instrument of reason is the reflective intellect, that of poetry is phantasy or taste, which ultimately are identical. Phantasy expresses, but does not analyse the passions. By this doctrine Calopreso protected the autonomy of poetry, imagination and taste; he tended, however, to fall into the correlative fallacy of conceiving poetic expression as immediate. This excess found its corrective in such observations as those of Giannelli[1] (Basileo Giannelli, 1662–1716), that mere expression was not enough, and that the greatest poets excelled not by the direct force of their expression but by the great clarity of their 'sentenze'; which was, in its way, a vindication of the mediatorial character of art, against mere expressive passionality.

Under the combined influence of cartesian methodology and the opposition which cartesianism aroused against an intellectualist aesthetics, the artistic theory of the baroque attained its highest expression. The concept of form which is both concrete sensuous image and idea was born.

The thinker in whom the new tendencies were conjoined with the traditions of the baroque age and of the Renaissance was Vico. In the synthesis which he achieved, all of these elements were raised to new power and efficacy. The genesis of his thought cannot be understood without reference to the great figures of the new spirit, Bacon, Descartes, Grotius. It becomes unintelligible, however, if it is forgotten that Vico retained contact with methods and concepts which the new rationalism disdained or ignored. His masters were as well the Italian philosophers of the Renaissance, Ficino, Pico deilla Mirandola and many more. His metaphysics and philosophy of nature recall the Renaissance; his gnoseology takes its point of departure in Ficino; his political theory retains the fine gold of Machiavelli; his aesthetic brings to fruition the veiled insight of Pallavicino, of Tesauro, of Calopreso. With Vico the baroque age was at once fulfilled in all its positive promise and transcended.[2]

[1] *Avvertimenti*; SEB, 219–20. Cf. *Con. Crit.*, III, 40–2.
[2] For Vico cf. Croce, *La Filosofia di G. B. Vico*, Bari, 1947; A. R. Caponigri, *Time and Idea*, London, 1953.

VI

THE MORAL LIFE

THE evaluation of the moral life of a period, Croce notes, is liable to two fallacies, and both are increased when the period under consideration is an era of 'decadence'. The temptation to make of the history of such a period the mere record of its shortcomings is understandably strong; this course, however, he points out, evades the problem of decadence as an historical concept. History is wholly positive. In the moral sphere, which, in his thought, embraces the whole of the life of spirit in its unity and integrity, history must seek out the positive ideals of an era. Even when this positive character of history is assured, however, a second danger appears. It is the fallacy of anachronism, the temptation to evaluate those ideals from the vantage point of a later age, and not to appreciate their significance and force in the context in which they were formed.

The principle which must guide the interpretation of moral history is clear: it must seek out the ideals which are on the ascendant in any period. The ideals which are withering away, which are moribund, form the natural foil for those which are emerging, but cannot of themselves constitute history's object. The decadence of the baroque age in Italy, he has already indicated, was in its actual character a depression of moral enthusiasm, of that power of which moral ideals are born and by which they are advanced. For this reason, its moral history cannot be a record of customs or mores, for these possess historical interest only as functions of an ideal. If that moral ideal is inferior, they must be accounted inferior; in dissolution, if it be in dissolution. They may become the obstacles against which a new ideal is seeking to define itself, impediments which it must overcome. Finally, they may be signs of that nascent ideality.

As Italy had lost the spirit of enterprise in poetry, in philosophy, in the quest of perfection, so it had lost the plastic force by which fresh ideals are shaped. The ideals which elsewhere in Europe were gaining rapid ascendancy, here evoked but uncertain echoes; and

164

this, despite the fact that not a few of these ideals had received their initial impulse from Italian culture. These were, in the area of religion, the ideal of a more 'profound' Christianity, a creed more in tune with 'reason'; in politics, the ideal of absolute monarchy; in economic life, the extension of commerce and industry spurred by the development of science and technology and the substitution of mobile capital for capital in land. Their rapid ascendancy had as its correlative the decline of the privileged aristocracy and the advance and numerical increment of the industrial and professional 'bourgeoisie'. In this vigorous new life, to which in many aspects she had given the initial impetus, Italy did not participate. She had become a 'conservative' country, that is, one living on the capital of ideals accumulated in the past, ideals which had lost their 'élan vital' to borrow the phrase of Bergson, because élan is the property of life only in its present actuality. She had become arrested at positions attained in the past and in many instances lacked the power even to maintain these. The Spanish effort at unification, whether by annexation or by federation, was resisted by the older local forms of autonomy. The great republics, whose exploits made epic four centuries, were afflicted with senile inflexibility. The concept of absolute monarchy, which was now the rising principle of political life in the rest of Europe, had found its first formulation in Italy; it was now received with reserve and equivocation. Where she could, she resisted it fiercely as in the last stand of the Florentine republic; where she could not, she submitted passively, permitting the monarchical establishment to be imposed upon her, as by the Spanish in Naples and Lombardy, but showing no power to assimilate its idea and make it her own. This imposition of absolute monarchy provoked, it is true, a rash of rebellions in the middle of the seventeenth century; but these cannot be called effective. They were rather the last, spasmodic movements of institutions already anachronistic, as the 'revolution' of Masaniello and of the Macchia proved,[1] and served more to advance than to retard the monarchical movement. The international power of the Italian states, before so aggressive and positive, now, in like manner, became conservative and defensive. Only Savoy offered an exception, participating, not wholly without effect, in the wider life of the continent. The Italians, like those legendary behemoths whose defensive armour immobilized them, now found themselves

---

[1] For the revolution of Masaniello, cf. SRN, 35–6, 130–1; for that of the Macchia, G. B. Vico, *Scritti Storici*, ed. Nicolini, Bari, 1939, 'De parthenopea conjuratione', 304 sqq.

impeded by the very forms from which they had derived their strength. They watched their fabled riches melt away, as their commerce passed into the hands of the Flemish, the Dutch and the English. They were effectively excluded from the trade of the New World, while politically bound to the declining fortunes of Spain.

Above the meagre and languishing political ideals of the particular states there gleamed from time to time, attractive and enticing, but fugitive and ineffective, the ideal of Italian unity, based upon the geographical configuration of the peninsula and its spiritual community of language and culture. A common territory and community of historical origins do not, however, suffice to generate an effective movement of unity, when moral enthusiasm is lacking. For this reason, that ideal of unity became the object of nostalgic and sentimental contemplation, without impulsive force upon the moral will. The power which had been Italy's in the Renaissance and which would again be hers in the Risorgimento, and which in either epoch rested upon her moral enthusiasm, had passed from her. Even her most ancient glory, the faith, suffered the same eclipse; for while the Counter Reformation was powerful to conserve and defend, it was impotent to advance the religious ideals of the past.

Where then, in this picture of gloom almost unrelieved, were there to be found the positive ideals which could give this age a history? To this question the whole fabric of his narrative is the answer. Laboriously, supporting the tedium of ungrateful matter, of pompous poetastering, of subtle, but unsubstantial, ratiocinations, he had winnowed the wheat from the chaff. The grains were few, but golden, for they were heavy with the promise of the future. In a handful of dust man had his beginning; and from such slight seeds as these, cultures have arisen anew.

In the weaving of this fabric, Croce has added a fresh dimension, a dimension in depth, to the conception of ethico-political. He has come closer to the essential movement of human history, by discerning the systolic and the diastolic moments of progress and decay. He had perceived, above all, that in the one moment and the other the same life runs, now languid and heavy, like the waters of a muddied stream, now with impetuous force, like the sonorous mountain torrent—the life of the human spirit, immortal in its idea.

PART THREE

THE IDEA OF LIBERTY: THE LIBERAL FORMATION OF EUROPE IN THE NINETEENTH CENTURY

INTRODUCTION

THE ethico-political conception of history was formed in the matrix of the matter of Naples. It was called forth by Croce's effort to penetrate to the human principle of that matter, the principle of its humanity, by which it might be lifted, from a narrative of the struggles, internal and external, of a minor state of Europe, to a record of the historical struggle of man himself to possess his eternal nature in time. To achieve this concept, he had found it necessary to reject all naturalistic presuppositions of history and to accept as its only principle the spirit of man, in its diverse moments and its multitudinous labours. In the history of the Baroque Age in Italy, this conception of ethico-political history had been extended and deepened. The problem of the 'negative' or 'decadent' period in history laid bare the essential rhythm of the life of the human spirit, the alternation of moments of moral enthusiasm and of moral depression which alone define such concepts as progress and decay. Materially, so to speak,[1] the concept had been extended to achieve that union of 'Staatsgeschichte' and 'histoire de la civilization' which Federico Chabod has noted,[2] a union which simultaneously transcends these limited concepts, reducing their unilaterality and abstractness to concrete identity.

The ethico-political conception remained, nevertheless, incomplete. It remained diffuse, in solution and suspension, so to say, with many other insights and ideas. There was lacking that single and unitary idea which could collect and fuse the diverse aspects of this genial insight, precipitating its pure essence. Croce, it is clear, at every stage of the history of Naples and of the baroque age is groping for this idea. It has its 'forma negativa', to recall the Vichian phrase, in the resolute rejection of all naturalistic, non-libertarian explanations of historical process. It has a more positive, but still abortive,

[1] For there can be in Croce's view no really material dimension of human history, of the life of the human spirit.

[2] 'Croce Storico' in *Rivista Storica Italiana*, LXIV (1953), 4, p. 505.

expression in the insight that decadence is but moral depression, the diminution of the moral enthusiasm which sustains the humanity and the ideality of history. These could not suffice, however; they were partial insights, needing to be gathered and fused in some larger concept. Their partial character must be traced to the relative poverty of the matter. Both the matter of Naples and of the baroque age had yielded their ideality; but this was limited. There was necessary, consequently, a wider and a higher matter, *paulo altiora*, whose inner character would evoke the higher concept alone able to penetrate and encompass it. This matter was furnished to Croce by the formation of Italy and of Europe in the nineteenth century, and the idea which it evoked, the ultimate informing idea of his historiography, is the idea of liberty.

The liberal formation of Europe and of Italy in the nineteenth century thus forms the third, the widest and most inclusive theme of Croce's historiography and yields its ultimate and informing idea, liberty. That these two, the Italian and the wider European experience, constitute one historical reality, seen in its diverse aspects of universal and particular, is the most profound conviction which animates the two histories. The positive and transforming ethico-political ideal and force is the idea of liberty and the liberal spirit or will, and the formation of Europe in the nineteenth century was essentially the work of this spirit. The Italian experience is integral to the wider experience of Europe as a whole; but it is even more. It exemplifies the liberal idea and will in their purity, that is to say, in the highest form and expression there were to attain. Modern Italy, in his view, is the purest type of the liberal nation-state which history has seen, just as, and because, the movement of which it was born, the Risorgimento, was the most nearly flawless example of the liberal spirit in operation. The ethico-political history of Europe in the nineteenth century must, consequently, be polarized about these two centres: Europe, as a whole, and Italy. It can be, however, only one history, for these centres represent the universality and the particularity of one historical reality, the liberal movement.

Some critics have remarked that Croce's treatment of this theme lacks the richness and warmth of the history of Naples and the elaborate refinement of particulars which marks the history of the baroque era.[1] Some material justice is reflected in this animadversion; differences in treatment do exist and are pronounced; no

[1] E.g. Cecil Sprigg, *Benedetto Croce*, Yale, 1952, p. 31; Federico Chabod, op. cit.; Nino Cortese, op. cit.

pejorative conclusion, however, can be drawn from them. These differences are to be traced to the diversity of materials and to the diversity of mood and insight which sustained him in these various themes. The treatment accorded each single theme, however, is strictly commensurate to the ideality and the spiritual attitude it could evoke. As a consequence, comparison between them can only be oblique. The dominant note of the history of Naples is one of tragic lyricism, even of elegy. This mood is dictated, we have already suggested,[1] by the intense identification which Croce felt with the tragic national experience of Naples. He was narrating the vicissitudes of the people and the land with which his sentiments bound him most closely, as a Neapolitan by election, and in whose sufferings he shared. In such matter, objectivity is almost more than can be demanded of the historian; but Croce achieves it, to a remarkable degree, at the cost of an almost heroic detachment. The baroque age, on the other hand, attracted him with much less elemental force. He once remarked to a friend, it is true, that when he permitted himself to dream of the life he would choose above all others, there came to his imagination the cloister of a seventeenth-century Neapolitan convent, with its white walls and silent walks, shaded by cypress, inhabited by studious monks united in silent spiritual communion.[2] When addressed historiographically, however, that age became for him a problem. It was a problem under its formal aspect, the idea of a period of decadence, a 'negative' period of history. It was a problem under its material aspect; while he saw it as the matrix of modern Italy, the elements of the new, of the future had most delicately to be isolated from the dead encrustment of the past. His attitude, consequently, was that of the inquirer before the problem. The mood of the work is detached, analytic, almost surgical, as with deft and probing scalpel, the cold edge of criticism, he seeks the elusive point where past and future, death and life must be distinguished. The delicate anatomy of the poetry of an unpoetic age, of the speculations of an unphilosophical era, of the religious proliferations of 'the most unreligious age Italy has ever known', these are not tasks to warm the cockles of a man's heart or lift his spirit. Particulars must be sought with care, almost with caution, for every distinction and evaluation is worth only the evidence which can be adduced in its support. More than once, the author is tempted to turn away in 'ennui' and is prevented only by the thought of the fruit to be won by this effort.

[1] Cf. *supra*.   [2] E. Nicolini, *Benedetto Croce*, Napoli, 1944, p. 18.

INTRODUCTION

The dominant note of the history of Europe and of Italy in the nineteenth century, in contrast to both those earlier histories, is at once positive and buoyant; it is written in a mood as near the epic as may be hoped for in the modern world. This mood again, as in the case of the history of Naples, is evoked by identification with the matter. In this instance, however, the identification is unqualified. It is not, as in the case of Naples, acceptance and rejection at once, but unqualified acceptance, identification, not with defeat, but with victory. The liberal experience and achievement is for Croce limited but wholly positive; and while reserving to himself the right and the power to distinguish these limits between fact and idea, his identification with the fact is complete. The style of the works in turn is dictated by this positive and buoyant mood. They are painted in broad, forceful strokes, the outlines clear, the colours bold, the movement vivacious. There is a preoccupation with the whole, an Olympian subordination of detail, reflecting confidence and certitude. The distinctions and oppositions may be, as de Ruggiero suggests, of that between speculative or philosophical romanticism and its practical or sentimental form,[1] even a shade too sharp. In this case too, however, as in the matter of Naples and in the baroque theme, the commensuration between mood, style and matter is complete. We are confronted by three autonomous historiographical achievements, which may not be evaluated in terms of each other, and can be contrasted only to heighten the values particular to each.

The identification which, in the history of Europe and Italy in the nineteenth century, exists between historian and matter bears closer examination. It reveals, as a matter of fact, the ultimate basis of this history, the basis upon which the massive reconstruction of a whole century of European experience rests. It is a maxim, perhaps the most celebrated, of Croce's historiography, that all history is contemporary.[2] The Crocean sense of this maxim is, in the first instance, that all history is written in answer to an urgent need of the present. In the widest sense, it answers to the need of ethical and moral action; these demand a plenitude of presence in the subject, a plenitude of which the past, secured by the historiographic act, is an integral dimension. Without this basis in the present history is at best irrelevant and redundant; at worst, it may become a mode of self-alienation for the human subject, which lessens his moral enthusiasm, as he has pointed out with reference to the baroque era, for overattachment to the past was a dimension of its own

[1] *L'Età del Romanticismo*, Bari, 1949, pp. 419–22. [2] Cf. FPS, 443–5.

'decadence'.[1] The contemporaneity of history is the basis for the identification of the historian with his theme in the histories of Europe and Italy in the nineteenth century.

The grounds for this identification are many and complex. The first is Croce's position as a member of the generation which was the direct and immediate heir of the Risorgimento. The Risorgimento must always mean more to the Italian than a mere phase in the history of Italy. It means the birth of Italy, for before the Risorgimento there was no Italy in the sense of an autonomous nation-state able to vindicate its claim to self-identity and historical existence and to contribute to the common good of humanity to which all nations must contribute.[2] The creation of Italy as a nation could never be considered a mere political achievement. It was an ethical transaction of the highest order, marking a true beginning rather than the rebirth which the appellation Risorgimento suggests. For this reason, every Italian must identify himself with the ideals and the forces which made the national aspiration of Italy an historical reality. In its simplest form, this identification meant the impossibility of any return to a situation resembling that which had prevailed before the Risorgimento; any step toward the undoing of the work of the Risorgimento must appear a desecration. Even more, however, it meant the ethico-political obligation of realizing the full ideality of the new Italy, its richest historical possibilities. This obligation was felt by the men of the 'Right', the direct inheritors of the Risorgimento in political power; it was felt by the men of the 'Left', the 'young Left' who displaced the Right in office in 1876, but adhered to its methods and ideals;[3] it was felt by the Catholics, torn though they were by conflicting loyalties. It was felt, finally, by Croce personally as a member of this generation, even as a 'purist' of the Risorgimento tradition, and becomes vocal in his history.

The acceptance of the Risorgimento implied the acceptance of the whole European movement of which it was a part. The rise of Italy as an independent nation was not an anomaly. It was the expression, in terms of the life and history of the peninsula, of a common movement embracing the whole of Europe. It possessed analogues wherever effective centres of such formation presented themselves. The community among the nation-states was based upon common principles and common ideals. This wider acceptance and identification is also a basic characteristic of Croce's position.

[1] Under one aspect only; under another, it exhibited contempt for the past; cf. *supra*, p. 161.　　　　[2] Cf. SE'800, 13.　　　　[3] SI'71, 2 sqq.

His was not, however, an acceptance and an identification with the fact merely. His history is not an apology either for the Risorgimento[1] or for liberalism and the Europe it created. It is, rather, a critical exposition of the ethico-political ideals and the ethico-political forces which achieved the fact. The purpose of this criticism is both to identify those ideals and forces in their historical actuality and to relate them to the present with its special problems and aspirations. The identification which marks his work, consequently, is born at the high level of critical reflection which is in turn the preparation for relevant historical action in the present. Its critical character renders the mode of identification and the historical narrative complex; but it also lends it new strength and clarity. Finally, his identification is born of the contemporary crisis in which the new Italy was caught up in the third decade of the twentieth century. Although Croce had been absorbed in the matter of these histories, under one aspect or another, from the very beginning of his career,[2] their composition was not undertaken until the crisis of the new authoritarianism and totalitarianism was well advanced and the path which lay before it well marked. The polemical character of these histories, consequently, cannot be overlooked. Croce saw in the developing trend of political life the destruction of the Italy of the Risorgimento. It detracts only a little, if at all, from his final vision that it was relatively slow in forming, or that he overlooked a countermovement, that of popularism, which might have rectified many of the long-standing anomalies of liberal Italy, while reaffirming the basic liberal insights. The tardiness of this vision is also compensated by the fact that it was born of a fundamental confidence in the resiliency of liberal Italy, its power to absorb and to domesticate such a movement as Fascism.[3] When finally the vision came, it was crystal clear. The polemic which it provoked was radical but took the form, not of a controversy *ad hoc* which in the circumstances would surely have proven less than useless, but of a synoptic and critical restatement of the basic ideals which were in danger of repudiation. In this sense, the history of Europe in the nineteenth century and that of Italy even more, in the period between 1871 and 1915, was a judgment upon Fascism. At the same time they con-

---

[1] That is, for the existence of modern Italy.

[2] A first sketch of a history of Europe in the nineteenth century is to be traced to 1914-15; cf. Franchini, op. cit.

[3] Cf. *Nuove pagine sparse*, Napoli, 1948, I, pp. 45 sqq. CCMS in FPS, 1172; R. Franchini, *Esperienza dello storicismo*, Napoli, 1953, p. 135.

stituted a judgment upon all Italians, himself included. Their polemical objective was to show that while it is true that the possibility of such a movement as Fascism may be traced in the structure of post-Risorgimento Italy, it is present there only as the possibility of moral failure is always present in human effort. Fascism cannot be conceived as following necessarily upon the course of events of that period. It must be traced to a moral failure in the Italians themselves. The histories possess consequently the character of a recall of Italy to the pristine ideals and moral volition of her national life.[1]

The central theses of these histories are unambiguous, stated in the same bold and positive tone which marks their style. The positive and effective ethico-political force in the nineteenth century was liberalism, which supplies both the ideality and the effective moral will of the century. Thus the basic thesis. The authentic idea of liberty[2] is to be found in the tradition of philosophical romanticism or classical idealism. Thus the second. The third concerns the relationship between the idea of liberty, as defining liberalism, and the concrete institutional forms into which that idea, in the course of the century, was translated: that there exists between them the essential incommensurability between idea which is always normative and the concrete existential form; so that their simple identification, as exemplified in the attitude of the Right in 1876,[3] must be recognized as erroneous. Finally, there is his thesis concerning the place of Italy in the liberal movement of Europe as a whole and concerning the fate of the liberal idea in the first crucial decades after the creation of the new Italy: that, in the first instance, the Italian experience of the Risorgimento represented the quintessence of the liberal movement of the nineteenth century; in the second, that the experience of the first decades of the life of Italy as a nation vindicates the liberal idea and establishes the positive achievement of the new nation which makes of any movement such as the Fascist 'adventure' an historical and moral anomaly.

In the liberty which is the sustaining principle of liberalism, the ethico-political conception, as we have suggested, is completed. In its original context, the matter of Naples, the ethico-political concept is primarily a methodological canon; it is a guide for the historian in his effort to find the living centre of the matter with which he dealt.

---

[1] Cf. on these points Chabod, op. cit., pp. 515 sqq.

[2] In terms of which liberalism is to be defined in contra-distinction both to alternate ideals and to limited or erroneous statements of its own idea.

[3] Cf. SI'71, 15.

The ethico-political insight, in this sense, is essentially the insight of Vico: 'in the night of thick darkness enveloping the earliest antiquity ... there shines the eternal and neverfailing light of a truth beyond all question: that the world of civil society has certainly been made by men, and that its principles are therefore to be found within the modifications of our own human mind'.[1] The living centre of history is discerned as residing in the will and the ideality of man himself. Vichian too is the attitude toward nature, specifically, toward the natural forces at work in history. 'Whoever reflects on this cannot fail to marvel that the philosophers should have directed all their energies to the world of nature ... and neglected the study of the world of nations or the civil world.'[2] The world of nature can but delineate the theatre within which the will and ideality of man are deployed; they are but limiting factors, bereft of explanatory force,[3] and engendering, when substituted for the agency of man, a false conception of historical necessity.[4] It becomes the historian's intent, according to this canon, to eschew naturalistic explanation in history in whatever form it may suggest itself, and to seek always, in Croce's own words, its 'vero moto e il vero dramma negli intelletti e nei cuori'.[5] The chief result of the application of this canon is to throw into relief, as Croce remarks about his own history of the realm of Naples, the human character of history.[6]

By the concept of liberty, this canonical sense of the ethico-political conception is converted into, and completed by, its ontological sense. According to that canon, the historian had been directed to the human centre of history and admonished to see there the true principles of explanation. He was instructed to see history as wholly the work of the human spirit. But no positive concept of the human spirit itself had been advanced; or more accurately, such a concept had been only adumbrated, and that negatively. For to say that man is not subject to natural necessity in historical action is, in a negative manner, to assert that he is free, but without indicating the positive form of his freedom. This lack is only partially remedied by the classical doctrines on the freedom of the human will; these are arrested wholly at the level of the psychological analysis of freedom and tend, as a consequence, to fall back into naturalistic dilemmas, or pseudo-dilemmas. Liberty is the concept which defines the human spirit in its ontological character; through this concept the human

---

[1] *Scienza Nuova Seconda*, 331.　　　　　　　　　　[2] Ibid.
[3] Cf. SRN, 269 sqq.　　　　　　[4] Cf. FPS, 495–9, 458–9, 1078, 1112.
[5] SI'71, vii.　　　　　　　　　　　　　　　[6] SRN, 272.

spirit is discerned in its ultimate quality of being, as the creative existential agent of ideal forms. Ethico-political history thus discovers its own positive character; it is the history of human freedom, because liberty is the constitutive form of the human spirit itself.

I

THE SPIRITUAL FORCES OF
THE CENTURY

THE historical drama of the nineteenth century, Croce suggests, opens with a complex situation, fraught with contradictions. The event which opens the era is the fall of Napoleon. His career, with its roots in the libertarianism of the great Revolution and its fruit in the militaristic imperialism of his last period, seemed to retrace the career of the idea of liberty itself, from utopistic promise of equality and fraternity to personal despotism. His overthrow was engineered by a coalition of forces openly reactionary and hostile to the notion of liberty whose motto was not equality or freedom but order, and which in the name of order envisaged the reconstitution of the old regimes and the maintenance of an armed peace. These circumstances should, logically, have ushered in an era of undisputed conservatism and reaction; this was not, however, the case. On every hand, the hope and the demand for liberty and independence were raised anew and, if anything, with greater force. The concrete and particular forms of this demand and hope were numerous and highly differentiated by the historical antecedents and the contemporary conditions of the various countries of Europe. In one they took the form of freedom from foreign domination and the nascent ideal of national unity, in another that of the substitution of constitutional for absolutistic government. In one place, it was a matter simply of the reform or the extension of an electoral system already established, in another the far more difficult task of establishing such a system *ab ovo*. Where, through the efforts of earlier generations, civil equality and religious toleration had already been established, the object was to open the paths of participation in government to wider social strata while elsewhere the battle against the political and civil privileges of persistent feudal classes had still to be won. In every case, however, these objectives, for all their specific diversity, appeared as the multiple images of one ideal, liberty, and

179

it was liberty which was sought in every specific diverse form.[1] How then, it must be asked, could this contradictory, or seemingly contradictory, situation arise?

The answer is, to Croce's mind, clear. The renewed aspiration, in a multiplicity of forms, toward the single goal of liberty is to be traced to the emergence of a new idea of liberty itself, or, more accurately, a new formulation of an idea and ideal both immemorial. The emergence of this new idea is not in contradiction with the disillusionment with the Revolution which swept over Europe, nor with the discredit, indeed the abhorrence, into which its ideal, the 'unchanging, eternal triangle' as the poet Monti called it, of liberty, fraternity, equality had fallen. On the contrary, this disillusion and abhorrence constitute its premise, its precondition, just as did every other limited, historical formulation of liberty. The new idea was not the refutation or the rejection of any of those earlier formulations; it was at once their deeper penetration and their transcendence so that, while new in the most profound sense of that term, it still was born of all those others, or, more precisely, of the one human spirit which formulated and criticized, by the harsh criterion of history itself, each of those earlier ideas in turn, while seeking always the principle of its own authentic historical existence. That same spirit, now, on the basis of its own complex historical experience, advanced this new idea, which became in this way a fresh motive force in history.

Nevertheless, this new idea did not spring, to invoke an honoured metaphor, as Athena full-grown from the head of Zeus, full-grown from the consciousness of the new age. On the contrary, it was wrought laboriously, by thinkers who, while aware of the novelty of the idea, yet saw only dimly the terms in which it must be expressed. Fallacious formulations were almost the necessary condition of its ultimate clarity. The first and most significant of the abortive efforts was the attempt to define liberty juridically, that is to say, in terms of the institutions in which it must be historically incorporated. Juridical distinctions, Croce suggests, are practical[2] and refer to limited and transitive institutions. They cannot be used, consequently, to define the idea of liberty. This fallacy was as old as Plato who, as Vico had pointed out, had sought to incorporate the idea of justice in an 'ideal' city where only philosophers could dwell, while spurning the admonitions of historical experience, which clearly suggested the incommensurability of the idea with any, or with the sum of, its

[1] SE'800, 2-4.   [2] Cf. FPS, 597 sqq.

historical incorporations.[1] It took contemporary form in the problem of the 'differential' between the ancient and the modern ideas of liberty, in which the experience of Greece and Rome and of the French Revolution which had followed the classical models was set in contrast with the present, that is, the new ideal of liberty which was struggling to achieve formulation. The problem in this form was poorly posited, and the comparative procedure it suggested proved less than useful as a means of discovering the quality of the new concept of liberty. Following this procedure, inquiry tended to dissipate itself in abstract distinctions, all of them juridical, such as that between political and civil liberty, between the individual and the state, and to define the old and the new concepts by attributing one or another of these abstractions now to the past, now to the present. Only gradually did it become apparent that the new concept of liberty which thinkers like Sismondi and Constant had sought to define in juridical terms could find adequate expression only at the philosophical or speculative level. When transferred to this level, the new concept is seen to be at the same time very old; that is, the resultant and the beneficiary of the speculative effort of centuries. It was the result and the fruit specifically of the stubborn effort to reduce the dualistic antinomies in which the concept of man had been involved since the days of classical naturalism.[2]

The most radical of these antinomies had been that between reason and history, most radical from both a logical and a humanistic point of view.[3] This dualism had its origins in the classical naturalism, in its permanentistic theories of being and its universalistic theories of science. It appears in its most violent contrasts in Plato; in Aristotle, while somewhat qualified, it was by no means resolved. The antinomy is profoundly alien to Christianity; for Christianity, by its central dogma of the incarnation and the soteric office of Jesus, is historiocentric. The gigantic labour of synthesis between Christian dogma and Greek naturalistic philosophy, which was accomplished by the great thinkers of the Christian tradition and above all by Augustine, aggravated the situation by compressing the Christian insight into an intellectual and theoretical framework alien to it. To say this is in no wise to minimize the genial character of that synthesis. It is simply to recognize what Augustine himself did not fail

---

[1] Cf. Vico, *Autobiografia*, Bari, Laterza, 1911, p. 12; *Scienza Nuova Seconda*, paragraphs 131, 253; A. R. Caponigri, *Time and Idea*, London, Routledge and Kegan Paul, 1953, ch. XI.

[2] SE'800, 9.

[3] SE'800, 8.

to recognize, even while the philosophical principles which he adopted militated against its accomplishment, namely, that the authentic theoretical development of Christianity lay in the direction of a theory of history. The antinomy between reason and history at the heart of the Christian-classical synthesis was obscured by the eschatological inheritance from Judaism, which was taken up into that synthesis. With the process of the 'secularization' of western culture, this antinomy stood out in even greater relief, until in the eighteenth century it became the hall-mark of the illuministic mentality, profoundly antihistorical, suspended, like Buridan's ass, between the truths of reason and the truths of fact. The 'philosophy of history' which had its origins precisely in the illuminism and in that process of the secularization of the traditional Christian structure of ideas, illustrates, rather than heals, this rupture; for its premises are precisely the propositions of a naturalistic rationalism. It could do no more than gloss the opaque 'facts' of history with a veneer of brittle reflection, a process of which Voltaire was the acknowledged master.[1]

The persistence of this antinomy was due to the failure of western thought to develop the logical instrument by which it might be overcome. Western philosophical speculation had rested wholly on the logic of contradiction; this logic was able to support only the ontological notion of nature. The need for a larger logic orientated toward an ontology and a methodology of history had been felt as early as the Renaissance; Bruno and Campanella alike strain at the tethers of the older naturalism. It is with Vico, however, and with Vichian gnoseology, summed up in the maxim 'verum et factum convertuntur' that the basic insight which would lead to the healing of the separation between time and idea, reason and history.[2] The theme is taken up with even greater clarity by Kant, whose theory of the synthesis 'a priori', while arrested in its immediate effectiveness by its phenomenalism, nevertheless both demonstrated the possibility and indicated the principle of a larger logic in which the logic of contradiction would not be negated but would be assigned its

[1] Cf. 'Il concetto moderno della storia', Bari, 1947; reprinted as appendix to *Filosofia e Storiografia*, Bari, 1949, 353–69; 'Il concetto della filosofia come storicismo assoluto' in *Il Carattere della Filosofia Moderna*, Bari, 1945, pp. 1–22; *Teoria e Storia della Storiografia*, 5a ed., Bari, 1943, xxi, pp. 223 sqq.

[2] Croce traces the antecedents of the Vichian gnoseology in the essay 'Le Fonti della gnoseologia vichiana', reprinted in *Saggio sullo Hegel*, 4a ed., 1948, pp. 235 sqq.; cf. also Manlio Ciardo, *Le quattro epoche dello storicismo*, Bari, 1947, pp. 25 sqq.; Croce, *La filosofia di G. B. Vico*, 5a ed., Bari, 1947, pp. 1–32; A. Robert Caponigri, *Time and Idea*, London, 1953, p. 155 sqq.

restricted function in the living process of thought. The reduction of Kant's phenomenalism was the work of that whole group of thinkers, culminating in the achievement of Hegel. The gradual dissolution of the thing in itself,[1] the ontologization of the human subjectivity, with the dialectic as its dynamic principle, a principle at once of thought and being, established the basis of the new historicism. As a result of this speculative achievement, in Croce's words, 'man . . . no longer appeared crushed (*schiacciato*) by his own history or as the vindicator of his own character against history, nor did he reject the past as the record of his shame, but as its true and indefatigable author, contemplated himself in his history as in his very life. History no longer appeared devoid of spirituality, and abandoned to blind forces, supported or rectified by extraneous forces, but was demonstrated to be both the work and the actuality of spirit, and since spirit is liberty, the work of freedom.'[2]

The speculative concept of history as the history of liberty is the summation and the expression of this entire process and of the new historicism which provided the philosophical basis of the new faith in and the new demands for liberty. The force of this concept has often been erroneously represented in later accounts, and made the object, consequently, of ungrounded criticism. Most frequently it has been represented as the repudiation of any moral dimension in history, as the unqualified vindication of the past by the equation of the rational and the real, or, as in the case of Hegel, the basis of an extreme political conservatism and statolotry. The instance of Hegel is specifically considered by Croce[3] and his position trenchantly criticized not only in its political but in its more radical speculative aspects as well.[4] He interprets his failings as the limits of the man, however, and not the intrinsic weakness of the speculative idea of history as the history of liberty. Even in the case of Hegel, however, the charge of amoralism is without foundation or significance, for the liberty which is here indicated is entirely moral liberty, that is, the freedom and creativity of the human spirit in its historical effort to realize existentially the ideals which sustain its life. The fact is that the notion of history as the history of liberty entirely displaces all the older notions of natural or fatal necessity in history and places in its

---

[1] This process is traced by Windelband, *History of Philosophy*, trans. Tufts, Macmillan, pp. 568 sqq.; and by de Ruggiero, *L'Età del romanticismo*, 3a ed., Bari, 1949. [2] SE'800, 8. [3] SE'800, 10.
[4] *Saggio sullo Hegel*; 'Differenza dello storicismo hegeliano dallo storicismo nuovo' in *Discorsi di varia filosofia*, Bari, 1945, vol. 2, pp. 116–28.

stead that moral and logical necessity which is the very essence of the freedom or liberty of the human spirit agent in history. When this point is appreciated, the charge of neo-fatalism in the equation of the real and the rational in history loses all its ostensible force. That equation simply asserts the transparency of history to the human intellect, for it is human reason working in history which imparts to history its existential form; at the same time it asserts that the existential principle of history is the human will whose informing principle is reason. Nor is it the abstract reason so adulated in the period of the enlightenment which is intended in this formula; it is rather, the concrete process of human thought, of which imagination, passion and judgment are all components. The coincidence of reality and rationality in history thus precludes both the fortuitousness of chance and the determination of natural causation. If anything, it is the apotheosis of the moral dimension in history.[1]

The formulation of the speculative notion of history as the history of liberty establishes the ideal character of the new faith in liberty as against the abortive efforts to define liberty in juridical terms. One effort of this latter character has proved especially persistent and in the long run contributed a major impetus to the decline of liberalism which Croce is presently to note and to open the door in modern history to the antiliberal forces of socialism and of twentieth-century neo-authoritarianism and statism. This is the effort to define the notion of the new liberty in economic terms, or, that is to say, in terms of the economic institutions of human society. This effort Croce calls, in contrast to liberalism, 'economic liberism'.[2] Its persistence is due, he feels, to the fact that it has both a common character and origin with the political liberalism, for it shares a common derivation from the concept of history suggested above. There is a strict parallel, he believes, between economic and political authoritarianism, and liberalism is opposed to authoritarianism under both these aspects. In the area of science, the principle corresponding to the idea of liberty is that of free research and free discussion. All are aspects of the common notion of liberty, and history narrates how consciousness of particular liberties has arisen and translated itself into juridical institutions as well as the fact that with these particular liberties and their corresponding institutional forms there has arisen the insight that they are not many but one, and that they cannot stand alone, but only together.[3]

[1] SE'800, 44 sqq.   [2] 'Liberismo economico' or simply 'liberismo'.
[3] 'Liberismo e Liberalismo' in Et. Pol., 316.

No opposition arises between ethico-political liberalism and 'economic liberism' so long as one sees them as specific operations of a common principle. Opposition appears when the latter is made the supreme regulative principle of social life, when the specific is made regulative of the general notion of liberty. Ethical liberalism alone can possess this regulative character for it is by definition a principle apt to specify itself in many particular directions. When this general regulative character is imputed to economic liberism, it is converted at one stroke from a legitimate (though by no means absolute, as must presently appear) economic principle into an illegitimate and invalid ethical theory; it generates a hedonistic and utilitarian morality which assumes as the criterion of value the satisfaction of desire or of interest as such, a satisfaction which becomes under this specious quantitative aspect the satisfaction of individual interest or of the interest of society conceived as the sum, and the means of the fulfilment of, individual interests. The apotheosis of economic liberism into a social law has given occasion for the denial of that principle itself. For it is manifest that moral and ethical exigencies oppose a legitimate limit to hedonic and utilitarian satisfaction of interest. Nor is it sufficient, in order to dissolve this opposition, to distinguish the proper spheres of each; for this effort tacitly reaffirms the fundamental error, that of counterposing the two principles on an equal level.[1]

The only solution is to recognize the undisputed primacy of ethical liberalism, as expressed in the theory of history as the history of liberty, and to treat the economic problems of social life only in relation to it. Ethical liberalism abhors the authoritarian regulation of economic life in so far as it sees in such regulation the mortification of an inventive and creative faculty of the human spirit. It cannot, however, accept the view that those things alone are good which satisfy individual interest, or that wealth consists only in the accumulation of means to this end. More precisely still, it cannot concede that such are goods at all unless they lend themselves as instruments to human ethical elevation. For the notion of liberty which informs ethical liberalism and which derives from its concept of history envisages always the promotion of man's spiritual life in its entirety and integrity, that is to say, precisely in its moral and ethical quality. It cannot tolerate any elevation of a specific aspect of that life to a regulative norm of the whole.[2]

The obligation of ethical liberalism, with respect to any economic

[1] *Et. Pol.*, 317–18.   [2] Ibid.

institution, is not to determine whether it be economically productive, but whether it is qualitatively valuable; not whether its quality be grateful to one or to a large number but whether it is salutary for all or for the whole, for man in his character and dignity as man. It may well be that in determining this question ethical liberalism countenances many or even the greater part of the institutions of economic liberism, and this has been the case, historically. This approval is accorded those institutions, however, not for abstract economic reasons but for ethical reasons; and for the same reasons liberalism is free to repudiate these or any others which, under a specious appeal of liberty, offer obstacles to liberty in its supreme ethical sense. On the other hand, since the ethical character of economic institutions can be judged only in the concrete, it results that all theoretical efforts to predetermine such judgments are abstract and lacking in consistency. Such issues can be handled only practically, *caso per caso* as the famous saying has it. Dispute frequently arises, for example, as to what should be left to individual initiative and what reserved to the initiative of the state. To resolve this dispute in the abstract is impossible. The issue must always turn about some specific economic institution under specific circumstances. Opinion is frequently exercised over the opposition between economic liberism and socialism and over the preference to be accorded one rather than the other. From the point of view of ethical liberalism this must appear a fatuous exercise. In the first place, these two 'systems' do not exist historically in opposition to each other. The liberistic institution inevitably exhibits certain 'socialistic' features, and the socialistic features of economic liberism. Here again the only real issue at stake is the ethical; and it is perfectly conceivable that ethical liberalism might approve institutions which the economists might label socialistic, so that it becomes possible to speak as Hobhouse does of a 'liberal socialism'.[1]

This distinction and dialectization of ethico-political liberalism and 'economic liberism' in Croce's thought is neither academic nor otiose. It has direct relevance to the history of Europe in the nineteenth century and to the fortunes of the movements contending for supremacy. If liberalism failed, he will presently make clear, and had to concede historical ground to one degree or another to the contending ideals of democratic socialism and communism and to the political authoritarianism with which both of these are fraught, it is

[1] *Et. Pol.*, 319–20; compare the discussion by de Ruggiero in *The History of European Liberalism*, trans. Collingwood, Oxford, 1927, especially p. 347 sqq.

precisely because this distinction was not made, or not made effectively. For ethical liberalism, precisely because ethical, preoccupied
with the whole man, in his human character, has power to assimilate
and domesticate all economic exigencies. If it exercises this power
unilateral forms of political economy will not arise in history. In
order to exercise this power, liberalism must be aware of its own
character, of its relation to any and all of the more limited forms of
life which may assert themselves in ostensible opposition to its central ethical claim. The failure to grasp its own character, as will
appear in reference to the specific problem of Fascism in Italy, must
be imputed to it as a moral failing entailing corresponding moral
responsibility.[1]

The concept of history as the history of liberty had as its necessary practical complement liberty as a moral ideal, that is, as an end,
the chief end, of all practical activity. Here, too, the dependence on
the past is apparent. The moral ideal of liberty had been present in
the whole movement of thought and civilization of the west, as
Hegel had indicated; in modern times it had passed from the concept of liberty as a complex of privilege through the stage of abstract
natural right to the spiritual liberty of the historical concrete personality characteristic of idealism and romanticism. At the same time,
the advance of the new idea of liberty upon the past is equally to be
noted. It is characteristic of the new concept that it transcends all
such limited notions to become identical with the historical process
of the human spirit as the inner law of its movement. Liberty is both
that by which spirit is and that according to which it must be, independently of all limiting conditions. This fact had been perceived by
Kant in his moral philosophy, and it had been developed by the
romantic tradition.

All limitations upon this radical and constitutive freedom must,
consequently, be accounted practical and empirical; and all attempts
to interpret empirical limitations ideally must be specious. Specious
was the objection that radical liberty could not be moral since it did
not envisage the entire exorcism of evil from the world of culture
but rather its eternal dialectic with the good. Specious, too, were
those utopian and hedonistic objections which complained that this
conception of human liberty, involving man in a never-ending
struggle, precluded him from that absolute and final peace toward
which he aspired, and which modern utopianism, having rejected
the transcendental elements of earlier religious belief, imagined

[1] Cf. on this point Chabod, op. cit.

might be attained within history itself. Specious, finally, was the argument, correctly called authoritarian, which, while recognizing the intrinsic claims of liberty, saw it only as a function of the privileged and the elect, delivering the remainder of mankind to subjection. Alternate forms of this exclusivism: racism, nationalism, culturalism, share this same specious character. The notion of liberty as moral ideal is qualifiable by no adjective, can be subordinated to no limit. The only limits or qualifications which it can tolerate are those which it engenders historically and which are the concrete existential forms of its historical being. These limits are reconcilable with, indeed necessary to, the radical concept of liberty because they are acts of the same free principle, limits which the spirit assigns itself in the interest of its historical existence. At the same time, spirit in its freedom transcends those limits ideally by the fact that it has generated them.[1]

This is the reason why the attempts to define liberalism juridically, mentioned above, necessarily proved fallacious. Institutions were interpreted as absolute limits upon liberty and not as contingent limits generated by the historical process itself. In the same manner, the particular structures which the liberal movement during the course of the century was to call into being have to be viewed as historical modes, answering to existential conditions, and not as defining or delimiting the idea of liberty itself. Thus nationalism, so closely allied with liberalism as almost to be identified with it during that age, answers only to existential conditions: though surely born of the liberal idea, it remains a transient and contingent embodiment of it. Nationalism arose, to a great extent, in opposition to the abstract humanitarianism and cosmopolitanism of the preceding age. Its positive intent was to promote humanity in its concrete form, the personality, both of men as individuals and as complexes of men bound by ties of common origins and memories, customs and attitudes, that is nations whether already historically existent or waiting to be awakened into historical life. The concept of nation in the liberal lexicon, consequently, is a spiritual and an historical, not a naturalistic and immobile concept. It is not intrinsically opposed to the notion of higher unities among 'nations', as some would maintain; on the contrary, it envisages in principle the possibility and even the historical necessity of such larger and more inclusive formations, with the sole condition that their formation be as much an act of freedom and liberty as the national formation itself. The translation

[1] SE'800, 12; *Et. Pol.*, 317; FPS, 486–523, 629–33, 637–40.

of the idea of the nation into any imperialistic movement is necessarily opposed to the liberal idea, for it violates precisely this condition. In the same manner, constitutions and representative forms of government are born naturally from the liberal idea, bringing into the circle of political activity, as they do, men and classes of greater capacity and of greater devotion to the common good. Neither are they, however, to be construed as definitive forms of the liberal idea itself. Freedom of the press, the two party system, regionalism, constitutional monarchism, all stand in the same relation to that idea of liberty.

Nevertheless, while transient and contingent with respect to the idea of liberty, these forms, Croce makes clear, possess their own inner, logical and ideal necessity. Radically, this necessity flows from the historical time structure of the human spirit, which dictates its existentialization in concrete historical moments of particular quality. It flows also, however, from the ideal affinity of these forms with the idea of liberty itself. Not all possible structures of historical life possess this affinity indifferently. It marks only those which are born of the moral will to liberty. While these forms are relative and contingent to the idea of liberty in the sense that they are incommensurate with its total ideality and cannot exhaust that ideality in the limited existential structures which they establish, they are not equally contingent or transitive with respect to other possible historical formations of human life and society, which may have other origins than the natural movement of the idea of liberty. With respect to such forms, of whatever provenance, the forms freely generated by the historical movement of liberty possess an indubitable necessity which makes it inconceivable that they should be compromised. It must still be clearly asserted, however, that the distinction between forms generated by the movement of liberty and those having other origins and hence other qualities cannot be established abstractly and apodictically. It can be established only historically; and the idea that this distinction can be achieved in any other way must be rejected as a subtle form of utopianism. The historical process of this distinction is a dimension of the total struggle between good and evil which is the ineluctable pattern of the life of the human spirit.

The formation of this radical concept of liberty and moral commitment to it was the supreme achievement of the nineteenth century, in Croce's view. Its commitment to the idea of liberty was complete, embracing all levels of thought and action. It is this total character of the commitment which leads Croce to speak in this context of a 'religion' of liberty and of a liberal 'faith'. The choice of these terms may appear of dubious propriety to some; but Croce's intention in their selection is clear. He has defined religion as a view of reality which involves a concomitant ethical commitment, and he has amply demonstrated that liberalism fulfils this definition, though the definition itself may be acceptable only with grave qualifications.[1]

While Croce conceived liberalism as the one positive and effective ideal of the nineteenth century, the only one to which may be traced the constructive form of European life, he did not imagine that it enjoyed an open and unopposed course. On the contrary, it was contested at every stage, not by one but by a variety of forces. Nor, from the standpoint of liberalism itself, can this opposition be considered an unmitigated evil; it was necessary, for only in opposition to conflicting ideals could the ideals of liberalism be clarified and actualized. Moreover, the opposing ideals were of the same character as liberalism; they were 'religious faiths' in the same sense as Croce had called liberalism 'religious'. For this reason alone they were able to contest the advance of liberalism. The history of the nineteenth century thus appears to Croce what his fundamental conception of ethico-political history has led him to expect: a struggle of wills in the service of conflicting ideals of reality and of man.[2]

At the same time, the conflict is not a simple and naked opposition of forces. The ideals and the ethics arrayed against each other were not abstractions, but historical realities. They sustained among themselves, consequently, all those ligatures which bind and relate the elements of a common historical process, even when these elements have entered upon a fatal contest. In the analysis and depiction of these ideas and forces and in the comprehension and penetration of the actual course which the struggle between them was to assume, and finally in evaluating the triumph of the one over the other, it is necessary to employ the method, not of violent contrast, but of a delicate balancing of affinities and oppositions. All of these ideals and forces arise within a common matrix, European culture; they sustain relations of origins, of common aims. Thus, for example, liberalism itself arose by way of the democracy of the eighteenth century, yet found itself in opposition to the form that principle assumed in the nineteenth. Similarly, it was impossible to forget that the first move-

[1] For the definition of 'religion', cf. FPS, 478–9; for other definitions of liberty and liberalism, cf. op. cit., 623 sqq.
[2] SE'800, 23 sqq., 55 sqq.

ments of the liberal life had been made under the aegis of the enlightened monarchies of the eighteenth century, as Croce had clearly
illustrated from his history of Naples. This memory determined its
unrelenting opposition to the form of the restored monarchies while
committing it to a monarchical idea. This segment of history demonstrates, Croce believes, that there is in history no simple opposition of
forces, of good and evil, of right and wrong, but a complex struggle
from which the victor emerges with the sense of having triumphed,
not over an alien principle but over one dimension of himself. This
holds good of the contest between liberalism and the idea most
radically opposed to it, communism.[1]

The most direct and logical, though not most radical opposition
was offered, in Croce's opinion, by Catholicism. At the ideal level,
this opposition would appear to be simple: liberalism conceives the
end of life, as life itself; man's supreme duty is the increment of this
life by the method of free initiation and of individual inventiveness.
To this, Catholicism, in its most abstract form, would seem to hold
that the aim of life, this life of man here on earth and in history, is not
itself, but a life beyond it for which this life is but a preparation: a
preparation for which man of himself is inadequate, and in which he
must be guided by the authority and discipline of an institution of
transcendent representation. Between ultramundane authoritarianism and historical libertarianism, there would seem to be no middle
way. Yet this simple and naked opposition, when examined historically and with the purpose of discovering the effective opposition between Catholicism and liberalism in the Europe and in Italy of the
nineteenth century, is subject to grave modifications. Catholicism
does not appear in history under the form of this unambiguous ultramundanism, as the negation of those values of the historical life which
would seem to be the primary concerns of liberalism. On the contrary, it appears through long periods of history as the mover, and
frequently the prime mover of the ends of civilization, of knowledge,
of custom, of political and social policy, of liberty and equality. If
the alleged ultramundanism of Catholicism were its ultimate character, this historical effectiveness could not belong to her. As a consequence, a community between the activity of Catholicism and the
preoccupations of liberalism manifests itself at the historical level
which contradicts any abstract opposition between them. Even more,
some of the basic values of the liberal programme, such as the notion
of the person, are derived from the body of ideas which Catholicism

[1] SE'800, loc. cit.

has fostered. This fact[1] Croce recognized most clearly in the late essay on the essential Christianity of the liberal tradition. This radical community lying immediately beneath the surface of a radical opposition is reflected also from the part of Catholicism and of the Church in the nineteenth century. It is reflected in the phenomenon of liberal Catholicism which arose from a profound and sincere insight into this community. Liberal Catholics felt the radical incongruity of setting themselves, in the name of their Catholicism, against such concepts as liberty or equality when they saw Catholicism and the Church as the historical seed-bed of these ideals. It was reflected in the official attitude of the Church toward the struggle for a free and united Italy: for the papacy felt strongly drawn toward placing itself at the head of that struggle. The effective opposition between Catholicism and liberalism must, consequently, be sought elsewhere.

Croce indicated unambiguously where, in his opinion, this opposition really lay.[2] It lay not between the radical ideals of liberalism and Catholicism, nor in their historical consciousness, but between liberalism and political Catholicism, or as it has been called, clericalism. Nor is this designation, 'political Catholicism', made in the name of the ideal of the abstention of the Church and of Catholicism from all political life. This idea would be in contradiction to the historical reality and effectiveness of the Church and the basis of her community with the aims of liberalism. The term clericalism here has a concrete historical reference and signification. It indicates that tendency of dominant elements in the Church to align themselves with retrogressive movements of political authoritarianism, with the monarchies of the restoration. The concrete image which Croce invokes of this clericalism is the Cardinal Ruffo invoking against the revolutionary forces of '99 in Naples, the horrors of the Sanfedism and making himself the executor of the reprisals of Ferdinand. Again, in another context, he invokes the stoniness with which the Church set herself against the liberal programme for the unification of Italy after she had lost, or better surrendered, leadership in that enterprise, or the manner in which Antonelli could for decades after that unification nourish dreams of its dissolution even at the cost of foreign intervention. The conflict was, therefore, between a definite historical attitude of Catholicism, an attitude which might well be

[1] 'Perché non possiamo non dirci Cristiani', Bari, 1944, reprinted in DVE, I, 11–23.
[2] SE'800, 24 sqq.

interpreted as opposed to its own historical civilizing energy, and a liberalism which recognized its historical solidarity with Catholicism. The opposition must, consequently, be stated in more limited, concrete, historical terms. It is also to be noted that this historical opposition was dissolved in part by later developments as Catholicism established its rapprochement with democracy and with social thought in much the same manner as liberalism. In this way it came again to occupy much common ground with liberalism in its political and social programmes, just as it had historically provided the seed-bed for the ideas and forces which liberalism was to claim for its own.[1]

The effective form of the opposition between liberalism and clericalism, it has appeared, lay in the attachment of the latter to the cause of the reactionary absolute monarchies which had led the resistance to Napoleon and which had stepped into the power vacuum left by his downfall. These absolute monarchies constitute the second of the forces which contested the nineteenth century in Europe with liberalism. Absolute monarchy, Croce feels, was ultimately 'religious' in character. The principle upon which it rested was that of the divine representation of the monarchical establishment. This was the idea which the absolute monarchies of the post-Napoleonic period, in their ideological formulations, sought to revitalize and to offer as basic justification of their reactionary programmes. There appeared here, however, as in the case of the opposition of liberalism and Catholicism, a discrepancy between the historical and the ostensibly ideal dimensions of the conflict. The ideal to which the absolute monarchies sought to return was an historical anachronism and represented a phase of the history of the monarchical institution which had effectively been transcended, bloodily, in the persons of Charles Stuart and Louis Capet, peacefully, in the inner transformations of that institution, in the period before the Revolution. As a result, the absolute monarchies of the Restoration were unable to live up to their ideological pretensions. In order to effect their programme (which was nothing more than a forcible restoration of an historically obsolete system) they had recourse to the machinery of the police state.

The attitude of liberalism toward monarchy was very similar to its attitude toward Catholicism. Again it was conscious of an historical solidarity for its own first advances had been accomplished under the protection of the enlightened monarchies of the eighteenth

[1] SE'800, 21-7.

century. It was aware of the services which the monarchical institution had rendered to European civilization. The abhorrence for the extremes of the Revolution, which was a marked characteristic of the new liberal faith, inclined it favourably to the more ancient institution. Its chief concern, consequently, was not the destruction of the institution of monarchy, any more than it desired the destruction of Catholicism or the Church. It desired, rather, the transformation of the absolute monarchical institution in the direction of constitutionalism; a transformation, the liberals felt, which would have the double effect of preserving the serviceability of this institution while ridding it of those elements abhorrent to the concept of liberty. Conflict ensued only when the absolute monarchies resisted this transformation and conspired instead to put down the new spirit of freedom. Where resistance did not arise, where, instead, the monarchical establishment not only submitted to, but itself led the way in, its own transformation, this institution proved its serviceability anew. Such was the case of the House of Savoy which became the leader in the liberal regeneration of Italy. Again an opposition which first appears as an abstract contradiction reveals itself historically and concretely as far more limited.[1]

The more cautious analysis of the opposition of liberalism to Catholicism and to absolute monarchy had revealed a continuity and solidarity which considerably modified the initial force of that opposition. Such is not the case, however, with the third of the ideals which contested the nineteenth century with liberalism, democracy. In this instance, the initial relation would seem to be direct affinity. Careful analysis, however, reveals a basic opposition. The democratic and the liberal ideals were associated even to the point of identification in an 'indissoluble dyad'. The points of agreement between them were not only negative, but positive. Negatively, they shared an opposition to clericalism and to absolutism. Positively, they shared the goal of individual liberty, of civil and political equality, and 'popular sovereignty'. The radical difference appeared in their interpretation of the very goals they held in common. For democracy, individuals were centres of equal force, possessing an equality of fact, as it was called. To liberalism, individuals were above all persons; their equality was only that of their common humanity, and hence a matter of right. To democracy, the 'people' was a sum of equal forces: to liberalism, a differentiated organism. The ideal of democracy was quantitative and mechanical; that of liberalism

[1] SE'800, 27 sqq.

qualitative and vital. To these ideal differences there accrued others of an historical character. The experience of the French Revolution and its aftermath had put to the extreme test the affinities between liberalism and democracy. Democracy had revealed itself in all its Jacobin extremism; the result had torn asunder the body politic and sacrificed its living actuality to the pursuit of unattainable abstractions. Out of that Jacobin experience, and the tyranny for which it had opened the way, the attitude of the moderate liberal was born: resolutely opposed to the method of revolution, to the cult of the 'people' (when the 'people' was identified abstractly and quantitatively with the vast unreflective portion of the population), and to the republican ideal. The type of the moderate liberal, by whom the programme of liberalism was to be effected, emerged directly from the test of the revolution. This type is studied by Croce in the figure of Giuseppe Poerio.[1] As the image of the Revolution receded, liberalism, republicanism and democracy were, at times, able to effect a working agreement. The radical difference of spirit between them persisted, however, so that their identification must always appear to the liberal consciousness as a confusion. The breach between them had been closed, where it has been closed, more by the initiative of democracy itself; it has closely approximated many of the ideals and attitudes of liberalism, renouncing its own early abstractions, so that in the twentieth century the very notion of democracy from which liberalism had to dissociate itself at the beginning of the nineteenth and with whose threatened recurrence it had to combat is scarcely a memory. Yet if that first democratic idea is not recalled in its clarity the whole dynamic of the nineteenth century remains obscure.[2]

Communism, the fourth of the forces which contested the nineteenth century with liberalism, was at the inception of the period also the weakest; history has proved it ultimately the strongest. This idea which, Croce warns, must not be confused with socialism, is an ancient idea which at this time was experiencing renewal in modern form. In its modern form, as it appeared at the beginning of the nineteenth century, it exhibited instead characteristics in common with liberalism: a mundane and immanentistic conception of life, the enjoyment of goods, the increase of wealth, science and technical advancement and other instruments of economic progress. Beneath this superficial affinity, however, a profound diversity lay concealed. This diversity was not, as some critics had supposed,

[1] Cf. UFP, 1 sqq., and *supra*.   [2] SE'800 31, sqq.; FPS, 1062.

based on the fact that communism contemplates the socialization and nationalization of the instruments of production, while liberalism was committed, supposedly, to the twin dogmas of private ownership of the means of production and unlimited competition. This notion is based on the untenable identification of liberalism with 'economic liberism'.[1] The conjunction of liberalism and 'liberism', or economic liberalism, is provisional and contingent. Liberalism does not reject in principle the socialization or nationalization of the means of production but must, as Croce has pointed out, judge such issues 'caso per caso', on ethical grounds. The opposition between it and communism could not rest on these grounds.

It proves to be a conflict of ideals, the most profound in which liberalism is involved, and which has grown with the passage of time and the triumph of communism in the twentieth century. It is the opposition between spiritualism and materialism. Liberalism, as it has been seen, is radically spiritualistic; the notion of liberty upon which it rests is itself inseparable from the notion of spirit; the terms define each other. Communism, on the other hand, is radically materialistic. Its principle is the conception of economics as the foundation and matrix of all other forms of life, which it considers as phenomena of that unique reality. In the philosophy of spirit, which lies at the basis of liberalism, the economic activity of life is itself a form of spiritual activity, arising from and leading to other forms. When it is isolated it is materialized. Matter is essentially sterile, incapable of bringing forth any other forms of life.[2] The materialism of communism reveals itself even in the first utopists of the nineteenth century; their faith in the regeneration of man all turned about the machine, and the society they tried to establish was itself a machine. Failing to grasp the notion of freedom in history, as it rests upon the idea of spirit, they interpreted liberalism as a mask for capitalist interests and conceived the political struggle as the conflict of economic classes. Since the utopian society which communism seeks to achieve is and can be nothing but a machine, and since machines, unlike the forms of life, are not active but must be moved by another principle, that society always demands regulation by a dictatorship, alien and transcendent. Thus there is introduced into the world an authoritarianism and a totalitarianism far worse in principle, as Croce points out in another place,[3] than any of those

[1] Cf. *supra*.
[2] Cf. R. Garbari, *Genesi e svolgimento storico delle prime tesi estetiche di B. Croce*, Firenze, 1949, pp. 56 sqq.; SE'800, 37.　　　　　　　　　　[3] FPS, 1061.

forms which earlier in history had relied on divine and supernatural sanctions. These had been spiritualistic in principle at least. The result of communism must be the total 'abétissement', of man, the opposite of that freedom with which liberalism recognized him to be endowed in every department of his activity. For this reason, between liberalism and communism there could be no meeting; there could be only a radical opposition, which no historical circumstances could modify.

In Croce's account of the 'religion' of liberty and of the conflicting 'faiths' which contested with it the emergent soul of the nineteenth century, the position of romanticism is peculiar and peculiarly important. If, as has been noted, the relationship between these conflicting faiths is not, in Croce's view, one of simple and nude opposition, but of intricate involvement, of complex affirmation and negation, this is especially true of romanticism and the liberal idea. These are the more intimately related because the more trenchantly opposed; they draw life and force from each other even as they emerge in mutual negation. For this reason, Croce suggests, their simultaneous appearance in history is no mere juxtaposition, but a vital coincidence.[1]

It is necessary to draw a distinction, Croce believes, within romanticism, between theoretical, or speculative, and practical, or sentimental, romanticism. This distinction, he feels, is fundamental and more nearly penetrates the essence of romanticism than do the multitude of superficial and empirical distinctions which have sprung up about it. It establishes that these 'forms' of romanticism were, in reality, two different things, two diverse attitudes of the spirit. It clarifies as no other distinction can, the complex relationship in which liberalism stands to romanticism.[2]

Theoretical or speculative romanticism Croce identifies as the revolt against the literary academicism and philosophical intellectualism which had dominated the eighteenth century, and their replacement by a new system of artistic and theoretical values. Against the devaluation of art in the enlightenment, its debasement to an inferior and extrinsic role in the economy of the human spirit devoid of any intrinsic principle of autonomy, theoretical romanticism awakened anew the feeling for genuine art and developed the concept of its autonomous and theoretical character in the new science of aesthetics. Against the apotheosis of the abstract intellect, it set the value and importance of spontaneity, passion and individuality and gave them

[1] SE'800, 43.   [2] SE'800, 43.

an adequate place in life, in ethics, in art and in politics. Against the anti-historicism of the enlightenment, which had rendered it contemptuous of the past, romanticism conceived the relation of the past to the present as a living unity and developed a theory of history and of historiography to express and embody unity. Against the cult of mathematics and of the abstractive sciences, it sought to thrust these disciplines back within their natural limits within the total economy of the human spirit. Its essential insight into life was that of its combative and dialectical structure; and thus it opposed the utopianism, both implicit and explicit, which was a dominant feature of that age of the enlightenment. Even in its exaggerated and mistaken manifestations, Croce suggests, in its acquiescence to irrationalistic tendencies, in its vain efforts to erect a philosophy of history over and above history or a philosophy of nature over and above the natural sciences, it displayed the elements of its power and vitality, for these extravagances, by an internal criticism, proved ultimately to be amenable to a reduction to positive and integral insight.[1]

Sentimental or practical romanticism presents an altogether different physiognomy. It exhibits a pathological quality which the greatest of the contemporary philosophical romanticists were the first to recognize and identify; a major evidence of the validity of the distinction he has suggested, proof that it is not a formula excogitated by retrospective criticism, but a real difference sensed and expressed within the historical form of romanticism itself. Thus Goethe appears as the keenest judge and the severest critic of sentimental romanticism in both poetry and morals, defining the one as 'hospital poetry' and expressing profound aversion for the character formed by the other. In the same manner Hegel, the greatest of the romantic philosophers, mercilessly excoriates sentimental romanticism in all its manifestations, relentlessly exposing its fatuousness and illusion.

The manifestations of sentimental romanticism were numberless. It appeared as romantic Catholicism, an attempt to return, by way of the imagination and the sentiments, to the harbour of that transcendent belief. The fatuousness of this effort was recognized by the church itself, so that the position of the romantic converts was always ambiguous in her eyes. By a struggle of centuries she had rid herself of similar tendencies and she was now alert to prevent their re-admission under this new form. It expressed itself in a new eroticism, seeking the redemption of man in love and the 'divinity' of the beloved woman, not in the spirit of the 'stil nuovo' of the thirteenth

[1] SE'800, 44.

century or of the Platonism of the Renaissance but with a refined and sublimated sensuality. It manifested itself at the political level (at the level of 'political fantasy', Croce suggests, rather than of politics, for a politics of the romantic malady is a contradiction in terms) in both utopian and primitivistic forms, envisaging now a return to an idealized middle ages and now in the projection of an idealized future to be reached by some magic force such as that of an idealized and deified science. Or again it fastened upon such explosive ideas as ethnicism, racism and divisive nationalism, weaving false and dangerous myths of group superiority. Finally, and most dangerously of all, perhaps, it manifested itself in an aestheticizing conception of life, a conception in which passion and imagination and spontaneity were not returned to a central and efficacious place in the structure of the human spirit, as theoretical romanticism had succeeded in doing, but were identified simply with life, so that its other forms were rejected or devaluated. In all these features, sentimental or practical romanticism revealed its pathological character, gave evidence that it moved, not in the central stream, but on the periphery of the constructive consciousness of the period.[1]

What then, in Croce's view, is the relationship of romanticism in both these forms (or rather of these diverse realities which are erroneously denominated by a common term, romanticism) to liberalism, to that 'religion' of liberty to which he ascribes central effectiveness in the formation of Europe in the nineteenth century? It is a complex relation, but unambiguous. In the first place, its relation to liberalism defines the essential character of practical romanticism. That romanticism had been defined as a loss of faith, and its source or genesis had been found by some critics in the dissolution of that vision and certitude which the older faith of the European tradition had apparently been able to offer men. To Croce it appears otherwise. To him the source of practical romanticism lies not in the loss of an older faith, but in an incapacity to lay hold upon a new.[2] The loss of an older faith, he notes, has never been attended by the pathological symptoms which sentimental romanticism displayed, when that loss has been but the first step in the translation to a new. In such cases, the transition is made with a sense of joy and release and with an unclouded consciousness, the reflection of the truth toward which one moves. A new faith offered itself at this

[1] SE'800, 45–6; for a critique of Croce's analysis of romanticism: cf. e.g. G. de Ruggiero, *L'età del Romanticismo*, where many contrasting analyses are also cited.
[2] SE'800, 47.

time, in an emergent form it is true, but in unambiguous configuration. The source of the pathological symptoms of sentimental romanticism lay in the fact that, relinquishing the old, it had no power to seize the new. Hence its fundamental ambiguities, its sporadic and impulsive movements, the contradictions and absurdities in which it became involved. The very essence of this romanticism is a lack of moral power, a fatal incapacity to make the spiritual transitions as history demands. This essential weakness can be comprehended in terms of the new faith to which romanticism proved unequal. That faith was precisely the idea of liberty and the insights upon which it rested.

The relationship between liberalism and philosophical romanticism is direct and positive. On the one hand, the remote preparation for the liberal ideal and the liberal 'faith' is laid in that combative vision of life which Croce has already noted in philosophical romanticism. More positively still, and more profoundly, the vision of liberty upon which liberalism rests is the speculative achievement of romanticism. This is the conception of liberty rooted in the idea of man as spirit, and of reality as the creative process of the human spirit; in the idea of the co-extensive character of reality with the ideality of history and at the same time its essential incommensurability in idea with that historicity in its concreteness, in the sense that the idea of liberty and the ideal possibilities and the spiritual forces which it encloses can never be exhausted in or abortively identified with, its historical moments. It is thus that spirit and liberty are identified with history, and, at the same time, released from abortive immanence to the mere concreteness of the historical process. Thus it becomes possible to accept the notion of human progress in history without succumbing to the fallacies of utopianism or progressivism, or to the despair which their unmasking infallibly generates. Liberalism is as intimately wedded to philosophical romanticism as it is alien to its spurious sentimental double.

The cross-influence of these 'forms' of romanticism upon each other and upon liberalism remains to be noted. Philosophical and sentimental romanticism did not, as has already been seen, generate totally diverse phenomena. They could not, since they were not equally positive forces. Sentimental romanticism appears in its most dangerous form when it imitates, and, at the same time, distorts and exaggerates the positive values of philosophical romanticism. At the same time, however, philosophical romanticism exhibits itself as the sole force of the century which can exercise a measure of restraint upon the excesses of sentimental romanticism. Every other force of the century is the victim of this sentimental romanticism and never succeeds in mastering it. This pattern of cross influence is continuously to be observed in the history of liberalism in the nineteenth century. Liberalism has constantly to combat its false double, as it were, as well as the positive forces arrayed against it.

II

LIBERTY AND ABSOLUTISM

THESE are the spiritual forces, the ideas and the ideals, in terms of which Croce understands the conflicts, discomfitures and triumphs of the history of the Europe of the nineteenth century. As presented at the threshold of his undertaking, these forces wear an abstract and formal aspect. In reality, of course, they are wholly immediate and concrete, immanent to and constitutive of the existential process of history. They are the thoughts and the ideals of men acting. The abstract and formal presentation serves only a practical, didactic purpose. The reader is put in possession, at the beginning of the historical narrative and exposition, of the ideal principles which the historian has discovered by the laborious analysis of documents. At the same time, it serves an aesthetic end; *ars nasconditur arte*. Croce eschews entirely that procedure which he so severely condemns in his critique of the 'philosophy of history':[1] the construction of a transcendent history in terms of which the concrete process of history is then interpreted, the 'history without documents' which he censures, for example, in Hegel.

The drama of European history in the nineteenth century opens, in his view, with the fall of Napoleon. The debacle of his imperial ambitions apparently left the field of European politics to the undisputed possession of the coalition which had brought it about. Conscious of the historic juncture at which they stood, the powers united in this coalition sought at once to give an ideal form and a transcendent representative value to the power which they apparently possessed. They set about the erection of the Holy Alliance, into which they wove the seductive theme of the political unification of Europe, the logical correlative of its secular cultural unity. This device could not serve, however, to mask the reality of that power. The Holy Alliance, Croce writes,[2] was but an imperialistic utopian dream, existing nowhere but in the imagination of Alexander, in which conservative, pacifistic, religious and even liberal (pater-

---

[1] TSS, 53 sqq.　　　　　　　　　　　　　　[2] SE'800, 59.

nalistically liberal!) motives mingled in surrealistic pattern. What really lay concealed behind that title was the concerted determination and the diverse designs of the restored sovereigns to conserve their systems of government and to impede any revolutionary or revisionist movement. The signing of the Declaration of Paris on 26 September 1815 was, in his view, only in tangential relation to the power situation. England, for example, and the Papacy did not, for very different reasons, append their signatures, but both co-operated in the repression of revolutionary movements. Austria, which did sign, altered her policy not a jot to support the lofty and vacuous declarations of that document; her programme of repression in northern Italy and of diplomatic intimidation in the Two Sicilies was not relaxed. Nor did any of the three signatories abandon, for a common end, any of their divisive particularist interests. The only unanimity discernible was the recourse of all to police measures for the repression of movements of liberty of whatever provenance.

This undisputed prepotence of the restored monarchical establishment was, however, no fact but an illusion. The reality of power, and the future, lay rather with the liberal ideal. The situation is not unlike that which Croce has depicted in his analysis of the Baroque Era. Where, he asks of the new age as he had demanded of the earlier, are the positive elements, where the seeds, however hidden, of the future? The reply is clear: with the liberal ideal. During this period of fifteen years, from the discomfiture of Napoleon to the July Revolution of 1830, liberalism opposed to renascent absolutism an unfaltering resistance, combated it at every point without quarter and in the end inflicted upon it a decisive defeat.[1]

There is a certain irony to be discerned in this new situation, in which absolutism and liberalism appear in immedicable opposition, and Croce's narrative reflects his constant appreciation of it. At an earlier period, as Croce had made clear in the history of Naples and again in certain sections of the history of the Baroque Era, these two forces had enjoyed a close relation of cross-germination. Liberalism had grown up in the protecting shadow of the enlightened monarchies; in the tranquil and ordered world which the monarchies were able to provide, liberalism first worked out its principles. In turn, the monarchies had been deeply influenced by the presence of liberal ideals; under that influence a transformation in the direction of constitutionalism and tolerance was initiated, in the course of which their pristine absolutism and transcendent representational

[1] SE'800, 59.

claims had begun to be modified. This situation was now completely changed, and the agency of this change had been the French Revolution. The overall effect of the Revolution on the monarchical principle and institution was to drive it back to that position of absolute and transcendent claims which in the eighteenth century it had begun to modify; it engendered, in a word, the reactionary absolutism of the Restoration. Such a return, in any literal sense, was, of course, historically impossible. Behind the ideological veil which it raised, the new absolutism stood revealed in its true character as an unqualified bid for power. In the presence of the forces of liberalism, this bid for power could be successful only by the assimilation of these forces or by recourse to the instrument of naked power, the police state. The restored monarchies exploited both possibilities with complete opportunism, but with a marked preference for the second. But any success it might attain must prove transient and illusory. Between a naked bid for power and the divine representational claim upon which it had rested, there was an infinite, ideal gulf; monarchism had lost all ideality. At the same time, its claim to civil serviceability was reduced to the vanishing point. A similar educative influence had been exercised upon liberalism by the Revolution and its Napoleonic sequel. By that experience, liberalism had been detached from the monarchical principle and from the libertarian and jacobin principles of the Revolution. In a sense, it had come of age. With respect to the Revolution, Croce had pointed out in the case of Naples and the movement of '99, how the liberals had abandoned the path of gradual reform upon which they had entered under the aegis of the enlightened monarchies, seduced by the siren voice of jacobin democracy. In this course, it was to be violently disabused, and Croce made a careful study of this process of disillusionment in the case of the Neapolitan patriot Giuseppe Poerio.[1] Yet for the liberal, too, the path to the past was closed. Because of the effect of the Revolution on the monarchical establishment, any idea of a return to the rather idyllic relation which had obtained between them had to be abandoned. From this doubly educative experience, however, liberalism emerged as an autonomous idea and force in European life. It must henceforth stand on its own feet and work for its own ends with greater self-confidence and self-sufficiency.

At first glance, as it has been suggested, the battle in which the forces of restored absolutism and of liberalism were to become locked

[1] UFP, 1 sqq.

seemed woefully unequal, heavily weighted in the direction of absolutism. It entered the contest fresh from its victory over the caesarism of Napoleon. It was in undisputed possession of all the instruments and organs of power, the armed forces, the police power, the administrative and legislative organizations, and it had at its service men of supreme political adroitness, swift to appreciate and to organize this advantage. Liberalism, by contrast, appeared powerless. To the alliance of powers which constituted the reality of the Holy Alliance, it could oppose no leagued powers of its own, as Protestantism had once been able to oppose league of princes to league of princes. It controlled no machinery of government, no system of propaganda. It was not concentrated in centres, but diffused throughout Europe in varying degrees of density and it was internally divided over issues arising out of this dispersion. Nevertheless, the actual balance of power, of historical leverage, lay with liberalism. And the secret of its power lay in this, that while absolutism looked to the past, liberalism looked to the future. The advantage of liberalism was wholly ideal and moral. Metternich, the genius of absolutism, proved his genius anew, for he sensed the situation with perfect clarity; the opinion of the age is against us, he is reported to have said, and in this sentence passed judgment on the movement to which he dedicated his life.[1]

In the same sentence, he identified the real source of the power, of the future of liberalism. At this stage, before it had opportunity to organize its forces for the acquisition of the organs of power, liberalism was a purely moral and intellectual force.[2] To the Holy Alliance and its league of power for the restoration of privilege and special interest, liberalism was able to oppose a league, not of states, but of free minds and spirits, a living union dedicated not to the restoration of ancient privilege but to ideals, to social and moral values of public life yet to be achieved. Because it was a living force, it manifested itself with the spontaneity of life and not with the ponderous mechanism of oppression to which absolutism had recourse. It flowed out effortlessly into free discussion, into oratory and poetry. It established spontaneous and generous bonds of sympathy between the oppressed and the intimidated everywhere. It inspired the formation of secret societies, or 'undergrounds', both national and international; but these, in Croce's opinion, were of relatively little importance compared to the great coalition, the 'spiritual conspiracy', irrepressibly apparent, of which liberalism

[1] SE'800, 83.   [2] SE'800, 62.

consisted.[1] The repression of secret societies was an easy task, one of
his ministers is said to have reported to Metternich; but it was quite
another thing to repress a true political party, composed of the most
enlightened elements of a people, and this was in fact the task which
confronted absolutism.[2] The pattern of political life throughout
Europe reflected this balance in favour of the ultimate victory of the
moral ideal of liberty. It is a pattern of intellectually and morally
united opposition to absolutism; an opposition which expressed
itself in terms of the particular needs and aspirations of particular
countries and regions, but which aspired in all its forms to a common
end, liberty.

France and England, quite naturally, led the advance of liberalism
during this period of its opposition to absolutism. England had, in
the heat of her opposition to Napoleon, inclined momentarily toward
absolutism; under Castlereagh, she had aligned her foreign policy
with the attitude of the Holy Alliance; at home, recourse was had to
exceptional laws, the writ of habeas corpus was suspended, the press
restrained, workers' demonstrations put down in blood. This lean-
ing was quickly corrected, however, by the inherent balance of her
constitution. Her realistic foreign policy quickly imposed a limit to
her participation in the machinations of the continental powers; the
debates of Parliament, the opinions of the law courts, the staunchness
of her other guaranteeing institutions limited or annulled the extra-
ordinary measures which were invoked. More importantly, the
liberal idea showed itself the constructive principle in British public
life. Her literature and poetry breathed the sentiments of the ideal
of liberty, and one poet, Byron, redeeming a frivolous life by a
magnanimous death, became its very symbol. The Benthamites and
the Radicals, though employing the dry instruments of statistics, and
invoking the limited ideas of utilitarianism and a hedonic ethics, still
promoted reforms in every branch of social life. The crisis of reaction
after Waterloo passed quickly and was succeeded by a strong liberal
movement finding voice and action in the ministry of Canning.
Between 1824 and 1832 a series of reforms was carried through
which indubitably placed England in the forefront of the liberal
movement, while in the area of foreign affairs, completely reversing
her earlier attitude of co-operation with continental absolutism,
Britain became the advocate of liberal policy, refusing to countenance repression in Spain, favouring a constitutional movement in
Portugal, recognizing the freedom of the South American colonies

[1] SE'800, 63.   [2] SE'800, 63.

from Spain, supporting the Greek fight for freedom and putting an end to the trade in slaves.[1]

In France, the pattern was different, but the principle identical. That country was already in possession of a constitutional charter, that of 1815; it was, however, a document filled with ambiguities and surrounded with a fog of reservations, for it had been accepted by the party in power with the intention of ruling not according to it but in spite of it. The problem of the liberal party was to win in actuality, in practice what had been granted nominally and formally in the charter, transforming it into a popular constitution. The opposition to liberalism lay in the forces surrounding the throne; their programme envisaged the customary restriction of the press, modifications of the electorate to favour the landed gentry, recompensation of the émigres, the commitment of education to the clergy. An enthusiastic, but dubious ally of liberalism appeared in the extreme 'left': the republican group of Lafayette and the French branch of Carbonari. Its real strength lay in the parliamentary centre. Here opposition to all reactionary movements was moderate, but firm and energetic. The real and effective ally of the centre was the extreme right, that is, the most intransigent elements of reaction, for it was the manifest impossibility of their proposals and demands which revealed the emptiness of the royalist and absolutist pretensions.[2]

In Italy the force of reaction, in the form of the presence of a foreign power dedicated to the vindication of absolutist claims, was felt in a manner unimagined and, indeed, unimaginable in France or England. The extirpation of the liberal idea and will seemed complete. Austria had destroyed the constitutional liberty of Naples, repressed constitutional revolution in Piedmont, foiled and savagely punished revolutionary movements in Lombardy and Venetia and encouraged her dependent princelings in similar programmes. Here again, however, the prepotence of reaction was an illusion. Where repression was most savage, the will to liberty burned with whitest heat. By the ferocity of their programmes of repression, the reactionary governments were forcing the growth of the liberal plant and preparing inevitably their own frustration. Preparation for the season of revolt went on first among the Italian exiles who, gathered in the relatively free atmosphere of London and Paris, meditated the Italian problem without end. Even more, this preparation went on among the very numerous patriots who remained at home and were

[1] SE'800, 66 sqq. [2] SE'800, 69 sqq.

thus forced to confront the problem in its more immediate aspects. Slowly, link by link, the liberal programme was forged between the anvil of alien imperialism and the hammer of the patriot will. Liberty meant, for Italy, above all the expulsion of the foreign tyrant; but it meant as well the settlement of accounts within Italy, that is, the unambiguous discrimination of those who stood for Italy from those whose interests were other than her freedom and deliverance. Dimly, the idea of her unity took form, though as yet in fantastic pattern, extending the notion of liberty to include freedom from internal conflict as well as exoneration from foreign dominion. These sentiments were almost universally embraced. There emerged the phenomenon of Liberal Catholicism, adding a powerful element to the liberal forces, winning over to liberalism large sections of the people at first opposed to it and freeing it from anti-religious and anti-Christian suspicions. The menace of the foreign oppressor, finally, was strong enough to draw into the liberal orbit the kingdom of Sardinia which, repudiating its absolutist past, was presently to provide the effective leadership of the Risorgimento.[1]

Germany presented a contrast to this heartening picture, a contrast fateful for the whole future of liberalism in Europe. Here the liberal formation was weak and without continuity. The ultimate reason for this Croce discovers in the Reformation and the mentality which it fostered, capable of entertaining a dualism between inner freedom and outer order, between the speculative and the political spheres. Research, criticism, philosophy moved in a realm of ethereal and detached 'freedom', while in political life, authority ruled. The effect was to render both sterile; the life of thought, lacking genuine contact with the movement of affairs, grew remote and pedantic; authority, lacking the inner check of a vital and committed criticism, tended to degenerate into the mere fact of power. One element of the liberal spirit did, however, exist: the nationalist impetus, the conviction of German identity and the desire to find its historical expression. This nationalist sentiment, like everything else in the German picture, was clouded by ambiguity; while demanding national status, it was not coupled with a clear demand for political liberty in the internal life of the nation; yet these elements, as the Italian experience had already demonstrated and was to demonstrate still more clearly, were inseparable. This ambiguity or incoherence made it possible for authoritarian forces, the very forces of absolutism and reaction, to place themselves at the head of the nationalist movement, as its

[1] SE'800, 71 sqq.

natural agents. At the same time, the ambiguity was compounded by this leadership; for the forces of authoritarianism saw clearly that the nationalist issue could not be resolved without recourse to war among the contending elements of the loose German group. Meanwhile, in the speculative realm, the concept of liberty was made the object of extensive debate and intensive meditation. Many of the ideas expressed concerning liberty were imitative of French and English reflections, frequently complicated by the German penchant toward pedantic transformation of simple insights; thus it was frequently asserted that to achieve political liberty Germany would have to run an historical course analogous to the experience of England.[1]

The speculative power of the German mind, though inclined to pedantry and to imitation, was nevertheless genuine and deep. Even its isolation from the movement of practical life gave it a certain advantage; its detachment, though illusory and unhealthy in the total view of social life, enabled speculation to follow an idea to its ultimate implications. This was precisely what German thought did, and so rendered a very great service to the liberal cause everywhere; for once the ultimate implications of liberty were made clear, the ethical unity of human life would reassert itself and inevitably bring these implications to bear upon the practical order as well. Thus it came about that liberalism, after the rejection of the jacobin trinity: liberty, equality, fraternity, discovered the solid speculative and historical basis of the idea of liberty through the office of German philosophy and scholarship. The romantic philosophy, distinguished carefully and sharply by Croce from sentimental or practical romanticism,[2] was the chief agent of this achievement. Its greatest cultivators, Fichte, Schelling and Hegel, though stopping short of its application to the political order, or even, in that order, falling into errant contradiction,[3] nevertheless established the cardinal principles upon which the modern idea of liberty rests. Whatever the situation in Germany itself, these ideas had immense, perhaps immeasurable, effect everywhere else. They found unambiguous expression and rich development in the new historiography, the clearest demonstration of how profoundly the idea of history had entered the European consciousness. The literature which it inspired is one of the richest the world has ever seen, embracing the finest talents of every nation.[4]

The German achievement was in the order of principles; it was France that gave liberalism its clearest doctrinal formulation.

---

[1] SE'800, 77 sqq. [2] Cf. *supra.* [3] SE'800, 10.
[4] SE'800, 76 sqq., 84 sqq.

Liberalism in France lay under the necessity of defending itself at once against absolutists, clericals, feudalists and republicans. It was prepared for this contest by the attention with which it had received the speculative and historical thought of Germany. The liberal protagonists in this contest came to be known collectively as the 'doctrinaires'. Many of them had lived in Germany and in Switzerland; others had become versed in the literature of German thought and historical science. In the theoretical and historical writings and in the political discourses of such men as Royer-Collard, Guizot, de Broglie, Jordan, Barante and de Serre, there is to be encountered, Croce feels, complete awareness and expression of what liberalism was and willed, and of the difference which separated it from other doctrines.[1]

Signs of the instability of absolutism and its reorganization of Europe were not lacking. Chief among these was the appearance, under liberal influence, of new alliances which boded little good for the absolutist idea or its power. The Catholic Church, for example, had early expressed its solidarity with absolutist regimes. Presently, however, it experienced a crisis in this commitment, and began to enter, in concrete situations, into understandings with liberal governments. In England, for example, it readily joined in the liberal proposals for reforms. On the theoretical plane it expressed the desire for its own liberty in the doctrine of political indifference, which to this day persists as its semi-official attitude; the theoretical basis for this doctrine may appear very weak, but it at least expressed and secured for the Church the opportunity of fresh reorientation. At the same time, liberalism entered into a fruitful relation with democracy; this was made possible by the internal transformation which democracy itself was undergoing. Its extremism was so modified that it became, under many aspects, the left wing of liberalism. Communism (the term under which, as has been seen, Croce, at this stage, treats all socialist doctrine) was not as yet strong enough in Europe to offer any real basis for relations with liberalism. It was already clear, however, to Croce's mind, what relationship would ultimately prevail between liberalism and socialism; it would be a relationship not unlike that between democracy and liberalism. Once the distinction between liberalism in its theoretical and moral aspects, and 'economic liberalism' in its practical and utilitarian character, had been made clear, the way would be open for the liberal assimilation of socialist elements, with the simultaneous reduction to contradic-

[1] SE'800, 98-9.

tion and extravagance of the extreme forms of communism, of which of course marxism would be the chief.[1]

The period of contest between liberalism and absolutism terminates with the July Revolution of 1830. Most various accounts have been given of this event. It was, some have held, the result of an error of judgment on the part of Charles X. In the opinion of others, it was an accident, in the strict historical sense, an event, that is, which has no place in the logic of history; for, they hold, the success of liberalism would have been assured in another fashion and without this recourse to revolution and bloodshed. Such explanations, Croce feels, are but expatiations on abstract possibilities. Genuine explanation must begin with the fact; the July Revolution happened. What then was its character, its rationale? To his mind, that character is clear and inescapable. It was the reduction to armed conflict of the contest between liberalism and absolutism which had endured for a decade and a half. This passage at arms between these forces possessed its own logic. It derived from the character of the contending forces, and especially that of absolutism. The logic of liberalism excluded recourse to arms as the regular method of social process and development; the logic of absolutism, by its intransigence, made such recourse, in the wide probability of events, unavoidable; in terms of its own logic, again, liberalism could not refuse such a reduction. In the course of this conflict, the quality of both movements, which had gradually appeared during that extended period of opposition, was made decisively apparent. As the result of that conflict, the energy of the one, liberalism, was immensely increased, that of the other dissolved and dissipated. The moral discomfiture of absolutism, as well as its physical defeat, was complete. After fifteen years, this movement which had demonstrated its weakness and its logical incoherence in the intellectual arena, was defeated in the field which had been most properly its own, that of force. The moral increment to liberalism was correspondingly great. To the indubitable elevation of its ideal and programme, there was added the evidence of its power to confront an adversary in the ultimate and irreducible terms of political life, to give its ideal the support of material force from which no political idea must draw back. At the barricades of the streets of Paris a battle of universal import was fought, from which a moral ideal of liberty emerged with new strength and new promise.[2]

[1] SE'800, 96.   [2] SE'800, 100–1.

III

THE PATTERN OF LIBERAL PROGRESS

ALTHOUGH the moral discomfiture of absolutism in the Revolution of July was complete, Croce believes, and the vindication of liberalism no less so, that event did not mark the disappearance of absolutism from the political arena altogether. Its result was rather a re-apportionment of dynamism and influence between liberalism and absolutism and between both these forces and other contrasting parties. The absolutist movement had been from the beginning, in Croce's view, a defensive operation; inspired by no fresh and wider moral vision, commanding no new source of moral action, it sought only to conserve, to protest, even to retreat. This defensive character was now, after the July Revolution, even more in evidence. The liberal movement, on the other hand, from its very inception had been an active movement, on the offensive. It represented fresh vision and new moral strength; it had nothing to defend, but all to conquer and achieve. This character was in turn, after that revolution, emphasized anew. The liberal movement now entered on the main course of its work in the nineteenth century. At the same time, however, and inevitably, within liberalism itself problems and conflicts began to appear.

Evidences of the new relations, the new apportionments of influence and force which had been created by the revolution are readily to be traced in its 'effects'. These 'effects' are, of course, in Croce's view, simply those new relations viewed in their concreteness. The first is to be seen in the independence of Belgium. The first impetus of the revolution was toward a simple readjustment of the relations between the Dutch and the Belgians; independence had not been envisaged. After the events of 25 August and of 23–26 September, however, the liberal sentiment of nationalism rose rapidly in Belgium and its independence was declared in November of that year. In England, the acceleration of the liberal reform programme, begun with the accession to power of Canning, was marked by the demands, on the part of manufacturers and working-men alike, for electoral changes; these demands involved the overthrow of the Wellington ministry in November 1830 and the electoral changes became law in 1832. Even in smaller countries such as Switzerland, Portugal and Spain reverberations of the Paris revolt were evident. In Switzerland, the patrician regime was overwhelmed, constitutions were granted in thirteen of the cantons. In Portugal the struggle between the constitutionalists about the young Queen Maria and the absolutists led by Don Miguel was resolved in favour of the former, despite the support which the latter received from Wellington, from Charles X of France and Ferdinand VII of Spain. In Spain itself, the queen-regent, Maria Cristina, after the death of Ferdinand VII, had turned to the liberals for support against the absolutists and as evidence of her good faith granted the 'estatuto real' of 1834; though not a genuine constitution, this charter exhibited marked liberal features. In Germany, many of the smaller states reflected the rising tide of liberal influence; Brunswick, Hesse-Cassel, Hanover, Bavaria and Baden saw reforms in a liberal direction either in the form of constitutions, or of legislative and juridical improvements.[1]

At the same time, however, evidence that absolutism retained a great deal of its power and still could exercise it effectively over large areas of Europe was not lacking. The most moving spectacle of this power was to be seen in Italy. Here the attempted insurrections on the Paris model, in Modena, Parma, Bologna, the Romagna and the Marches, with the establishment of liberal regimes as their aim, were swiftly and ruthlessly repressed by Austrian action. Central Europe contributed evidence to the same effect. Prussia, in conjunction with Austria and Russia, lost no opportunity for repressive and constrictive measures; the dispersion of the convocation of Hambach in May 1832, as well as the swift action after the *coup de main* at Frankfort in August 1833, witnessed their determination and ruthlessness. In the Treaty of Berlin these powers reiterated their rights of intervention, while, finally, the pitiless revenge by Russia upon the Polish insurrectionists of November 1830, sealed the immobility of the central powers' purpose. These victories of absolutism aroused a widespread feeling, naturally enough, that the July Revolution had been a failure. In Croce's opinion, the historian, viewing the movements of those years more dispassionately and with greater command of the evidence, cannot agree. In the historical perspective, the true balance is discernible, and that it lay with liberalism is a judgment vindicated by the event.

[1] SE'800, 105–6.

This judgment is strengthened by the fact that after the repression of Poland legitimism as a political principle was dead, and legitimist uprisings such as that in the Vendée were galvanic and not vital. Appreciation of this fact was reflected in the polemics and the publicism of absolutism; their bitterness and vindictiveness were evidence of a sense of defeat, in complete contrast to the serene assurance of an eventual victory which breathed through such liberal testaments as *Le mie prigioni* of Silvio Pellico.[1]

That conflicts and differences should appear within the liberal ranks was inevitable. The most widespread was the general disillusionment with the liberal leadership of France. That nation was the natural leader of the liberal cause, to whom the liberal spirits of all other areas looked. In the days after the July Revolution she proved unable to carry out this natural function, to supply the guidance for which all looked to her. This inability was the more marked in that those expectations rested upon the protestations and the gestures of France herself: upon her committees for the emancipation of Italy and the reconstruction of Poland, for example. The reason for this inability lay within her, Croce feels, in the discrepancy between the generous impulses of the French people and the government through which alone those impulses might be transformed into effective action, but which was neither ready nor able to respond to them. The disillusionment of her liberal allies was great; but the disillusionment, even the delusion of France herself, was greater.

This disillusionment was not, however, an unredeemed evil; it had many salutary consequences. In Italy, for example, it contributed enormously to the formation of the insight, at once spiritual and political, to which that country would eventually owe her regeneration: that she must act for herself. It enabled Italy to see that she stood in need of a twofold liberation, from the incubus of Austrian domination, and from the illusion that liberation would come through any external agency. Cavour was to crystallize this insight for all time in his celebrated dictum: 'Italia farà da sè'. The first perception of this truth was the real greatness of Mazzini: although practically all other elements of his plans for her liberation and unification had one by one to be abandoned as fallacious, this insight won him indubitable stature as the father of modern Italy. From this time forward the liberal movement in Italy was never to lose sight of this twofold end. Within Italy, two centres of absolutist influence confronted the liberal movement; but fortunately both, though for

[1] SE'800, 109–10.

different reasons, proved far from indomitable. The two peninsular monarchies, Sardinia and the Two Sicilies, were absolutist in principle. The first, Sardinia, was eager for aggrandizement; in this way, she was led into the orbit of Italian nationalist feeling. Presently, she was to assume its leadership and in this character was herself to become liberal. The other, the Two Sicilies, was eventually to disappear, precisely because it could not rise effectively to the vision of a free and united peninsular nation. The papacy seemed to offer a third centre of absolutist power. Its position was, however, veiled in ambiguity or, possibly, neutralized by the pull of opposing desires. For a time the papacy seemed eager to place itself at the head of the Italian movement of liberation and national unity. This came about through the influence of the remarkable movement of Catholic liberalism, or neo-guelfism. This movement hoped to unite the two most powerful forces in Italy, the liberal idea and the Catholic Church, in the programme for national liberation. This purpose was symbolized by the image of a papacy which with liberal intent would place itself at the head of the national effort. For a time this persuasive image swayed even the imagination of Pius IX to the consternation, it is said, of Metternich, who confessed that the only political possibility which he had not anticipated was a liberal papacy. The image was soon to lose its attractive power. Liberal Catholicism or neo-guelfism was to lose its identity in the movement of social democracy. The papacy was to retire into that position of 'non-expedit' which was to raise the Roman question and to divide the Italian nation so profoundly even after its external unity had been achieved.[1]

A problem similar to that of Italy, but destined to be resolved in a far different manner, confronted Germany at this same period. Here the two elements of the liberal programme, nationalism and political liberty, which in Italy had appeared inseparable, stood in apparent opposition. The national movement in Germany was as old, if not older than the corresponding movement in Italy. As Croce had already noted, however, the national sentiment had taken form in opposition to, rather than in terms of, political liberty.[2] Not all of the principals were united in the nationalist purpose. The larger units of power within the German complex saw that the national issue must ultimately be resolved by war, internecine war. Time proved them right, and more; for the expected war proved also to have as its inevitable issue, not political liberalism, but

[1] SE'800, 115 sqq.   [2] Cf. *supra*.

imperialism. Liberalism, thus, in Germany died aborning. This fact is rendered the more poignant by the consideration upon which Croce has dwelt at length: philosophically liberalism was the achievement of German romantic thought. The Germans themselves, however, never drew from their own premises the liberal conclusions which others intuited so clearly. Instead, by a devious course they arrived at the concepts of state monism, of paternalism and even imperialism, averse to the liberal idea and will.[1]

While its victory over absolutism appeared ever more secure, while it confronted and, when possible, adjusted conflicts within its own ranks, liberalism was entering upon a new conflict with a fresh opponent. The new antagonist of liberalism was social democracy. The name itself is not unambiguous; in order to make clear the terms and the significance of this conflict, Croce deems it necessary to trace the historical genesis of social democracy.

As its name would indicate, social democracy represents a fusion of elements. The first, present in this appellation under the ambiguous term 'social', Croce identifies as communism and prefers, on the whole, this latter designation. The material basis of communism, he indicates, was the industrial revolution, with the type of finance and capitalism it called into being and the problems this revolution occasioned. These problems, which in their ensemble came presently to be known as the 'social problem' but which in their concreteness were highly diverse and scarcely to be merged into an amorphous unity, were not, Croce suggests, new; they differed neither in principle nor in substance from the problems which had always confronted society. They are constant elements in the problematic of human history. As such they demand solution, and it is the political task of the present, as it has always been of the past, to address them. Two attitudes toward these problems are, however, possible; and it is about this difference of attitude toward the 'social problem' that the distinction (and the statism and totalitarianism with which socialism is pregnant) turns. The first may be called the problematic. It is the attitude of liberalism and suggests that these problems be solved in terms relevant to the time and the form and the availability of moral, material and political forces. It recognizes that these problems are constant; that they inevitably recur, *mutatis mutandis*, and that the very solutions proposed for them from time to time tend to contribute to their recurrence. They must always be solved anew. The other attitude, represented by communism, is the utopian. It believes

[1] SE'800, 124 sqq.

that the social problem, or the complex of diverse problems which it gathers under this single name, may be stated and resolved, 'once for all'. This utopianism toward the problems of society is, in Croce's view, the indelible mark of communism or socialism, the element from which springs all that is specific in its character and which bears the seeds of its opposition to liberalism. There can be, he asserts, no material difference between them; liberalism is as conscious of the issues veiled by the term 'social problem' as communism; if one consults its history, it will quickly become evident that these problems have always been its central concern. In its approach, however, it is problematic and historical, avoiding the illusion that the 'social problem' can be stated definitively in trans-historical terms, or that it can be solved by a single world-transforming gesture which would create a situation of historical stability immune from further change. Communism, by contrast, imposes on this complex of problems a false unity and a false simplicity; it is ready prey, consequently, to the illusion and the fallacy that such a terminal solution and such a state of stability can be engendered.[1]

The early stages of its history (the stages with which he is concerned, since they belong to this period of the history of Europe) demonstrate the constitutive utopianism of social democracy and its immedicable opposition to liberalism. The term 'utopian' was to be hurled at the earlier communists by Marx himself, although his own pretended transition to a 'scientific' phase is in its turn illusory.[2] The antithesis between liberalism and communism appears very early, in the manner in which St. Simon and his follower Enfantin, for example, while planning the social rejuvenation of the world, dismiss the concept liberty as vague and metaphorical. It is revealed in the preoccupation of the same writers to secure the transcendence of the whole over the individual and the part; it is apparent in the fallacious parallels they establish between social and natural process. It is revealed in the words of Louis Blanc who wrote that liberty is bait for the ingenuous and that the only true liberty is that which is to be obtained in the state by the organization of labour. The sympathy which the St. Simonians showed for certain autocratic tendencies in the Catholic Church and their readiness to amalgamate with the ultramontanists (to the embarrassment, it should be noted, of the

---

[1] SE'800, 136 sqq.
[2] 'L'immaginario passaggio del comunismo marxistico dall'utopia alla scienza' in *Filosofia e Storiografia*, Bari,1949, p. 270 sq.; 'Il materialismo storico di Marx e il presunto passaggio del comunismo dall'utopia alla scienza', FPS, 55 sq.

more discerning within the ecclesiastical establishment), illustrate the same antithesis, while St. Simon's readiness to seek absolutist aid for the realization of his socialist and utopian projects, or that of Babeuf to seek their instrument in the impulsive movements of the 'masses' constitute evidence scarcely less compelling. Finally, the vast gulf between liberalism and communism is made clear by the dedication of the latter to the elaboration of vast and mechanistic programmes of social reform illustrated by the philosopher of early communism, Auguste Comte, whose vision depicts the prototype of the pseudo-religious organization of a materialistic utopia with which later history is to become all too familiar.

From the very character of communism, or socialism, Croce feels, any union it might contract with democracy must lack logical and sympathetic coherence, must be a union only of convenience. This in fact he discovers to be the case. That union was born of the desire of communism, at that time still without a political organization of its own and disillusioned with extra-political action, to find a political organ by which to exercise influence upon the state. The intimate contradiction of the union was made clear by later communist thought; after it had mastered the political situation and created its own organs for political action, communism made it abundantly clear that democracy could have no place in the monolithic society it envisaged. For this reason the terms of the basic contest of the century were altered. The opposition was no longer between absolutism and liberalism, but between liberalism and a democracy which had become the political vehicle of communism. In a deeper sense, this was but an extension and reaffirmation of that earlier opposition which had appeared between liberalism and democracy. After the revolution, it will be recalled, liberalism had reason to re-examine its earlier alliance with jacobin democracy. This it had done and as a result had shed those affinities to adhere more closely to its own basic insights.[1]

The years 1848–51 constitute, in Croce's interpretation, a period of especial importance in the liberal formation. These were years of revolution, and since of revolution, also of reaction; for it has become clear to Croce that these phenomena are intimately and dialectically related in history and that any separation of them reflects that utopianism for which he has only disdain. Europe, wearied by six decades, yearned to be delivered from the revolutionary cycle, but seemed unable to advance on the path of social and political progress

[1] SE'800, 142 sq.

or to realize the moral and ethical ideas which drew her on save by these means. The revolutions of this period were of two kinds, liberal-national or social-democratic. These years are forever important because they witnessed the final eclipse of authoritarianism as it had existed under the banner of the Triple Alliance. In the second place, they saw the clarification of the lines along which liberalism was to effect its organization of Europe: the formation of liberal-national structures embodying to a greater or lesser degree the liberal idea. Finally, they witnessed the maturation of that force, social democracy, with which liberalism had already come into conflict. That force now assumed the form to which its inner logic destined it, authoritarian and totalitarian communism. In this form it was to prove resistant to the assimilative and transformative power of liberalism and was presently to challenge liberalism's dominion over Europe.

The same ambiguity which, in the eyes of succeeding generations, had clouded the character of the July Revolution seems to Croce to hang over the 'year of revolutions', 1848. The revolutionary movements of that year have been condemned as failures, because they did not actualize the goals which they had set themselves and because they provoked certain anti-liberal and anti-national reactions. On neither score, Croce contends, can the positive character and achievement of the national-liberal revolutions of that year be denied. As to the first criticism, every event in history is, in this sense, he points out, a failure, for no historical project ever existentially achieves the fullness of its motivating ideal. At the same time, no historical project can be called a failure in the ethico-political view of history so long as it does not betray its principles. This surely the liberal-national revolutions, and for that matter those of social-democratic colouring, did not do. On the contrary, they remained firm in these principles and, even more, created new instrumentalities for their realization. The term failure cannot be applied to them. Again the historian's task is to identify the positive achievement, surrounded though it be by all the limitations which circumstance all human effort.[1]

In Italy these were years of profound disillusionment; at the same time, they were years of a fresh and more realistic affirmation of her national and unitary goals. These were the years in which the Risorgimento was born in its effective form, the form in which, as has been suggested earlier, it was to become identical with the new

[1] SE'800, 164–5.

Italy as the root with the flower.[1] The element of disillusionment came in the collapse of the neo-guelf movement and the failures of the federative and republican ideals. These were not, as the event was to prove, actual failures. They were, rather, clarifications of the actual historical premises of the liberal-national programme in Italy. They revealed certain contradictions and incoherences, certain false hopes and false conceptions, which had to be eradicated before that movement could become historically effective. For this reason, to conceive them as failures in any absolute sense is sentimental. The re-affirmation came as a result of the clarification effected by the neo-guelf and republican disillusionment. Both the form and the agency of the liberal-national Italy stood revealed, in the ideal of constitutional monarchy and the House of Savoy.

That year of revolutions opened in Italy, ironically enough, with the apparent realization of the neo-guelf dream. The papacy, which Machiavelli had defined as an insuperable and intrinsic hindrance to the liberation and unification of Italy, now seemed to have become instead its instrument. The same papacy, which from the beginning had seemed the natural enemy of liberalism, now for a moment stood out as its collaborator and protector. A liberal pope seemed to be realized in the person of Pius IX, 'Pio nono'. The young Hegelian philosopher and statesman, Silvio Spaventa, sang a philosophic paean to this miraculous transformation, asserting that the abstract infinite of the Church was now united with the living infinite of the nation and the state, the infinite of religion with the infinite of society, by the work of one man recognized to be infallible. Under the spell of the papal example, the King of Naples was induced to grant the revolutionary demands; constitutions were granted in Turin, in Tuscany and in Rome itself. The Milanese rose and in five days of fighting obliged the Austrians to withdraw and to abandon all Lombardy. Venice proclaimed itself a republic again, Carlo Alberto crossed the Ticino and declared war on Austria. The pope sent his troops to the frontier and the King of Naples dispatched a corps to the valley of the Po. Rejecting every vestige of foreign influence or aid, as the vision of Mazzini bade her, Italy seemed to have taken up with serious intent the work implicit in the motto 'Italia farà da sè': Italy will act on her own.

The intrinsic contradiction which was latent in this situation was, however, quick to reveal itself. It revealed itself in the Roman constitution of 29 April 1848, 'a hippogriff', as it has been called, since it

[1] Cf. *supra*.

tried to combine the vote of the chamber, reduced to a mere consult-
ative status, with the veto of the college of Cardinals, the freedom of
the press with ecclesiastical censorship. It revealed itself in the under-
standable reluctance of the Pope to take the ultimate step of war
against Austria, announcing, as his universal office compelled him,
that the head of the Church could not take up arms for one people
against another equally Catholic. Finally, it was revealed in the
action he was to take in the following years, summoning to the
defence of the papal temporality foreign arms, Austrian, Spanish,
French and Neapolitan, against Italians. It was the complete and inevitable collapse of the neo-guelf dream. With this collapse, the
Italian national movement was deprived of its original point of
support in an existing internal power.[1]

The collapse of the neo-guelf dream was by no means, however,
the failure of the Italian national movement. Another 'point d'appui',
in another existing power, revealed itself, a power which was capable of unambiguous commitment and free to carry out the national
programme with vigour and logic. With the collapse of the neo-
guelf movement, Carlo Alberto of Savoy was left alone; and he
chose to stand alone. He refused to enter any alliance either with the
princes of the north or with the King of Naples and of the Two
Sicilies. In this manner the hegemony of Sardinia in the Italian movement was established. By this gesture it became the natural and
indubitable agency of the Italian national aspiration. Immediate
failure was Carlo Alberto's lot. His attempt to press the issue against
Austria ended in the defeat of Novara, while in Naples reaction to
the neo-guelf enthusiasm had begun. But the leadership of the Kingdom of Sardinia and the House of Savoy remained intact.

The year of revolutions in Italy thus seemed to end in stalemate
and defeat. Under the ethico-political aspect, however, the situation
was far more hopeful. In these days the ethos of the new Italy was
formed. The passing of neo-guelfism was the passing of an illusion,
an illusion which was to be mourned, for it too had done its work
for the movement of Italian freedom, but an illusion nonetheless.
The Mazzinian dream was passed, with its vision of a popular war
against the foreigner and the emergence of an Italian Republic from
the Alps to the Straits of Taranto. Mazzini's real contribution to the
Italian movement, however, his vision of her free activity in her
own deliverance, endured. Finally, a new fulcrum had emerged in the
Savoy monarchy, now bound to the liberal-national cause of Italy.[2]

[1] SE'800, 167.　　　　　　　　　　　　[2] SE'800, 166 sqq.

The experience of Germany during this 'period of revolutions' provides, in Croce's opinion, an instructive contrast to that of Italy, a contrast which will grow sharper with the advancing decades and which is filled with portent for the fate of the Europe liberalism was shaping. Constitutions were not unknown in a number of the German states and under pressure of the February revolution of 1848 others were extended and, almost immediately, conservatively amended or withdrawn. But the great effort of the German revolution of 1848, Croce believes,[1] lay, not in these constitutional manœuvres, but in the attempt at unification through liberal and parliamentary means. This effort was the work of the Frankfort Assembly, proposed in March and convoked in April of that year by a group of journalists, men of letters, political figures and members of the opposition in various German chambers. Its guiding genius was Gagern, who summed up in his person and character both the nobility of intention and the debility of will in the assembly. Steering a careful course between the conservative proposals which would have left all decisions concerning unification to the princes, and the republican desires for a federation of states somewhat on the American model, the assembly declared for a constitutional monarchy envisaging a union of states about Prussia and the exclusion of Austria: the 'little-German' proposal. The crown was offered to Frederick William of Prussia, who spurned it as infringing upon the absolutist prerogatives of his crown. This marks the first point of contrast with the Italian experience; for Carlo Alberto of Savoy was able to rise to the liberal vision and to set aside absolutist claims to place himself at the head of the national-liberal movement of unification. Needless to say, the king's refusal was a severe blow to the assembly and, at the same time, a clear indication of the path German national unification was to follow. Thus rebuffed, having no secure political support, the assembly signed an act of renunciation and dissolution. In time, many of its members, like the scholar Droysen, were to lose this initial liberal aspiration and to become converted to absolutism and its plan for German unification. For Frederick William supplemented his rejection of the offer of the Frankfort Assembly by a proposal of unification on his own terms, that is, by an agreement among princes. To implement this proposal, he called into being the 'Pact of the Three Kings'. His effort foundered, however, upon the rocks of Austrian opposition, for the Dual Monarchy could not support the idea of a German unification exclusive of her-

[1] SE'800, 172.

self. The result of this discomfiture was not, however, deleterious to
the interests of Prussia; on the contrary, it enhanced them. For by a
process of logic too subtle to be readily comprehended the conclusion was drawn, and expressed by the crown prince of Prussia,
that the unification of Germany must come by conquest: an utterance as close to prophecy as modern history knows. Here again,
Croce emphasized the contrast with Italy.[1]

The Austrian experience of '48 differed again both from that of
Germany and that of Italy. Unlike the one and the other of these
countries, Austria was almost completely without ideal preparation
for liberal action. Again, her internal problem was most dissimilar.
It was neither the problem of independence from an external power
nor of liberty nor state unity; it was rather the problem of the internal strife of nationalities, each seeking at once independence and
hegemony. The only path open to the ruling dynasty, since it lacked
the spiritual force to unite the component elements of the empire,
was to play them off against each other, keeping the balance of power
in its own hands; this procedure, certainly instinct with no ideal
principle, sums up the internal policy of the government. The effect
of the infiltration of liberal ideas was to inflame the latent national-
isms, and to encourage separatist movements such as the Hungarian
under Batthyanyi and Kossuth.[2] Thus Austria presented to the world
the aspect, not of a league of states, nor of a great federation which
might serve as a model for the unity of Europe, but of an armed
camp ruled entirely by the force of the military and the police, a
model for nothing at all in a world that could engender the liberal
idea and die for it and deserving, in the observation of Mazzini, the
dissolution which was her transparent destiny.

Meanwhile, England remained immune from the revolutionary
wave (save for the Irish incident), not through lack of sympathy, but
because within the terms of her own constitution she was already far
advanced on the liberal path. Immune to the revolutionary currents
stood Russia also, but for reasons diametrically opposed to those
operative in England's case. The Czar had warned that the revolutionary tide would fall back at the frontiers of his empire and this
was indeed the case. To the severe regime of repression within he
added a constant readiness to lend military and diplomatic aid to
reactionary movements elsewhere. Beneath the hard shell of reaction
and absolutism, a cultural and political vacuum was created. Isolated
from the intellectual life of the west, the minds of the young were

[1] SE'800, 179. [2] SE'800, 180-1.

turned to turgid day-dreams and abstract and simplifying rationalism. Innocent of the discipline of liberal action, they were silently
being prepared for every type of violent and impulsive undertaking.
Thus it became apparent to a man like Herzen that when revolution
came to Russia it would be 'integral revolution'; again a note of
prophecy is sounded.[1]

Unequal as had been the liberal achievement in the year of revolutions in the various countries he has noted, it was still not without
positive achievement everywhere. Only in France, he writes, is it
possible to call the '48[2] retrogressive. Under the first impetus of
revolution, she turned again to the old jacobin dreams and abstractions. But the jacobin fervour was turned into new channels: those
of social democracy or social republicanism. France embarked upon
a period of social experimentation which, from the point of view of
a realistic economics and politics, could only be called fantastic. The
'ateliers nationaux', Croce writes, 'in no way resembled a serious
economic enterprise'.[3] The success of Louis Napoleon in the plebis-
cite over his republican rival Cavaignac, demonstrated that the
revolutionary tide had begun to ebb, and that of reaction to rise. The
coup d'état of 2 December 1851 was strictly in accord with the logic
of the situation, tracing again the classical cycle from democracy to
tyranny. With Louis Napoleon, however, a new type of absolutism
appeared in Europe (not entirely new, of course, but not seen since
the days of the Greek tyrants), an absolutism resting upon flattery of
the populace rather than upon the invocation of a divine right. The
results of this experience were readily apparent. During this and the
following decades of the Second Empire, France was troubled at
home and impotent abroad, prone like every despotism, and especially a despotism which appeals not to heaven but to the populace,
to military and political adventure.[4]

[1] SE'800, 185.   [2] SE'800, 191.   [3] SE'800, 194.
[4] SE'800, 191 sqq.

IV

POETRY AND POWER:
ITALY AND GERMANY

B Y the moral discomfiture of absolutism, the liberal idea had established itself as the dominant motive force of European life at the mid-century. In that contest, its strength and the purity of its idea had been tried even by violence and bloodshed. The severest trial still lay before it, however, a trial in which its power was to be measured, not with reference to the strength of another principle, but by the creative force within itself. Liberalism had shown itself heretofore as a principle of reform within the European nations. The question still was unanswered: had the liberal idea and the liberal will the power to create a state in its own image? The answer which history provides, Croce is sure, is affirmative. That answer in its concreteness, as an historical fact, in the richest sense of that term, is the kingdom of Italy, called into being precisely at this hour and this juncture and by no other force than the liberal idea and will. He writes: 'If it were possible in political history to speak of a masterpiece as we do in dealing with works of art, the process of Italy's independence, liberty and unity would deserve to be called the masterpiece of the liberal-national movements of the nineteenth century.'[1]

Italy presented on the eve of the revolutions of '48 the classical situation for the testing of the liberal idea. Every element, every force, against which the liberal idea had sought to define itself during the last fifty years, was present here, not merely in fact, but almost in caricature, that is, in a form in which its worst features are forcibly projected and exaggerated. The idea of liberty had appeared in its earliest form as resistance to external domination, of the presence within the nation, as defined by the spontaneous and historical national consciousness, of an alien power. Italy was the supreme theatre, with the possible exception of Poland, of such foreign domination. In the north, the hand of Austria lay heavily over the

[1] SE'800, 220.

225

richest expanses of the peninsula. In the south, the Bourbon monarchy, shorn of every vestige of moral right by the reprisals of 1799 and 1820 and by its perfidy to the constitutions given and revoked on more than one occasion, was garrisoned, rather than enthroned, in the largest single state in the peninsula, the Realm of Naples. In the papal states, where for a brief moment the alternate visions of a republic and of a federal Italy under papal guidance had promised in turn to take historical form, foreign bayonets were the fulcrum of power.

The expulsion of alien force was, however, only the *via negativa* of liberalism. It could not define the liberal idea. Beyond it rose the image of unity, a national unity which would be the political expression of the spontaneous oneness welling up in a people from the shared experience of history. The image of this unity had hovered upon the horizon of the Italian consciousness for a hundred, perhaps a thousand years; but it possessed the awful character of a dream which men scarcely dared recall. Yet it lay in the logic of the situation that the acquisition of liberty merely in the sense of deliverance from foreign domination would be a hollow victory. It would serve only to throw into relief the fragmentation which centuries of foreign dominion had imposed upon her. Consequently, while men, even Cavour, scarcely dreamed of that unity as a thing to be effected deliberately, so deep did that unity lie in the logic of the Italian situation that scarcely had the first step been taken in the direction of the expulsion of foreign power than the awakened consciousness of the peninsula swept on to this further fulfilment. Finally, the idea of liberty had expressed itself in the vision of the ordered constitutional and parliamentary life of the nation, held together by spontaneous bonds of historical sentiment and free of all alien intrusion upon its life. In divided and subjugated Italy, the possibility of such order and efficiency in administration and legislation seemed beyond the wildest imagination. Misrule was synonymous with foreign occupation, while in the Realm of Naples the spectacle of maladministration of justice and legislation without reason had elicited the shocked reactions of Europe. In a word, if ever a theatre was apt for the display of the creative power of the liberal idea, it was Italy at the mid-century.

To this material situation, as it may be called, there accrued another circumstance of vital importance. This may be called the relative impoverishment of ideals, other than that of the ideal of liberalism. This was not an impoverishment in the sense of an absence of ideas; it was rather an impoverishment produced by the successive disillusionment of Italy with every other possibility of deliverance. The earliest had been her disillusionment with the French Revolution, in so far as it had touched her; this disillusionment Croce had anatomized in his study of the Neapolitan Revolution of 1799 and its 'sequelae'. The second had been the disillusionment involved in the failure of the neo-guelf movement. This movement which embraced the twin elements of federation and papal leadership had received its death blow precisely in the transactions of the year of revolutions, 1848, and consequently persisted most vividly in the national memory. Finally (though perhaps weakest, since the republican idea had never really found root in the Italian consciousness) the dissipation of Mazzinianism, which had contributed so much to the formation of the Italian national consciousness, into internationalist and demogogic schemes after the failure of the Roman Republic must be counted an impoverishment of the ideal resources of the Italian effort. There remained alone, as still rich with promise and alive, the idea of liberalism. This idea, in turn, in order to be transformed into an existential, ethico-political force, needed embodiment in a political agent.

That agent was not lacking, Croce points out. It was Piedmont, or the Kingdom of Sardinia. Here, he writes, the liberal and national movement had suffered no interruption; on the contrary, in the very midst of the whirlwind of reaction it had cleansed and purified itself. it was, he adds, the only nation, tiny though it was, in Europe which was truly revolutionary, in the liberal sense of that term, able and ready, materially and ideally, to translate into action the elements of the liberal idea against the oppressive forces which weighed upon Italy. For the identity between Piedmont and Italy, he feels, was complete. Piedmont had received from the whole of the peninsula 'the cry of sorrow', the cry for deliverance, and if she were to act, it was only in the Italian theatre, and not in any narrower arena, that action was possible. The geographical situation of Piedmont had contributed much to place her in this position of leadership; but even more had the long ideal preparation of her princes and her statesmen. Her princely house had most spontaneously and most steadfastly accepted and adhered to the liberal idea; there was in her history no record of that perfidy toward her own subjects which marred, for example, the record of the Bourbons of Naples. To this had been added a remarkable succession of statesmen who had firmly established the elements of liberal rule in the kingdom: Balbo, Thaon di Revel and, above all, Massimo d'Azeglio. This last, who formed his first cabinet in 1849, under the constitution of that year, was more conscious than any other before him, perhaps, of the revolutionary potentiality of Piedmont and set himself to protect and to fructify this potentiality. His efforts to consolidate the position of the monarchy against democratic or republican extremists, his control of the electoral process to insure a moderate and balanced representation and his courageous programme of internal reform made it possible, when the time came, for Piedmont to place herself at the head of the national movement without fear of cavil and recrimination.[1]

The true guiding genius of Piedmont's leadership in the peninsula, however, was Cavour. It was he, in the first place, who carried on the work of D'Azeglio in the internal renewal of the kingdom. His first concern was the formation of an orderly parliamentary life as the only instrument and organ of a liberal government. His work during the decade 1850–9 was to make of the Piedmontese kingdom the working model of the Italy which he was to create: a coherent nation, firmly moulded by liberty and order and capable of reducing the idea of liberty to actuality in its own life. And all this was done without conscious plan or intent on his part; for Cavour was most typical of his time even in this, that the idea of a united Italy, while it hovered on the horizon of his consciousness as an ultimate dream, did not enter into his plans and calculations as a genuine possibility. The Italian character of the Piedmontese leadership was also attested by the large numbers of exiles from other portions of Italy who flocked to her capital. These exiles made clear how profound was the disillusionment with every other ideal and indicated the fervour and unanimity with which the rest of Italy looked to the leadership of Piedmont. In a certain sense, these exiles saw the end to which that leadership must ultimately tend, national unity, more clearly than Cavour himself. The Neapolitan exiles, for example, spurned a project for the liberation of Naples under the possible protection of Louis Napoleon on which Cavour was inclined to look favourably; they declared it abortive, for a free Naples was meaningless without a free Italy.[2] Similarly, Manin in Venice and Garibaldi on his return to Italy in 1854 repulsed all other projects because of their assurance that the path of Italian unity lay only through Turin.

Cavour's first task was to bring the case of Italy before the attention of Europe and to justify, in anticipation, the revolutionary programme he nurtured. To this end, he took a path which many of his

[1] SE'800, 205–7.   [2] SE'800, 209.

later critics have condemned, but in which Croce sees an example of that astuteness in the service of a higher ideal of which the very essence of ethico-political wisdom consists. Cavour committed, or more accurately perhaps, intruded the Italian contingent into the Crimean war, a war which had little of the lustre of a liberal cause. This was the price he paid for a hearing at the subsequent Congress of Paris, an opportunity of which he made good use. In addition to presenting the situation in Italy most adequately, he made it clear that Piedmont spoke for Italy. Austria, naturally enough, challenged this claim of Piedmont to Italian representation; but the fact vindicated it. Still, something more palpable was necessary. In addition to representation before the court of European opinion, Cavour sought also concrete alliances. This brought him directly into conflict with the lingering Mazzinianism of certain elements which had interpreted the motto 'Italia farà da sè' to mean abstention from foreign alliances in the cause of Italian freedom. Cavour, however, saw clearly that such alliances were necessary and, rightfully managed, offered no threat to the independence and autonomy of Italian action.

The first overt act in the revolutionary programme of Piedmont was the war of 1859.[1] Its object was the expulsion of Austria from Lombardy and Venetia and the constitution of a kingdom of northern Italy. The formulation of this objective illustrated the diffidence of Cavour toward the idea of peninsular unity; he accepted without hesitation the view of Louis Napoleon (who, while ready for his own motives to concur in the expulsion of Austria from Italy, did not contemplate even remotely the idea of a new nation-state embracing the entire peninsula) that Italy should be divided into four states, leaving the Two Sicilies and papal Rome intact and forming a kingdom of central Italy.

The war of 1859 was more easily successful in its primary objective than even Cavour dared hope. It held a surprise even for him, however, for the 'sequela' of events it set in motion certainly fell outside the scope of his project. Tuscany, Parma and Modena rose, driving out the dukes whose rule had rested on Austrian support. Revolution raised its head in the papal states. Most surprising of all, however, was the cry for annexation to Piedmont which followed upon these revolutions. Her representative position in Italy, and the magnitude of the forces she had awakened could not have been impressed more clearly upon the consciousness of Piedmont. It was, as Croce remarks,[2] Italy indeed 'acting for herself' and

[1] SE'800, 209 sqq.   [2] SE'800, 218.

expressing her will, which was for peninsular unity under the leadership of Piedmont. From this moment on, Cavour was more drawn on by the new spirit of Italy, than its leader; but he responded quickly to what he was pleased to call the 'improvisation of history'.[1] The fact was, of course, that the idea of Italian unity lay dormant in his mind and will also, and needed only this indication of its historical possibility to leap to life.

From this moment onward, the movement of Italian unity ceased even to have its vital centre in Piedmont alone. The will to unity sprang up spontaneously everywhere. In the south, the movement against the Bourbon monarchy crystallized swiftly; in a few months Sicily was liberated and the lower peninsula to the frontiers of the papal states. For a moment, the danger of a dualism of political tendencies threatened. It was averted by the quickness of Cavour's decision; his arms completed the liberation of the papal domains and that of Naples in the siege of Gaeta. The Risorgimento, in two short years, had flamed out over the peninsula and called the new Italy into being.

Yet the severest test lay ahead. Freedom from external dominion had been assured, unity was a fact. But the quality of the new state had yet to be determined. It had been born in the surging flame of liberty; but there had still to be created the actuality of a free state. For this reason the years 1860–5 were more important even than the 'heroic' years of armed uprising. They were years of legislative, administrative economic and financial construction. These years also gave proof, if further proof were needed, that the new Italian state was truly the creation of the entire nation and not of a single man or power. For this work was carried out without the guidance, though wholly in the spirit of Cavour. The state which arose as a result of the effort of those years vindicated the liberal character of the entire movement of the Risorgimento. This vindication was clearest, in Croce's view, in the manner in which the new government dealt with the problem of the papal temporal power. This was a problem which had no parallel in history; for this reason Croce rejects as hypocritical the protestations of other nations. They demanded, he remarks, that Italy execute alone a duty which was incumbent on all Catholic nations, namely that of insuring the freedom of the papacy to exercise without political interference its sacred office over all Christendom. But the new Italy was strong enough to confront even this demand, however exorbitant. By the legislation then enacted, it

[1] SE'800, 218.

insured that freedom in fact and in principle, in a manner consonant with the nationhood of Italy itself. How well it succeeded was demonstrated but a few years later when an oecumenical council of the Church convened in Rome with the greatest order and quiet. The Roman Question was not solved in those days; but by its attitude the new Italy gave evidence of its desire to employ every means, short of national suicide, to insure its just and liberal resolution.[1] So convinced, indeed, was Croce of the essential rightness of this solution, that sixty years later he was alone in protesting in the Italian senate the Lateran accord, while still later, in his last address to that body, he protested anew the inclusion of that accord in the constitution of the Italian republic called into being after the second world war.

The liberal movement had, therefore, in his view, vindicated itself in ultimate terms. Italy was the living proof that the liberal idea and the liberal will, in persons imbued with that faith, could create a nation, and if a nation, ultimately a world, at once civilized and free. For this reason in his history of Europe in the nineteenth century he does not hesitate to assign to Italy this signal place. But in this he is not guilty of a narrow chauvinism. It is not Italy in any narrow national character that he exalts. It is Italy in her ethico-political, her liberal character. Under this aspect, Italy is but an historical concretion of the universal ideal and will of liberty, generated not by any special breed of men, but by the human spirit itself and consequently available to all men according to the disposition and the capability of the persons and the hour. The experience of Italy is simply the guarantee of the universal validity of the liberal ideal, both in its principle and as a goal of ethico-political action. For Croce does not forget, as Ruggiero reminds us,[2] that in the overall picture the liberal experience of Italy is both small and, in a sense, imitative. The achievement of the Italian people lies in the purity with which it lived that ideal, and this secures its place in history. The ideas which were concretized were born elsewhere, were born of the human spirit itself. Croce, always most cosmopolitan or at least European in his outlook, is careful to draw from the Italian experience no narrow chauvinistic, but ethico-political conclusions; above all the conclusion that the idea of liberty is an idea of historical force; and that the desire of men for freedom need never again despair.

The unification and liberation of Italy, Croce writes, in a phrase that echoes Vico, was a lyric poem; the unification of German power

[1] SE'800, 200.   [2] *History of European Liberalism*, p. 90.

under Prussia, the construction of a powerful machine.[1] Thus he establishes a basic contrast, filled with the greatest portents, in his narrative of the liberal formation of Europe in the nineteenth century. In the contrasting and opposing spiritual attitudes which these images figure forth, lies the key to the subsequent progress of European life, the fate of liberalism and the character of the spiritual regime destined to supplant it. The general persuasion, he notes, is not sensitive to this contrast. It is customary to cite the formation of the German empire and of the Italian kingdom as parallel cases of a single movement, nationalism. To do so, however, is to evince no appreciation of the qualitative diversities within that common movement. These spiritual differences, the qualitative diversity of spirit in which an apparently common end is pursued, he holds (consistently with the ethico-political conception of history he has expounded), transforms both movement and product alike. Only preoccupation with extrinsic resemblances can obscure this fact; and, in the case of Germany and Italy, also the fact that the one marked the end, the other, the initiation of diverse ideal epochs.[2] There had indeed, for a time, been a certain affinity between these lands, expressed in the sympathy which the Italian patriots expressed for the German aspirations. In the actual process which developed in Germany between 1862 and 1870, this affinity was deleted. That movement was not, like the Italian, a movement for liberation from foreign oppression and the spontaneous expression of a common nationhood. It consisted in the formation of a centre of political power for the purpose of exerting political influence and preponderance in Europe. And the process, in certain aspects, was entirely the reverse of the Italian; for it involved in part driving out of the union of German states the one state, Austria, which had represented the Germanic nation to the world for centuries, and its substitution, as the centre of the new union, by a state of more recent origin, Prussia. Of importance above all, however, in establishing the character of the new German empire and the portent it held for the future of Europe, was the appreciation of its spirit, the spirit in which that process of unification and consolidation had been pursued. This spirit, in the case of Germany as of Italy, Croce finds distilled and incarnated pre-eminently

---

[1] SE'800, 248; Vico called ancient Roman law, and by implication, the commonwealth it sustained, 'un serioso poema', *Scienza Nuova Seconda*, paragraph 1027, where the sense of 'serioso' is, in line with the Vichian aesthetic, to be understood as 'lived through'.

[2] SE'800, 240-1.

in one man. In Italy, that man had been Camillo Cavour; in Germany, it was Otto von Bismarck.

The man who almost single-handed forged this new centre of power which was the German Empire, he writes, was, unlike Cavour, a purely political genius; a man, that is to say, impervious to ideals, a 'realist', a man of will; a practical man, inclined to hold in contempt those who were moved by phantoms such as a love of liberty, a faith in its power to create a common good in its own image. His devotion to the monarchy which he served and whose power he extended and imposed upon a whole galaxy of lesser states, was not an expression of moral ideality, of faith in the intrinsic idea of that institution and the ideal power which must therefore reside in it. It was, in Croce's terms, affection for the instrument of his will and purposes, the affection of a soldier for his sword.[1] The one concept which dominated all his thought and action was political utility; in relation to this, and this alone, he viewed and evaluated all the forces and factors which presented themselves and regulated his conduct toward them. They were all means to his end, to be used or discarded as the case might be: Austria and her Germanic tradition, liberalism and its institutions, the feudal princelings, who formed his entourage, democracy, Lassallean socialism, rebels and revolutionaries, all were on an equal plane, the plane of pure utility, now to be caressed and fostered, now to be rejected and opposed. As Von Moltke sought to make 'war and nothing but war', so Bismarck sought to make politics and nothing else. He carried out his policies in no mean spirit, but rather with far-sightedness and grandeur of vision on the political plane; his calculations were sure, at once cautious and bold, surrendering the lesser for the greater profit with sure instinct, discerning the lasting from the transitory, firm and flexible, changing with changing conditions, but remaining constant in his goal, the creation of a centre of power. Thus does Croce etch the soul of Bismarck.

Utilitarian and political opportunist though he was, and sure of his goal, Bismarck still had no clear design for its achievement. His creation, as Cavour had said of Italian unity itself, was an 'improvisation of history'. Not that Croce discovers in this fact a derogatory character. For 'grand designs' in history, he remarks, are fictions, corresponding more to the popular imagination than to reality. The politician, like the poet in the creation of beauty and the philosopher in quest of truth, is rather moved by 'una tendenza incoercibile', an

[1] SE'800, 242.

incoercible tendency, than drawn by a luminous goal.[1] In retrospect, the unity of design emerges with greater clarity; it is not, for this reason, to be assigned to prevision, but to be recognized as the existentialization of that incoercible impulse. In historical retrospect the pattern of Bismarck's political activity possesses the cold clarity and precision of a military campaign. His first step was the humiliation or debilitation of Austria; this, he perceived, was the absolute condition for the establishment of Prussia as the unquestioned centre of German political life; and since it was inconceivable that Austria might willingly renounce the German hegemony she enjoyed, this decision meant war. A pretext for war did not, however, exist; it had to be created. The war against Denmark in 1864 over Schleswig though waged with Austria as an ally, was, in the longer view, the creation of an occasion for conflict with her, a conflict which would bring her traditional authority to an end. The possession of this miniscule duchy became a bone of contention, and the logical sequel was the war of 1866. This war revealed, as much as anything else, the unpopularity of Prussia among the states she was to weld into an empire; for most sided with Austria, moved by suspicion of Prussian tyranny, by affection for their native dynasties and independence and, in the vast Catholic portion, by repugnance for the hegemony of a Protestant state. All this, however, proved impotent to thwart Bismarck's resolution. The defeat of Austria was effected. Its aftermath was the formation of the North German Confederation and alliances with the South German states with a view to their ultimate amalgamation with the confederation. In the conduct of this war, Bismarck had enjoyed the co-operation of the new liberal kingdom of Italy. The reasons why Italy was willing to lend her aid, to the limited extent that she did, were two: the memory she entertained, historically justified, of Austria as tyrant and usurper, and the affinity still felt by many of her patriots for a movement bearing many resemblances to her recent experience but whose real quality had not yet been revealed.[2]

Opposition to this political creation of Bismarck's appeared from another quarter, France. From the first, France had opposed the Austrian war, threatening military intervention, and after that country's defeat, offering obstacles to the desired entrance of the South German states into the newly established confederation. As a consequence of these and other manoeuvres on the part of the Second Empire, Bismarck came to consider war with France as in any case inevitable and from the Prussian point of view desirable as well, for success in that venture must endow her with eminent political status in central Europe. While military preparations for this enterprise were under way, Bismarck set about the systematic isolation of the future adversary by diplomatic means. The possibility of a triple alliance between France, Italy and Austria was precluded by encouragement of the Garibaldian expedition against Rome, to whose defence France was committed. A rapprochement with Russia was established condoning her efforts to open the Black Sea to commerce and shipping, contrary to the provisions of the Peace of Paris. When war came in 1870, it was an uninterrupted series of military successes. The new eminence with which it endowed Prussia and her satellites was signalized by another great and imposing historical improvisation, the proclamation of the German Empire, which went beyond the original programme of the confederation to evoke anew the imperial memories of mediaeval Germany, though this concept of Empire, Croce remarks, was understood by Bismarck in a sense far removed from the earlier conception.[1]

Croce's purpose in re-narrating the oft-told tale of Bismarck's strategy and triumph is not to review political and military history, but to set in relief the inward spiritual character of this movement, its portent for subsequent developments and above all for the liberal idea and movement. The unification of German power, he has already remarked, opened a new ideal epoch;[2] it signalized a general transformation of the European spirit, which boded ill for the liberal idea. It is only metaphorically that this transformed spirit can be called a new ideal movement, a figure of speech by which opposites are designated by a common nominative. In truth, from the liberal point of view, the Prussian movement ushered in a period of un-ideality, a period in which the whole moral impulse of the romantic movement[3] was negated and reversed. Nor was it displaced, as he was later to remark,[4] by an alternate positive deal, able to displace it by moral superiority. On the contrary, the fresh orientation of the European spirit represented a new emphasis upon those very elements of moral and civil, of intellectual and literary life, which the

[1] SE'800, 247.   [2] SE'800, 241.

[3] The movement of philosophical romanticism, it is needless to repeat, according to the distinction within romanticism which Croce has already established, SE'800, 43 sqq. and *supra*.

[4] CFM, 104 sqq.

ideality of liberalism had transcended. It was a reversal of values, so to say, and the Prussian movement was its bellweather. In the political order, the national idea, which in the liberal and romantic movement was the vehicle of spiritual values in their concreteness and specific diversity, that is, as they must necessarily manifest themselves in the process of historical existence distinct from that of ideal and logical delineation, was perverted to a vehicle of undisguised military and political power. The institutions of liberalism, which represented to the liberal mind ideal values, existentializing and corporealizing, under specific conditions, the ramifications of the idea of liberty itself, were reduced to the status of implements of power, to be used or discarded as political cunning dictated. Since, as Croce has repeatedly noted, the life of the human spirit is one and integral, this declension from the ideality of liberalism in the political order could not fail to be accompanied by a similar decline in the other orders of the spiritual life. Not, it is clear, that any determinate causality exercised by political life could induce such corresponding movements, but simply that a reversal in spiritual attitude irrepressibly finds expression in all the moments of the spiritual life of the individual or the group. The liberal movement had its source, as he has noted, in the maturation of idealistic and historical thought in the opening decades of the century.[1] The new spiritual orientation of Europe was marked, on the contrary, by a fresh adulation of science. That this must, from the liberal point of view, constitute a retrograde movement is evidenced by the fact, adduced earlier by Croce, that the constriction of the natural sciences and the philosophy allied to them within their proper limits had been one of the chief accomplishments of the romantic philosophy.[2] The rehabilitation of science was the natural accompaniment of the reversion to force in the political order; for science can, on the basis of its presuppositions, consider nothing but force or forces, physical force or vital force innocent of any moral, aesthetic or intellectual qualifications, and must treat those forces deterministically. The naturalistic philosophy which began to gain fresh influence in the last third of the century was simply the transposition of this attitude of science to the whole of the life of the human spirit. Its fruit was a host of pseudo-philosophical theories, touching every dimension of the life of spirit and contaminating them all with the same constricting scienticism. Historical determinism replaced the idealistic view of the movement of the human spirit in historiography. Taine represents a particularly

[1] SE'800, 249, 41 sqq. and *supra*.　　　　[2] SE'800, 44; cf. *Logica, passim.*

trenchant statement of this attitude, as well as a persistent execution of its principles. The conception of art as spiritual creation was replaced by naturalistic theories, or 'psychologies' of the artistic process. Ethnic phantasies, such as that of Gobineau, gained acceptance and were received as peremptorily binding in the name of science. Finally, the principle of force, of sheer vital force, impatient of any ideal qualification, was lifted to the status of the supreme rule of life and expressed itself in the attitude of activism, the valuation of action simply as action, predicated on the fact understood simply as fact. So great and imposing was the influence of this new attitude, signalized, as had been noted, in the political triumph of the Prussian movement, that it awakened doubts in the ranks of the liberals themselves. Liberals were intimidated for the moment, reflecting that perhaps too much weight had been given to thought and criticism, to the moral will in history, and not enough to the 'forces' of history and with historical prepotence as against the vital instinct and the sheer will to power. Most deeply of all, the mordant fangs of doubt penetrated even to the idea of liberty itself, awakening the suspicion that the benefits which this idea, translated into moral will, could insure were neither as great nor as secure as those which authority and force could guarantee. Finally, the economic development of Europe conspired to weaken men's faith in moral will and the sentiment of liberty, and to strengthen the appeal to authority and force. Liberalism in its economic aspects had created vast economic potentials; but signs were developing that, in accord with the spirit, though not the letter, of Marx's prediction, capitalism and liberal society might not possess the moral virtue to dominate the productive forces which it had let loose.[1]

Thus the period of liberalism's greatest activity and influence, and the period which witnessed, in Croce's view, the creation of its 'masterpiece', the Italian state, saw, at the same time, the emergence of a spiritual attitude, of a philosophy and an historical will directly opposed to it and ended, consequently, not on a note of unclouded triumph, but on a note of doubt, of trepidation and diffidence. Neither this doubt, however, nor the strength of the opposing 'ideals' was strong enough to compel the historian to deny to the succeeding period, the decades between 1871 and 1914, the appellation 'The Liberal Age'. At the same time, it is anything but a liberal 'Utopia' which this age presents to the view. It is a period, rather, of mounting and multiplying tensions, in which the liberal

[1] SE'800, 249 sq.; SI'71, Cap. IX passim.

237

idea is more and more compelled to justify its concepts and its works, and to prepare its strategy for an impending period in which it would no longer constitute the dominant ideal of European life.

V

THE LIBERAL AGE

THE logic of liberalism might seem to many to imply a golden age, a utopian fulfilment of its ideals. Certainly, in its initiation, whether in the form of economic liberalism (which Croce, as has been noted (cf. *supra*), reduces to a secondary status) or in its ethical form (which he recognizes as primary), enunciated by philosophical romanticism, the idea of liberty was not innocent of such associations. The economic liberals were ready, in the name of progress, to promise such a fulfilment even when, after the crisis of 1815, the shortcomings of their programme became manifest and a tone of pessimism infected some of their reflections.[1] The foremost philosopher of the romantic movement, Hegel, to whom the idea of liberty owes more, perhaps, than to any other man, was led by his theory of history both to harbour such a utopian notion and abortively to identify the Prussian state as its historical form, a development of his thought which leads Croce to stigmatize his position as *servil*, rather than *liberal*.[2] The fact, in Croce's view, is that ethical liberalism, by its very ethical character, precludes that notion. Liberty appears not as an *ergon* but as an *energeia*, a quality of the ethical will. It is depicted in constant dialectical tension with its opposites, and as subject to the fluctuations of the ethical will itself which, he had noted with reference to history of the baroque age, suffers moments of strength and moments of depression. In history, that age of gold ought to have appeared in Europe after 1871, for liberalism seemed to have overcome the forces against which it had struggled for the better part of the century. His conception of ethical liberalism, however, renders Croce immune to that illusion. His treatment of this period is realistic, sensitive at once to the authentic work of liberalism and to the forces and ideals which, inevitably, arose to challenge it.

The real question for Croce is not whether the liberal movement

---

[1] For this crisis and its effects, both on economic liberalism and on socialism, cf. e.g. Élie Halevy, *Histoire de socialisme européen*, Paris, 1949; and Guido de Ruggiero, *History of European Liberalism*, London, 1932.   [2] SE'800, 10.

had created a 'liberal utopia'; it is whether liberalism had exercised a spiritual and institutional influence upon European culture which was decisive in history, in the sense that, whatever movements might arise to challenge it and whatever depression the liberal spirit itself might suffer, its ideality remains normative and its achievement positive. To this question, the answer appears indubitably affirmative. The evidence is to be found first in the fact that the liberal form of government was, for the decades after 1871, as he expresses it, 'proper to the society of Europe';[1] even more in the fact that the movements which arose in opposition to liberalism as these decades advanced, did not constitute an ideal transcendence of liberalism, but drew even their active strength from the strength of liberal institutions which they assimilated to their own purposes. Thus liberalism was vindicated even in its adversaries. This is the thesis of the last chapters of the *History of Europe in the Nineteenth Century* and of the whole of the *History of Italy from 1871 to 1915*.

The continuing efficacy of liberalism is to be noted first, Croce indicates, in France. That nation had become almost synonymous with political instability. It was there that the weakness and failure of the revolution of 1848 had been most apparent, the demon of jacobin democracy leading inexorably to the reversal of the second of December. Yet, after the disturbances attendant on the Franco-Prussian war and the harrowing experience of the Commune, France turned again to liberalism. The Third Republic appeared as a temporary form, but it proved, not only lasting, but irreplaceable. From the first it was confronted by adversaries, but its strength was both tested and demonstrated by the manner in which it met these threats. Its earliest conflict was with the Commune, which Marx praised, but which Croce characterizes as a 'convulsive movement',[2] in which historically discredited ideas again rose to the surface. The threat of a monarchical restoration was removed by the action of the monarchists themselves and above all by the anachronistic pretensions of the Count de Chambord. These pretensions made clear, in Croce's words, 'what such a return would have brought with it and measured the abyss which had opened between the past and the present'.[3] At the same time, a danger presented itself, that of an over-rigidification against radical movements, which would have arrested her liberal growth at the constitutional stage, preventing parliamentary development. She had, too, to endure the attempted *coup d'état* of Boulanger and the conspiracy of the anti-Dreyfusards which,

[1] SE'800, 210.　　　　　[2] SE'800, 262.　　　　　[3] Ibid.

beneath the cloak of a moral and juridical issue, concealed a fresh attempt upon the republic and its liberal institutions. The republican and socialist forces united to resist these latter dangers and the liberal order issued from the conflict not only intact but strengthened.

In Italy, the advance of the liberal idea and the growth of its institutions was attested by the development of parliamentarism. The original constitution had been more markedly monarchical. In 1898, however, a movement which had for its motto 'back to the constitution' was stigmatized as reactionary and vigorously and universally opposed. This and the subsequent period also witnessed the extinction of programmatic anti-clericalism. This sentiment had from the first been radically opposed to the liberal spirit. It was to be justified in liberal Italy only by the tension between Church and state, as a regrettable accompaniment to an explosive situation. The idea of liberty embraced of necessity religious liberty. With the gradual relaxation of that tension and the return of Catholics to political life in a purely civil character, that sentiment was gradually purged from the Italian institutions. (Don Sturzo, who led the return of Catholics to public life, signalized this civil status of that return under the formula 'Catholics who are deputies, not Catholic deputies'.[1])

The clearest mark of the continued strength of liberalism, however, lay in its gradual assimilation and 'domestication' of socialism. Croce had from the first considered such a relation between liberalism and socialism as theoretically sound and practically desirable. It lay in the logic of both ideas and movements. By the careful distinction between ethical liberalism and economic 'liberism' and the subordination of the latter to the former as a practical, and hence transient, movement to an ideal, such a rapprochement had been theoretically prepared. Even more, however, the ethical character of liberalism by implication embraced and adumbrated the socialist idea. 'Socialism,' he writes, 'if we leave out of consideration the Utopias which grew up around it of redemption or transhumanization of humanity by means of a purely economic and therefore material or materialistic upheaval, is a movement of ascension or an impulse given to the ascension of those social strata, of those multitudes which had remained passive rather than active in public life. Inasmuch as it is a movement of ascension, it is social and not anti-social, historical and not anti-historical. And since this ascension

[1] Cf. A. Robert Caponigri, 'Don Luigi Sturzo', in *Review of Politics*, XIV, No. 4 (April, 1952), pp. 147–65.

implies that the number of citizens who share and take an interest in the state must grow and the directing class be enriched and enlivened by new men, new passions and new capacities, socialism has a noble political character.'[1] In this political character, however, it had been anticipated by the idea and the movement of ethical liberalism. Liberalism placed the real dynamism of the state and of society in the 'directing class', which was, as he remarks and as he had noted clearly in the account of the history of Naples, in no sense an 'economic' class, but the university of men who bore the public conscience, exercising both its executive and critical function. By the logic of the idea of liberty and the ideal of reason upon which it rested, this class had necessarily to be enlarged, its social basis extended until co-terminous with society itself. Ethical liberalism foresaw the elevation of the inactive classes to full and unrestricted participation in the life of the state. This elevation included necessarily the economic, juri-dical and ethical amelioration of those classes, not in any mood of benevolence or of charity, but in the strict order of justice, and not for the distinct advantage of those classes but for the benefit of the whole. As a consequence, he could conclude that socialism and liberalism lived by the same idea, liberty. 'Socialism without liberty', he writes, 'or not effected by liberal means is not true social-ism.'[2] Socialism inspired by the idea of liberty, like liberalism itself, could never descend from above, as the Bismarckian socialism, or be a 'state socialism' in the narrow sense of that term, that is, a pro-gramme of the state for the amelioration of the masses which did not envisage their political education, but only relief by technical and legislative means. It had, like liberalism, to find its resonance in the popular conscience and popular action. As a consequence the union of socialism, in this sense, and the liberal movement possessed logical, ethical and historical cogency.[3]

This union was achieved by a spontaneous movement of critic-ism within both liberalism and socialism. Within liberalism, this critical movement had been going on, in fact, for more than a cen-tury. It consisted in the disengagement of the liberal movement from the implications of jacobin democracy. This was the 'moder-ate' liberalism of which Croce had given a case study in the person of Giuseppe Poerio.[4] In the second place, it consisted in the dis-

---

[1] SE'800, 291–2. [2] SE'800, 292.
[3] Cf. A. R. Caponigri, 'Ethical and Sociological Bases of Italian Politics', *Ethics*, LIX (1948), I, 35–48.
[4] Cf. *supra, sub nomine.*

engagement of liberalism from the limitations of economic liberalism, from ideal commitment to the limited conceptions of that programme. More positively, it consisted in the evocation of the social dimension of the idea of liberty, by which it envisaged a universal, popular resonance of its idea and programme. Within socialism, it consisted in the gradual disengagement of the socialist idea from its historical limitations; from its narrow economic significance, from its revolutionary and anarchistic associations, and from its abortive internationalism. This critical progress within socialism marked the end of the dominance of Marxism in both its 'scientific' and its programmatic aspects. It meant the association of the socialist idea to the life of liberal institutions. This movement was naturally enough excoriated by the extreme or 'bolshevik' (to employ the cacophonous Russian designation) element, which was to achieve a triumph for its view in the aftermath of the first world war. But this excoriation represented no ideal criticism, just as the eventual success of those elements represented no real progress but engendered inevitably the most reactionary and retrogressive programmes, social, political and cultural. The success of these elements is to be traced, in Croce's view, to the peculiar development of Russia, where the intellectuals, cut off from the general movement of European culture, the matrix of the idea of liberty, fell readily into revolutionary and abstract rationalistic attitudes.[1]

In its practical and effective forms, this liberal conversion of socialism (which was, at the same time, the social extension of liberalism) was seen first in Germany. The conciliation of the Marxist and Lassallean associations, in the Gotha congress, provided the basis for an effective socialist party. This party immediately and without the reservations characteristic of Marxism, began to participate in the activity of the few, weak liberal institutions existing in Germany, sending its deputies to the parliament of the Empire. At the congress held in Switzerland in 1880, German socialism broke definitively with the anarchists. 'With that expulsion of anarchism', Croce reflects, 'socialism purged itself, though without full advertence, of communism itself.'[2] Italian socialism followed, in general, the pattern of the German. After a first period, between 1870 and 1880, of anarchistic fermentation, Bakuninian insurrectionism and an evanescent Marxism, a party was formed which, in 1892, achieved disengagement from revolutionism and anarchism, sent deputies to the Chamber and committed itself to legal avenues for the effectuation

[1] SE'800, 220, 271, 293.   [2] SE'800, 295.

of its programme. The socialist party in Italy encountered its share of external opposition and internal division; these were presently resolved, the first by the strength of liberal institutions in Italy, which recognized the illogicality of this opposition, the second by the definitive success of reformist socialism in the party congress of Bologna in 1908.[1] Giolitti, remarking to the Chamber that the Italian socialists had effected the discomfiture of Marx, sought actively to draw the most able among them into his government. The influence of Sorel caused some disorder in its ranks and subsequently weakened its effectiveness in the crisis of 1914; but its best elements had already been assimilated by the liberal movement.[2] In France, the confluence of liberalism and socialism proved easier. The ideas and programme of Marxism held little attraction there. The insurrection of Blanqui, which represented the revolutionary tradition of French socialism, was in disrepute. With the consolidation of the Third Republic even the republicans of the extreme left included in their political programme a 'social programme'; as a consequence, the socialist found natural allies in those republicans. There arose in the ranks of socialism the party of the 'possibilists' who proposed to ask and to obtain reforms which were practical and possible in a foreseeable future. England had offered a cold reception to Marxism. From the beginning liberalism there had spontaneously included in its programmes the problems confronting labour. Fabianism was liberal in spirit, while the Independent Labour Party early gave evidence of reformist and non-Marxian spirit.

The socialist movement in its turn contributed, though not of set purpose, to the establishment of the all-important distinction between ethical liberalism and economic liberalism and to the dissolution of the identification between them. That identification really represented an adolescent phase of liberalism; with changing economic conditions, its promise of a spontaneous resolution of the 'social question' was dissipated. Liberalism, watching the emergence, in its midst, of the monster of monopolism, realized that it was faced with social problems which it could not meet by means of free exchange, but which demanded ethical and political vision and

---

[1] SE'800, 299; cf. for an account of this same movement from another point of view, the popularist or Christian socialist, A. R. Caponigri, 'Don Luigi Sturzo', *Review of Politics*, XIV, No. 4 (April, 1952), pp. 147–65; also Mario Einaudi and François Goguel, *Christian Democracy in Italy and France*, University of Notre Dame Press, 1952.

[2] SE'800, 298–300.

action. This clarification of the liberal idea was attested by the rapid decline of the Manchester school of economics, and by the extension of state activity in the social order.

The same decades witnessed a constant extension of liberal institutions. Parliamentarianism, which constituted a very mature phase of liberalism as compared, for example, with constitutionalism, became more general. The directing class of society was constantly incremented from the wider ranks of the people. Suffrage was granted to wider and wider ranges of the population; juridical reforms in the liberal spirit appeared in many countries. These phenomena could not but be assuring. At the same time, however, Croce reflects, juridical and institutional reform is not the true sign of the level of liberty to which peoples have attained, nor of the reality of liberty itself; these forms may remain empty and ineffective. Nor is the constant enlargement of suffrage unequivocal testament. England, for example, with a more restricted suffrage than France or Germany, still gave evidence of a livelier spirit of liberty. In Spain suffrage was almost universal in principle; in fact, however, political life centred in the king, who found his support in the army and the clergy. Germany, the best instructed and the most orderly and laborious of European peoples, could not be called free. Where then does the reality of liberty lie? It lies, as he has indicated before, in the force of public opinion, in the quality of the directing class and, ultimately, in the firmness and strength of the ethical will illuminated by the idea of liberty. This is true of the liberal movement as a whole; its reality and truth lie in the strength of the ethical will and not in any programme or limited actualization in specific institutions which never can adequate the idea. In the midst, consequently, of this rapid extension of liberal institutions, he senses the actual weakening of liberalism. It was a weakening of the spirit, of the liberal faith, as he had called it, and was portentous for the future.[1]

In what did this weakening of the liberal movement consist? It resided in the fact that its practical activity was no longer joined with a lofty and clear understanding of the spiritual principle of that activity.[2] The ethical impulse was weakened, the capacity of ethical invention was lessened (a phenomenon he had noted with respect to the decadence of the baroque era);[3] the inner life of the conscience was mortified. Germany had been the 'philosophical Athens' of the

[1] SE'800, 310. [2] SE'800, 311.
[3] Cf. *supra* and specifically SEB, 43.

liberal movement; from philosophical romanticism, as he had indicated, liberalism had drawn its guiding ideas and above all the idea of liberty and of history as the history of liberty. It was expected, naturally enough, that her rise as a great national and political power would enhance this intellectual leadership; in fact, however, the manner in which that stature was achieved was anything but liberal in spirit, and her intellectual and spiritual leadership declined. She was the 'lost leader' of Browning's poem for the liberal cause. In the country of Kant and Hegel, positivism, with its narrow specialization of interests, initiated its reign, represented elsewhere by such men as Spencer and Ardigó. The theoretical defences and explorations of the idea of liberty which were undertaken were illiberal, empirical and superficial. This is Croce's judgment on the famous work of John Stuart Mill.[1] Nostalgic lamentations arose for the figures of the 'heroic age',[2] the Garibaldis, the Cavours, the Mazzinis and the Lincolns (for the American had caught the imagination of the Risorgimento), lamentations which constituted a calumny on the very able, though 'prosaic' men of the period. There was a dearth of poets, thinkers, and seers among the liberals; this could not be denied, and their place could not be filled by physicists, sociologists and naturalists. The loss of mental energy and courage, with consequent temptations to pessimism, was evidenced by a lack of resiliency in the face of inevitable change. The disillusionment with free trade was illogically transferred by some to ethical and political liberalism itself, a concept, obviously, of a higher order. Men were made doubtful and fearful by the apparent shortcomings in the concrete institutions of liberalism, the franchise, the party system, the parliamentary form. They did not reflect that such shortcomings inevitably manifest themselves in all historical structures, when these are measured by the ideal.[3]

The most baleful influence on the last decade of the nineteenth century was the Marxist doctrine of history and of the state. The career of Marxism had been chequered enough. About 1890, Croce notes, it achieved a European resonance. The Marxian doctrines, he recognized, performed a certain service in that they forced attention back to the fundamental issues of society. In themselves, however, whether in the economic or the political area, the specific Marxian theses could not hold their ground. In this context, Croce is speaking autobiographically, in a certain sense, for at this time he, too, had felt

[1] SE'800, 311.   [2] The phrase is that of Victor Emmanuel II; SI'71, 2.
[3] SE'800, 312 sqq.

the necessity of 'settling accounts with Marxism', that is, of facing up to its possible truth or error. One result had been the essays in *Dialectical Materialism and the Economics of Marxism*. The refutation of the Marxian theory of the falling rate of profit was recognized as definitive by Charles Andler, the editor of the *Communist Manifesto*. Another result had been Croce's confirmation in the ethical and spiritualistic romanticism and of which he discerned in the Marxian doctrine of historical materialism an illegitimate offspring. His refutation of the principal Marxist theses has remained one of the immovable barriers to an *intellectual* or *theoretical* Marxism in Italy.[1] Unable to sustain itself intellectually, Marxism still left a certain impression upon the times, principally the inclination to think of the active forces of history as 'economic classes' and to treat political problems as a conflict of the interests and forces of these classes. This inclination was, of course, directly against the liberal and ethical view of history and of the state as well, for this latter recognized the moving force of history in a 'directing class' moved by ethical ideals, the vehicle of the common conscience of society.

If, Croce concludes, this age, this liberal age, appears narrow and prosaic, this was due, not to the facts, but to the narrowness of vision which contemplated those facts. The impulse of the preceding age was still vital. It still possessed the power, in spirits rightly disposed, to rectify its own limitations and to press on to fuller accomplishment. But it was these spirits precisely which were lacking. It was an age when the spirit was weak, the ethical will depressed, and the social body, the body of European culture and society, disposed to consequent, but by no means immedicable, ills.

[1] Cf. the essay 'Come nacque e come morì il marxismo teoretico in Italia', printed as appendix to his edition of Labriola's *La concezione materialistica della storia*, Bari, 1947, pp. 267 sqq.

VI

FASCISM, THE DOUBLE

THE experience of Italy holds, for Croce, a special place in the history of Europe's 'liberal age', not for any chauvinistic reason but because it exhibits in a peculiarly heightened manner the features of that period, its strengths, its tensions, its ambiguities. The Risorgimento, the process of Italian liberation and national formation, had, by Croce's account, more nearly realized the liberal ideal than any similar movement of the century. Italy was the especial creation of the liberal spirit, its lyrical expression, in his own words, a poem. If utopian expectations might attach to the liberal idea in general, they might be expected to arise with peculiar force from the Italian experience. Should not Italy, with the occupation of Rome, with the establishment of the Eternal City as her capital, with the renewed echo of the Roman dictum 'Hic manebimus optime' have entered upon her golden age? The utopian expectations of liberalism, it has been seen, were explicitly rejected by Croce; they violated, in his view, the essentially ethical character of the liberal ideal and of the historical drama which it inspired. Yet it is not too much to say that though fortified against the future, not even he could have foreseen the actual career Italian life was to follow. The reference is, of course, to the emergence of the Fascist 'dictatorship' (the Italian associations of the term 'tyrant' are, perhaps, closer to the reality), from the midst of the purest creation of the liberal spirit in Europe.

Confronted with this phenomenon, the historian instinctively looks to its antecedents. But the antecedents of Fascism could lie only in the liberal age. The problem posits itself, precisely, succinctly. How was it possible that the Italy of the Risorgimento, admired through the length and breadth of Europe as 'libera e civile', could breed civil slavery, engender its own opposite, appear in the mirror of time as the demoniacally distorted double of itself? Does not the fact argue to the illusory character of the Italian liberal achievement? Did not the work of the Risorgimento, so solid in appearance, a veritable 'kateima eis eiei', stand revealed as the flimsiest of structures,

248

resting not on the solid ground of a universal liberal will, but upon the determination of a few, its heroes, with whose passing that structure must collapse? And was not the face of Fascism the face of the real forces, the real will, which lurked behind the liberal façade? Was it not possible that here, in the terminal fact of Fascism, and not in the liberal illusion, the public spirit of Italy is revealed? These, and other like questions, could not but crowd in upon the historian who, like Croce, undertook to contemplate and to narrate the history of Italy from the unification to the fourth decade of the twentieth century. Nor could the possibilities those questions suggested fail to arouse in him immediate and spontaneous protest. But spontaneity, he had long since decided, was the privilege of the artist, the poet; to the historian belong deliberation and judgment. His *History of Italy from 1871 to 1915* is the answer he offers to those questions, and it is a document remarkable not for lyricism but for the controlled passion with which it sifts the evidence on a problem to which its author as historian and as citizen is entirely committed.

Nor is the central idea of this history difficult to discern; on the contrary, it is limpidly apparent. The work proves in its most salient character to be a vindication of the Risorgimento and of the 'liberal age' which it opened. By the same token, it is an unequivocal refutation of fascism, and of the possibility that it, and not the liberal will, expressed the basic spirit of the Italian people. In his own words, fascism, on the evidence of history, could only be conceived as an 'adventure', as an historical 'sport', which proves nothing concerning the Italian spirit save that, like the human spirit everywhere and at all times, it is subject to ethical lapses. It cannot seriously be placed in the balance against the accumulated evidence of a century and more of the heroic and the sacrificial will of the Italian people to liberty and to civil life. At the same time, however, the sincerity of his historical judgment admonishes him that in a very real sense which he had long since recognized, history has no sports, the human spirit no adventures. Everything in history has its *raison d'être*. And if that *raison d'être* be in fact a lapse of the ethical will in an individual, a nation or a period, that too must be sought out and its specific quality determined and revealed. His history becomes, consequently, as well as the vindication of the 'liberal age' and a repudiation of fascism, an examination of conscience, in the name of the whole Italian nation, intended to fix that ethical and historical lapse of the liberal will, not for the purpose of morbid contemplation, but of spiritual purgation.

Croce's vindication of the 'liberal age' in Italy may be synthesized as his replies to the three major charges brought against it: it betrayed the Risorgimento, it was a prosaic age, innocent of positive historical achievement, it bred the seed of which Fascism was the logical and necessary fruit.

The feeling (for it is a feeling rather than a specific and reasonable accusation) that the liberal age was a betrayal of the Risorgimento had its origin, Croce believes, in the situation immediately after the unification, a situation, he notes, not without historical parallels. The liberation and unification of Italy had been a heroic effort, engaging the whole spiritual force of the Italian people and lifting them to a pitch of exaltation, which for its very intensity, must be rare in historical experience, associated only with undertakings of the greatest moment. That a nation should persist in this state of exaltation, of united effort, of spiritual fervour after the immediate object of that effort had been attained is hardly to be expected. On the contrary, a period of spiritual depression, of lassitude, of doubt and hesitancy must inevitably succeed. This is precisely what transpired in the case of Italy. A universal sentiment that an heroic age had passed, accompanied by nostalgia and by diffidence toward the future, descended upon the nation. The heroes were dead, the opportunity for heroic action past; nothing remained to be done. The future stretched bleakly before the new generation, filled with an endless succession of petty tasks which those who had known, even by association, the exaltation of the past could only disdain. It was the mood which Croce encountered in the house and, to a degree, in the person of Silvio Spaventa, his maternal uncle, when he took up residence with him in Rome in the early 1880's in order to pursue his university studies. Spaventa had first been active in 1848; he had participated in the enterprise of the Risorgimento in its final and decisive phase; he had known personally the enthusiasm and exaltation that movement had inspired. But now ennui, nostalgia, diffidence, cynicism filled his soul.[1]

This transformation of spirit, this 'betrayal of the Risorgimento' had become symbolized in the transference of political power from the liberal Right to the Left in the elections of 1876. The examination of this transfer constitutes for Croce the first link in the chain of arguments refuting that pretended betrayal. What, he demands, was its significance? The Risorgimento had been the work of the liberal Right. Did the transfer of power imply the undoing of its work, the abandonment of its political principles? Not, he concludes, if one

[1] Cf. CCMS in FPS, 1144 sq.; SE'800, 311 sq.; SI'71, 1 sqq., 133 sqq.

looks to the facts. On the contrary, in the light of the facts, that transfer meant the consolidation of the work of the Risorgimento and of the liberal Right, the continuance and the prosecution of its political concepts, adopted by the very men who had appeared in the election as its adversaries. The Right had stood for adherence to the monarchy as the bond of the new Italy with its past; the men of the Left, by tradition republicans, relinquished all republican aspiration to adhere in their turn to the throne. The Right had stood for a 'lay' state, that is a state without clerical dominance, resting upon universal principles of civil equity; the Left, not only took up this ideal but by diplomatic sincerity and finesse began to dissipate the aura of militant anti-clericalism which hung about it. The Right had stood for a strong state authority as a protection against all elements of reaction; the Left, if anything, was firmer, more resolute in this conviction than the Right itself. The Right had stood for a foreign policy at once wise and cautious, conducted wholly through diplomatic channels, repudiating all interference of irresponsible agents; the men of the Left, who had been Garibaldians and, consequently, exponents of the 'direct method', conducted a policy so cautious that it led to an alliance (which Italy was to repudiate with the World War) with the conservative powers of central Europe. Finally, the Right had taken as its principal objective, after unification, the consolidation of the financial and economic structure of the kingdom; the leader of the Left, on assuming office, announced this objective as the principal aim of his government. If, consequently, every portion of the work of the Left is passed in review, one will discern the principles of the Right at work. The parliamentary 'revolution' of 1876, consequently, could signify, not the betrayal, but only the continuation of the work of the Risorgimento and of the Right, the adaptation of its principles to new circumstances and new tasks.[1]

The prosaic character of the age, the absence of the poetry of national life, of great *imprese* would be a charge too trivial to elicit serious reply were it not also the kind of charge most damaging in many eyes. It is based, on the one hand, on the lingering contrast with the heroic age which had preceded it and, on the other, on lack of reflection, for reflection admonishes that every age has its own task. The task which confronted the new Italy was one of national consolidation. The work of unification, carried forward swiftly with sure inner logic enabled Italy to present a united front to the world; at the same time, it left in its wake an internal task of the greatest

[1] SI'71, 6-8.

importance and difficulty. For the great diversity of conditions, of interests and of tendencies, which had characterized the various portions of the country in its divided state could not be altered, resolved and reconciled at once. Even more, in the very course of unification explosive situations had been created which, some confidently predicted, would prove the undoing of the new nation. One of these, Croce notes, was the financial situation of the country; 'it was necessary to give the lie', he writes, 'to those both within and without Italy, who judged that though Italy had been aided (in the unification) by political ability and good fortune, it would be shipwrecked on the rocks of finance'.[1] This was as prosaic a task, to all appearances, as one might conceive, devoid of all appeal to the imagination or the emotions. Yet it was a task of the highest spiritual importance to the new nation. And Italy possessed men who were able to see the problem in this light, and to address it in a spirit inwardly no less heroic than that of the Risorgimento. Sella, Lanza, Minghetti, he believes, the men who achieved the financial consolidation of the kingdom, performed a prosaic task in an heroic spirit and enabled Italy to weather the first dangers of her new life.

The Risorgimento had been a liberal movement, the purest example of the liberal nationalist movement in Europe; but there remained after unification the task of establishing a liberal order in civil life. This again could only be a prosaic task when compared with the movement which had preceded it; yet without this achievement, that earlier must have remained without fruit. The decades after 1871 have to their imperishable credit both the quality and the extent of their accomplishment in this direction. True enough, despite centuries of division and oppression the Italians possessed a millennial tradition of civil life upon which they now could draw. This did not, however, lighten the specific tasks confronting them, the reform of the administration (or rather its creation), of the judicature and magistrature, the creation of an enlightened electorate. These tasks too, the post-Risorgimento generation accomplished, without fanfare, zealously and conscientiously. The 'social' question was more acute in Italy, perhaps, than anywhere else in Europe. To all appearances, the new nation offered a fertile field for revolutionary social reform movements. In this context, however, the strength of the liberal movement which had created Italy proved sufficient to meet the issue. The liberal conquest of the social movement, that is to say, the reduction of the social problem to its just status and the

[1] SI'71, 47.

application to its resolution of the procedures of liberty remains, in Croce's view, its greatest achievement after unification itself. The men of the Right, he notes,[1] were the first to recognize the social problem; they were not impeded by any uncritical identification of liberalism with economic liberalism despite the fact that some of the great figures of the Risorgimento had received the impress of the Manchester school.[2] This fact was itself sufficient to draw its revolutionary sting from social reform. In this, again, the continuity of the Left with the Right which it succeeded in political power was evident. Minghetti had in his youth received the impress of Sismondi's criticism of economic liberalism and now asserted that the liberal state 'had courageously to take the initiative in all reforms', becoming thus an exponent of 'transformism'.[3] Berti, as minister of agriculture under Depretis, laid out a plan of social legislation which received the support of Depretis as well as of Crispi. Sonnino and Franchetti gave special attention to the knotty 'southern question', perhaps the most extreme of the social issues confronting the age. Social reforms of a more technical and restricted nature were multiplied; social insurance for the aged and those injured at work, restriction of child and woman labour, the juridical recognition of societies for mutual aid. And Croce notes, as a sign of the health of these sentiments, the social questions occupied the artistic consciousness as well, finding expression in the powerful works of Verga, Serao, Patini and Dorsi.[4] Lest these reforms appear, as well they might, to have the character of mere 'adjustments' and 'accommodations', Croce points out that the logic of liberalism implied the constant extension of the social basis of the state; and that such extension necessarily implied the resolution of all the problems, sometimes so diverse, grouped under the epithet social. Consequently, the new liberal Italy was committed to the resolution of these questions in the spirit of liberty by her own historical principle and was not led to their consideration by external pressures. In this also, therefore, the liberal age shows its continuity with the logic of the Risorgimento. The civil education of the people, as preparation for entrance into the full life of the citizen, necessarily involved the resolution of social problems.

[1] SI'71, 80.
[2] Cf. G. de Ruggiero, *History of European Liberalism*, ed. cit., p. 10.
[3] Minghetti, M., *Attinenze della economia politica con la morale e il diritto*; cited by Croce, SI'71, 80.
[4] SI'71, 82–3.

A civil consciousness of this character could find support only in a quick and sensitive life of the spirit, and the evidences of such life readily multiply in the liberal age. A reform movement in education led by Manzoni and De Sanctis had, during the period of the Risorgimento itself, sought to strip Italian intellectual life of its traditional rhetoricism, and to substitute ideal of simplicity and sincerity. Of this movement, the *History of Italian Literature* of De Sanctis, when compared, for example, with the earlier work of Tiraboschi offers a clear example. This work was taken up and extended, and prepared the ground for a general purification of taste which rendered the classic works of that literature available and comprehensible as perhaps never before. In scientific research, a new austerity was apparent, cold to all facile generalizations, faithful to the study of fact and document. This referred not only to the so-called 'natural' sciences but even more to historical studies. A new periodical literature inspired by a similar spirit aided in the popularization of both the content and the discipline of higher studies. More important than these, however, though dependent upon them, was the formation of a common Italian life, that is to say, the overcoming of regional differences, within which the various areas of the land had remained closed. This common cultural life at once drew strength from and lent strength to the political life of the new kingdom. Apart from a common language and literature the state was the only matrix within which such a common life might develop; at the same time the creation of that common life was the sole guarantee of the stability of the new political unity. The manner in which this transformation was accomplished can only be appreciated by direct contact with Italian life. While the richness of variety remained, a new spirit of unity and communion arose, so that it was possible for the first time since the Roman empire to speak of Italy as one in spirit and in fact. The reduction of regional differences was accompanied by an analogous reduction of class tensions; this too was in the logic of an ethical liberalism, which could only thrive if all classes co-operated in the work of the state. Even in respect to the severe trauma which had appeared in Italian life as a result of the 'Roman question' great improvement took place. That trauma had consisted in the alienation of a vast portion of the Italian people from the life of the new state and it could not in the nature of things endure. Nor did it endure; for the passing decades witnessed the return, not only of the Catholic laity, but even of the clergy to public life. This was an immeasurable gain, and was provided for in the logic of liberalism. The liberal state provided a framework within which all groups could co-operate for a common purpose without the suppression of real diversity and without recourse to means of violent contrast. In all, the period presents to the historian a panorama of modest but positive and persistent work and improvement, sufficient to guarantee the civil and liberal character of the new nation and to refute any charge of prosaicness and negativity.[1]

This positive achievement of the liberal age in Italy would seem, at first glance, to offer substantial refutation of the charge that this period harboured the living seed of Fascism. The fact of Fascism, however, diverts the potential force of this argument. In order to exonerate the liberal age completely it would seem to be necessary to deny the continuity of Italian national life. This Croce seems to have been tempted to do, in calling Fascism an 'adventure'; such an 'adventure' would necessarily appear as a deviation from the line of continuity. This is not Croce's final attitude, however. He is sensitive to the fact that this characterization of Fascism is weak; that even if true it would not excuse the historian or the citizen from rendering an account of that phenomenon. This is precisely what he seeks to do, and this account constitutes a serious modification, if not the complete abandonment of the 'adventure' theory of Fascism. Croce's considered opinion is complex and completely consonant with his liberal theory. The seeds of Fascism, its conditions, the attitudes favouring its emergence, do not however constitute the central effort of that period; that lies indubitably with the positive achievement he has recorded. Nor did these conditions imply any necessary development such as Fascism. The latter could only appear as a free choice reflecting those conditions. For this reason, while condemning Fascism in a matchless criticism extending over three decades, Croce never exonerates either the Italian people or himself from the fact of Fascism. On the contrary, he assumes a just share of responsibility for it and with this responsibility the obligation of ethical rectification as historical circumstances might permit. His position is summarized concretely in his attitude toward the person of the King after the debacle of 1943; Mussolini he could dismiss a 'provero diavolo' seeking his own fortune; but the King could not escape so lightly, for he had been educated in the liberal tradition of his ancestors and had ruled over an Italy 'libera e civile'.[2] It is also reflected brilliantly in the course of action he undertook after the collapse of Fascism and during the trying

[1] SI'71 passim.   [2] Cf. *Per la nuova vita d'Italia*, Napoli, 1944, pp. 31, 20-9; cf. also *Pagine Sparse*, Napoli, 1948, I, 72 sqq.

period of readjustment; it was the course of action of one who felt the full weight of historical responsibility.[1] In what then did these predisposing, though by no means necessitating attitudes and conditions consist?

Despite the definitive character of the Risorgimento, its historical irreversibility, and despite the indubitable liberal achievement of the post-Risorgimento generation, the liberal age was laced with a strain of self-doubt. Croce had come into personal contact with this mood of self-question, it has been noted, during his first stay in Rome. It preoccupied him from that moment and became the object of much scrutiny and analysis. If ever an historical movement might be traced to clear ideals animating the wills of men of strong personality, the Risorgimento would seem to be that movement. Scarcely, however, had that achievement been realized, when a tone of diffidence appeared in Italian life: that achievement was due more to 'fortune' than to the virtue of the leaders and the people.[2] After the positive work of that age had progressed to the point where Italy could now speak of herself as a nation in the fullest sense of the term, possessing not only an external unity vis-à-vis the other nations of Europe but an internal structure and order able to sustain that external unity, internal criticism, sometimes sharp and bitter, arose among the very groups which had contributed most to that achievement. The poverty of the economic resources of the country were felt with new acuteness. The cultural deficiencies: illiteracy, widespread and obstinate, the persistence of 'secret' societies within the national structure, with a strong hold over the agricultural classes, the high criminal rate, the lassitude of large sections of the population toward political life, all of these were felt with greater keenness and conspired to strengthen the mood of doubt.[3] Especially discouraging was the response in general to the new opportunities for participation in public life opened by such liberal projects as the expansion of the electorate. The party and parliamentary systems, which had appeared vigorous and effective in the first decade of unification, seemed rapidly to decline, to degenerate into conflict of narrow and partisan interests. Together, these circumstances conspired to arouse the suspicion that the Italians did not possess the capacity for parliamentary life and self-rule.[4] There began the process, not uncommon in history, of denigrating the very heroes of the Risorgimento, especially those who, like Garibaldi, lived on into the new age but added nothing to their

[1] Cf. *Quando L' Italia era tagliata in due*, Bari ,1948, *passim*.   [2] SI'71, 29.
[3] SI'71, 100-1.   [4] SI'71, 101.

stature by their new attitudes and enterprises.[1] To all this was added the scandals of the present, the vindicativeness of the policy of Nicotera, the revelations of private and public corruption under Crispi and De Pretis, the conversion of the chamber of deputies, by this latter, into a vast 'provincial council'. Spaventa—the same Spaventa with whom Croce had taken up his first Roman residence —voiced the opinion of a wide and restless group when he wrote that the level of government is daily debased, falling more and more below the mean of the governments and civil administrations of the rest of Europe.[2]

This contrast with other nations was itself a dangerous symptom indicating the uncertainty and festering sense of inferiority and inducing false evaluations of foreign institutions. Thus there arose a wave of adulation for the German national achievement and for the internal prosperity and the external aggrandizement which that nation enjoyed. This adulation indicated clearly that the Italians had to a great extent lost sight of that qualitative difference between their own national achievement and that of Germany, a difference which Croce has taken great pains to emphasize. The qualitative superiority of the Italian achievement, from the liberal point of view, made such adulation an act of self-abasement without historical or ethical justification. The characteristics of Germany which marked her qualitative inferiority were precisely those selected for admiration: efficiency, aggressiveness, forcefulness, ruthlessness. Her tremendous material advance, compared with the poverty and technical ineptitude of Italy, heightened the contrast.[3] Closely associated with this adulation of Germany, and suggested by German 'scholarship' itself in great part, was an anti-Latin bias which suggested that the Italians were a people who long since had 'spoken their piece' in history, an old and decrepit people, little attuned to the movement of modern life. It was suggested, and this in the face of the history of Roman law, that liberty was born in the forests of Germany, that only the Germanic peoples might truly be free. Subjection was the natural lot of the Latin peoples, subjection to the Church in the spiritual order and to the institutions of absolute government in the political. The prepotence of German science and historiography intimidated the intellectuals of Italy; they lost the power to examine these claims calmly and critically, to pierce the veil of pedantic demagogy and chauvinism which surrounded them, to appreciate the irony that they should emanate from the people whose modern political formation was,

[1] SI'71, 102.   [2] SI'71, 103.   [3] SI'71, 104.

with the exception of Russia, the least liberal, the least enlightened of any people in Europe. And the diffidence and the pessimism of the intellectuals inevitably seeped down to the wider circles of opinion, to foster the common sentiment that the Italians were an aged race whose only possession was the past and whose future was without promise. In vain certain calmer minds sought to combat this pessimism, pointing out the spiritual and qualitative superiority of the Italian national achievement, reminding Italy that rather than old and decrepit, she was young, that her ills were not those of age but of adolescence, especially in regard to the institutions of liberal government, that, as a matter of fact, her life was wholly in the future.[1]

His purpose has been to throw into relief the positive tone and the positive achievement of the liberal age in Italy; yet under one aspect Croce does not hesitate to apply the term 'decadent' to this age. He had examined this concept at length in another context;[2] and had fixed its essentially ethical connotation. It is in this same sense that he now invokes it anew. The decadence of the liberal age was a crisis of faith and of ethical ideals, 'si assommava in una crisi di fede e d'ideali etici'.[3] More specifically, it was a decadence, a crisis of faith in the ethical and political ideals of liberty, rooted in a weakening of the theoretical and moral justification of those ideals. The philosophical root of the modern idea of liberty, in Croce's view, was the modern concept of history, the product of philosophical romanticism.[4] Historicism in turn, in his view, was the culmination of a millennial European experience passing through the successive phases of humanism, rationalism, criticism and the dialectic.[5] Precisely this current, however, at end-century, found itself impeded by materialism, whether scientific or historical, but even more by naturalistic agnosticism. As a result of the logic of naturalism, human values, ideas and ideals were denied all justification; will, faith, love, goodness, beauty, the very desire for God were treated as facts of psychological associations, sometimes stigmatized as pathological. For the naturalistic vision there no longer existed man in his true and integral character, in which the opposition of body and spirit is resolved, but man wholly 'animalized', whose occasional illusions of generous impulse and sublime vision were demonstrated to be the effects of nervous disturbances. Naturalism came to Italy tardily and met with firm opposition especially in the south where spiritualistic and idealistic traditions were very strong. But even here, that resist-

[1] SI'71, 106 sqq. [2] Cf. *supra*. [3] SI'71, 133.
[4] Cf. *supra*. [5] SI'71, 134.

ance was not able to turn back the new tide and to re-establish and vindicate the older claims. Symptomatic were the rapid spread of the reputation and influence of Herbert Spencer, and his English and French disciples; the pervasive influence of Bismarckian Germany, all philology, technology and scientism, on the Italian educational establishment; the elaboration of a positivism more rigid than its models by an Italian, Ardigó, and its rapid dissemination.[1] To ascribe to philosophy so principal an efficiency in social life, Croce notes, may appear extravagant to some; but this, he believes, is the place due it, and the consequences of the philosophical decline are visible in every dimension of intellectual and public life. He notes its effect on historiography which descended to the level of mere erudition, after a civil tradition extending from Giannone to Troya; in the theory of art, which from the achievements of Vico and the spiritualist school, now descended to the psychological and socio-logical and even physical analysis of the creative process and the work of art; on educational theory which, setting aside spiritual and ethical values, was filled with technical and scientific concerns; in political theory, where the loss of philosophical insight suspended judgment in the apparent dilemma of liberalism: the crisis of its contemporary institutions and the impossibility of substituting for them institutions of any other provenance without a manifest loss of ethical ideality; in the quality of university life which, from philosophical and speculative, now became all professional and technical; and above all in literature and art, especially the literature and art of amenity or diversion, which has by far the widest resonance in the public mind.[2] Literature and art became infected with the spirit of naturalism, under the rubric of 'verism'; so seductive did this poetic 'experiment' prove that even an artist of Verga's stature could not resist it entirely.

With respect to all this Croce's thesis is clear: a political and social order, a nation, is only as strong as its ideal and ethical faith. With the decline of these, the avenue is open to any eventualities. The specific crisis in the liberal age was, paradoxically perhaps, a crisis in the faith and the ethical ideals of liberalism itself. As a consequence, the avenue lay open to deviation from the liberal norm and the liberal programme in any number of forms. At the same time, however, he insists that there is no necessity driving the nation down this avenue. The remedy for loss of faith is in the ethical will itself.

[1] SI'71, 134–7.
[2] For these concepts in Croce and his view of the social resonances of literature cf. SI'71, 145–6, *Poesia*, 31 sqq.

Consequently, loss of faith is itself a free act, and the excursion into any deviation from ethical ideality is itself a free choice. Fascism lay at the end of one of these beckoning avenues; but there was no force driving the Italian nation to that goal. A lapse of liberal faith explains, but did not necessitate it. Experimentation is characteristic of moments of ethical depression; in Italy this experimentation took many forms even before Fascism; experimentations in authoritarian government, as of 1896-7 (quickly overcome by the native vitality of the liberal establishment), in colonial adventure, in activism, in verism, in moral gigantism, all of which may be construed as proto-types of the Fascist 'adventure'.

Since the remedy of ethical depression lies in the ethical will itself, as Croce has indicated, the evidence of this self-renewal of the Italian spirit is of the greatest moment. Nor is this evidence lacking. The period of 1901-14, the period of deepest liberal crisis, saw a strong movement of spiritual and cultural revival. In narrating the course of this revival, Croce cannot entirely escape the autobiographical tone for he was, after all, one of its moving spirits. This revival took the form of a frontal attack on positivism and even more importantly of an attempt to make fresh contact with the sources of the spiritual and intellectual life. It was an attempt to enclose the positivist phase in an iron parenthesis. This renewal manifested itself in both the speculative and the practical areas. The restoration of the claims of philosophy against the encroachments of scientism was especially forceful; the purification of literary and artistic taste, the restoration of historical studies, the spiritualization of education were among its other objectives. In the practical order, it set about combating all those extravagant attitudes which were suggested by the influences of irrationalistic scientism: the new cult of force and action, the new adulation of authority and 'leadership', the whole movement called 'activism' with its many complex elements ranging from sorelian violence to dannunzian sensualism, egotism and gigantism. Above all, it set as its objective the resuscitation of the liberal faith itself, not dogmatically, but critically, by a re-examination of its philosophical and historical bases, its disengagement from transitive historical concretions and associations and its reorientation toward the future, not under the term of a fatuous élan, a vacuous 'futurism', but of a restatement of the ethical character of history itself and its dependence upon the ethical will, whose central dimension is always the future, the real area of action.[1]

[1] SI'71, cap. X, *passim*.

The claims of this renewal are as strong as its features are incisive. Historically, however, the one and the other are overshadowed by the fact of Fascism. The question arises peremptorily, therefore: Why did this movement lack the force to forestall that development? Croce's answer is complex and circumstantial, as the situation necessitates. At the theoretical level, little responsibility, from his point of view, can be imputed to liberalism. This period saw a fresh clarification of the theory and concept of liberty in all of its dimensions; as to its constitutive principles: spirituality and creativity of the human spirit, as to its ethical character as the form of human wisdom, as to its political and economic ramifications, as to its modes of expression in art and in custom, its relation to law and to language. Particularly, the fatal conjunction between the idea of liberty as a philosophical concept and a moral ideal and the basic assumptions of 'economic liberalism' or 'liberism' had been resolved. At the same time, in the practical order, he notes, liberalism in Italy, as largely elsewhere, had fallen into a too complacent identification of its own principles with the institutional forms it had created, an over-readiness to assume that these forms definitively realized its idea and that they were, in a sense, endowed with an immanent dynamism which could function independently of a constantly vigilant ethical conscience and will. This complacency is easy to understand but, in its consequences, difficult to condone. The liberal idea and the ethical will which can sustain it in practice are intrinsically independent of the concrete institutions they generate historically. This is not to say that the liberal spirit may with indifference generate such institutions or not; on the contrary, they are existential imperatives. Nor is it to say that it is indifferent to the institutions through which it achieves historical existence, as though it could inform indifferently institutions qualitatively diverse.[1] Certain institutions possess a transcendental affinity to the liberal spirit; thus, for example, the parliamentary structure in legislation, the free press, etc. At the same time, however, he recognizes that the liberal idea and spirit transcend these very forms which it generates and for which it has a transcendent affinity, in the sense that it can never become substantially identified with them in their historical character.[2] It must maintain this independence which,

[1] Croce had criticized this 'indifferentism' in the policy of the Catholic Church toward political forms since the Counter Reformation, SEB, c. 3, *passim*.

[2] He has already pointed out this independence of the juridical structure and the ethical quality of political will in the controversy with Cenni over the history of Naples. Cf. *supra, sub nomine*.

concretely, takes the form of a constant inward criticism by liberalism of its own institutional creations, guided by a vigilant ethical will. It was this criticism within liberalism which became dormant in the very course of the liberal age. And again, Croce is wont to impugn, in a mood of self-examination, the over-confidence of liberal elements in the power of the liberal idea and the liberal movement to domesticate movements counter to it in spirit. The shining example of this had been, of course, socialism.[1] Liberalism had drawn the sting of antistatist and revolutionary socialism by demonstrating in principle and in fact that the aims of socialism were well within the scope of the ethical will of the liberal state and that those aims were best insured by the liberal procedures. Toward alternative forces which arose to dispute its path, liberalism could scarcely be expected to take a less confident view of its own assimilative and rectifying powers, especially as few of these alternatives exhibited the force of the socialist idea. Specifically, with respect to a return to authoritarian forms, the easy ascendency of the liberal movement over the recrudescence of authoritarianism in Italy during the social crisis of 1896 tended to justify this confidence.[2] In the turmoil of forces and ideas after the World War, this confidence which had arisen with regard to a movement of the left was readily extended to a movement of the 'right' such as Fascism was interpreted to be, as it actually was in 1920. The emergence of such a movement might provide a healthy tension within a state whose liberal tradition and will had been strong enough to domesticate socialism. This was Croce's personal stand by his own account.

In the final analysis, however, no accumulation of circumstances, however well it might illuminate the process by which a countermovement such as Fascism might have arisen, can establish a causal and necessary nexus between it and the liberal movement. The weakening of the ethical will and the critical vigilance of liberalism and the emergence of that countermovement remain only contingently related. Such a contingency is indeed foreseen by liberal theory. For that theory is completely innocent of utopian overtones. It contemplates, as inexorably implied in the character of history as ethical struggle, the dialectic of ethical wills of diverse quality and

[1] The neo-communism of post-war Russia and the west necessarily appeared to Croce anachronistic, a product quite directly of that cultural lag which he had noted between Russia and the west. SE'800, 82-3, 113-14, 188-90, 214-15, 235, 238, 276-9, 356-8.

[2] Cf. SI'71, 207 sqq.

a consequent modification of the historical quality of human institutions. For this reason, his original judgment that Fascism must, from the liberal point of view, be considered an 'adventure', a 'sport', received fresh vindication, and expresses a solid insight. The liberal spirit, reviewing the recent past, can impute to itself its proper faults, whatever these may be; it is, however, laid under no compulsion to assume responsibility for the alternatives of history. These alternatives are implicit in the nature of historical movement. The only meaningful self-criticism can be a renewal of the spirit,[1] and a fresh seizure of opportunities for historical action.

[1] Cf. the address to the re-established Liberal party in FPS, 1073.

VII

LIBERALISM AND INTERNATIONALISM

THE Italian experience could by no means be considered anomalous; on the contrary, its value lay in the fact that it was typical of European experience. In this wider theatre its correlative is the anarchy at the level of international relations. Croce had recognized that historically and ideally a unified Europe was implicit in the liberal ideal. The national movement of liberalism during the nineteenth century was, in his view, in no wise counter to this ideal. On the contrary, it was a preparatory movement toward its realization. For any unification of Europe must rest, in his view, not upon an abstract, but upon a concrete homogeneity; a homogeneity which at the same time rests upon the wide and wholly desirable diversities reflected in the national structures. This concrete homogeneity ideally might consist in the realization of a common ideal and spirit within the diverse contexts of national cultural and political forms. The liberal idea was such a principle of concrete homogeneity in diversity precisely because of its ethical quality. The idea of liberty being not metaphysical and abstract but concrete and historical had naturally to find its existential realization in diverse historical structures. In this very process, it was laying the foundations for a higher synthesis of international life, which would rest upon that concrete homogeneity, the diverse realization of the liberal idea in the institutions of the various nations.[1]

The ideal of a 'United States of Europe' had been firmly grasped at mid-century as, for example, in the thought of Mazzini, and it seemed implicit in the logic of events, the unification of Italy, the national formation of Germany, the dissolution of the Austrian empire, the independence of Poland, the modernization and Europeanization of Russia. Obstacles soon presented themselves, however. The chief was a development clearly not implicit in the ideal and the logic of liberalism, that of nationalistic imperialism. This movement replaced the idea of expanding co-operation congenial to

---

[1] SE'800, 319 sqq.

liberalism with the idea, historically and theoretically obsolete, of hegemony.

At first appearance, consequently, liberalism seemed in conflict with its own logic. On closer examination, however, this conflict proves unreal. For the seats of nationalistic imperialism proved to be precisely those countries in which the liberal spirit had laboured under the shadow of certain ambiguities, Germany and England.[1] England presented the strange picture of a nation in which a strong liberal tradition and establishment were intimately associated with imperialism. Indeed, it would appear, the growth of liberal institutions at home had rested upon imperialistic policy abroad with respect to colonies and to allies as well. English liberalism was a product not for exportation or for very limited exportation only. This was an ambiguity whose consequences history alone could reveal, as it has done, in the course of the twentieth century. For England has found herself placed in a progressively more equivocal and compromising position, as this century has advanced: her historical status as the champion of liberalism in ever more exasperated conflict with her colonial policy as the tensions of two great wars put their strain upon the imperial structure. Germany, on the other hand, had revealed the anti-liberal character of her governing principles in the very process of her national formation. Imperialism was implicit in that process and this fact was the chief reason why it could not, by any stretch of the imagination, be identified as liberal in spirit. Hegemony was the principle of German consolidation; it was the principle of the conflict with France.

Any attempt, consequently, to characterize the international conflicts which mark the twentieth century as a sign of liberal failure, must be rejected. Here again it is a matter of the conflict of ethical wills of diverse quality. The liberal ethical will in Europe did not prove, *ipsis rebus dictantibus*, strong enough to bring about the pattern of international co-operation which was implicit in its idea. This is quite another thing, however, from placing upon it responsibility for the historical development of an alternative idea, which in turn rested upon an ethical will for its realization. The national imperial conflicts arose from the presence within European life of elements which the liberal spirit had never, or only partially, informed.

The full expression of the national imperialist will was the first World War. In the same conflict the alienation of that will from the

[1] SE'800, 324.

liberal will stood revealed. Indeed, the logic of the liberal idea, international co-operation resting upon concrete homogeneity, an internal development of institutions informed by a common liberal idea and well expressing itself in the specific qualitative circumstances of national life, was vindicated completely. That it remains but a desideratum far from realization testifies only to the co-existence of conflicting ethical wills of diverse quality. But this in turn is but to underline, from Croce's point of view, the basic structure of human history. A unified Europe, or a unified world, informed by the liberal spirit, would necessarily be a delicate structure, to be maintained only by a moral vigilance, directed against alternate wills of diverse quality and predicated on their existence. Such a unity would be completely free from utopian illusions, as must every historical structure of liberal provenance.

APPENDIX A

REFERENCES

Principal relevant works of Benedetto Croce are cited under the following symbols and in the following editions. Other titles are cited as occasion demands. The publisher is Laterza of Bari, unless otherwise noted.

RN'99: La Rivoluzione Napoletana del 1799. Biografie, racconti, ricerche, 5a ed., 1948.

Teatri: I Teatri di Napoli dal Rinascimento alla Fine del Secolo.

TH: XVIII, 4a ed., 1947.

SVI: La Spagna nella vita Italiana durante la Rinascenza, 4a ed., 1949.

FPC: Filosofia, Poesia, Storia Ricciardi Milano-Napoli, 1951.

CCMS: Contributo alla Critica di Me Stesso (in FPS).

SRN: Storia del Regno di Napoli, 3a ed., 1944.

SI'71: Storia d'Italia dal 1871 al 1915, 9a ed., 1948.

SE'800: Storia d'Europa nel secolo XIX, 7a ed., 1948.

SEB: Storia dell'Età Barocca in Italia, 2a ed., 1946.

NN: Napoli Nobilissima (1892–1906; 1920–23).

ASPN: Archivio Storico per le Provincie Napoletane.

Crit.: La Critica (I–XLII, 1903–44).

QC: Quaderni della Critica (1945–52).

Est.: Estetica come Scienza dell'Espressione e Linguistica Generale, 9a ed., 1950.

Logica: Logica come Scienza del Concetto Puro, 7a ed., 1947.

Pratica: Filosofia della Pratica, Economica ed Etica, 6a ed., 1950.

TSS: Teoria e Storia della Storiografia, 6a ed., 1948.

VAFP: Vite di Avventure, di Fede e di Passione, 2a ed., 1947.

UCVI: Uomini e Cose della Vecchia Italia, 2 v., 2a ed., 1943.

AVL: Aneddoti di Varia Letteratura Ricciardi Napoli, 1942.

LI'700: La Letteratura Italiana del '700, 1949.

NSLI'600: Nuovi Saggi Sulla Letteratura Italiana del Seicento, 2a ed., 1949.

REFERENCES

SLI'600:   Saggi sulla Letteratura Italiana del Seicento, 3a ed., 1948.
SLN: Storia e Leggende Napoletane, 4a ed., 1948.
PS: Primi Saggi, 2a ed., 1927.
SH: Saggio sullo Hegel seguito da altri scritti di storia della
            Filosofia, 4a ed., 1948.
Et. Pol.:   Etica e Politica, 3a ed., 1945.
UFP: Una Famiglia di Patrioti, 3a ed., 1949.
Con. Crit.: Conversazioni Critiche 1a, 2a serie, 4a ed., 1950; 3a, 4a
            serie, 1932; 5a serie, 1939.
SPA: La Storia come Pensiero e come Azione, 4a ed., 1943.
CFM: Il Carattere della Filosofia Moderna, 2a ed., 1945.
Poesia: La Poesia, 4a ed., 1946.
DVF: Discorsi di Varia Filosofia, 2v., 1945.

APPENDIX B

BIBLIOGRAPHY

Note: The following list of books and articles represents only titles which have been useful for the present study. Extensive bibliographies concerning Croce's life and works are available in: *Bibliografia filosofica italiana dal 1900 al 1950* (Rome, Delfino, 1950), and Francesco Flora (ed.): *Benedetto Croce* (Milan, Malfasi, 1953). A definitive bibliography is in preparation under the care of the Associates of the Italian Institute for Historical Studies in Naples.

I. BOOKS

ABBAGNANO, N., *et alii: Il problema della storia*, Milan, Bocca, 1944.

ANTONI, C. (ed.): *Cinquant' anni di vita intelletuale italiana*, Naples, Edizioni Scientifiche Italiane, 1950, 2v.

et alii: Omaggio a Benedetto Croce, Edizioni Radio Italiane, 1953.

Considerazioni su Hegel e Marx, Naples, Ricciardi, 1946.

Dallo storicismo alla sociologia, Florence, Sansoni, 1940.

BATTAGLIA, F.: *Il valore della storia*, Bologna, Zaffi, 1948.

BONTADINI, G.: *Dall' attualismo al problematicismo*, Brescia, La Scuola, 1947.

BRUENELLO, B.: *Il pensiero politico italiano dal Romagnosi al Croce*, Bologna, Zaffi, 1949.

CALOGERO, G.: *Studi crociani*, Rieti, 1930.

Estetica, Semantica, Istorica, Turin, Einaudi, 1943.

La conclusione della filosofia del conoscere, Florence, Le Monnier, 1938.

CARR, H. W.: *The Philosophy of Benedetto Croce*, London, Macmillan, 1917.

CIARDO, M.: *Le quattro epoche dello storicismo*, Bari, Laterza, 1947.

CIONE, E.: *Benedetto Croce*, Milan, Perinetti-Casoni, 1944.

COLLINGWOOD, R.: *The Philisophy of History*, London, 1930.

The Idea of History, London, 1946.

CORSI, M.: *Le origini del pensiero di B. Croce*, Florence, La Nuova Italia, 1951.

DE RUGGIERO, G.: *Il ritorno alla ragione*, Bari, Laterza, 1946.

FLORA, F. (ed.): *Benedetto Croce*, Milan, Malfasi, 1953.

FRANCHINI, R.: *Esperienza dello storicismo*, Naples, Giannini, 1953.

GRAMSCI, A.: *Il materialismo storico e la filosofia di B. Croce*, Turin, Einaudi, 1949.

LOMBARDI, A.: *La filosofia di Benedetto Croce*, Rome, Bardi, 1946.

MAUTINO, A.: *La formazione della filosofia politica di B. Croce*, Turin, 1941.

MENDELBAUM, M.: *The Problem of Historical Knowledge*, New York, Liveright, 1938.

MUELLER, F.-L.: *La pensée contemporaine en Italie*, Geneva, 1941.

NICOLINI, F.: *Benedetto Croce: vita intelletuale*, Naples, Cacciavillani, 1944.

PETRUZELLIS, N.: *Il problema della storia nell'idealismo moderno*, 2a ed., Florence, Sansoni, 1940.

SCHMITT, B. (ed.): *Some Historians of Modern Europe*, Chicago, University Press, 1942.

SPRIGGE, C.: *Benedetto Croce*, Cambridge, Bowes and Bowes, 1952.

TROELTSCHE, E.: *Der Historismus und seine Probleme*, Tübingen, Mohr, 1922.

II. ARTICLES

ALFIERI, V. E.: 'I presuppositi filosofici del liberalismo crociano', *La Rassegna d'Italia*, Feb.-Mar. 1946.

ANTONI, C.: 'Croce historien et philosophe de la liberté', *Preuves*, Paris, Dec. 1952.

'Die Flucht vor der Freiheit', *Ordo*, Zurich, 1950, 272–9.

'La dottrina dialettica della storia', *Nuova Antologia*, Jan. 1948, 46–57.

ARANGIO-RUIZ, V.: 'Dialettica delle distinzioni e dialettica delle opposizioni', *Annali della scuola normale di Pisa*, 1941, fasc. 1–2.

'Concetto moderno della storia', *Leonardo*, April 1950.

BARBAGALLO, C.: 'Storia e storiografia nel pensiero di B.C.', *Nuova Rivista Storica*, 1920, n. 6.

BATTAGLIA, F.: 'Il problema storiografico secondo il Croce', *Rivista storica italiana*, 1939, n. 3.

BOBBIO, N.: 'Croce e la politica della cultura', *Rivista di filosofia*, 1953, 252 et seq.

BONFANTINI, M.: 'Per una storia d'Italia dal 1871 al 1915: le premesse e l'equivoco crociano', *Società nuovo*, 1945.

BOUGIN, G.: 'B. Croce', *Revue Historique*, April–June 1953.

BRAMSTEDT, E. K.: 'Croce and the Philosophy of History', *Contemporary Review*, Nov. 1945.

CALOGERO, G.: 'Intorno al saggio del Croce: Giudizio storico e azione morale', *Archivio di filosofia*, XI (1949).

CAPONIGRI, A. R.: 'Ethical and Sociological Bases of Italian Politics', *Ethics*, Oct. 1948.

'Italian Philosophy: 1943–1950', *Philosophy and Phenomenological Research*, July 1951.

CHABOD, F.: 'Croce storico', *Rivista storica italiana*, LXIV (1953), fasc. 4.

CHAIX-RUY, J.: 'Benedetto Croce', *Revue de la Meditéranée*, Algiers, n. 52, 1952.

'L'historicisme absolu de B.Croce', *Revue Philosophique*, June 1950.

CHIAROMONTE, N.: 'Croce and Italian Liberalism', *Politics*, June 1945.

COMOTH, R.: 'L'humanisme de B. Croce', *Revue de Culture Européenne*, III (1953), n. 5.

DE NEGRI, E.: 'Per un' interpretazione del pensiero crociano', *Civiltà Moderna*, 1929, n. 4; 1930, nn. 1–2.

FRANCHINI, R.: 'Idealismo e storicismo', *Atti dell' Accademia Pontaniana*, II (1949), n. 2.

'Conoscere e fare nel secondo tempo dello storicismo crociano', *Historica*, I (1949).

FRANK, N.: 'La pensée de B. Croce', *Mercure de France*, 1 May 1953.

GENTILE, G.: 'I primi scritti di B. C. sul concetto della storia', *Frammenti di estetica*, Lanciano Carabba, 1921.

'Storicismo e storicismo', Annali della scuola normale di Pisa, 1942; reprinted in *Il problema della storia*, Milan, Bocca, 1944.

'La distinzione crociana di pensiero e azione', *Giornale critico della filosofia italiana*, 1941, n. 3.

GILBERT, K.: 'The Vital Disequilibrium in Croce's Historicism', in *Essays in Political Theory*, Konvitz, M., and Murphy, A. (eds.), Ithaca, Cornell University Press, 1948.

GOFFREDO, A.: 'La storia nella filosofia di B. C.', *Rivista di filosofia neoscolastica*, 1927, n. 6.

GOULAY, G.: 'B. Croce philosophe et historien', *Suisse contemporaine*, Lausanne, May 1946.

GUZZO, A.: 'Il pensiero e l'opera di B. Croce', *Filosofia*, IV (1953).

La Fiera Letteraria, Rome, 15 Feb. 1953—special issue in honour of Benedetto Croce.

La Rassegna d'Italia, 1946, nn. 2–3, Feb.–Mar.—issue dedicated to Benedetto Croce on occasion of his 80th year.

LEMEERE, J.: 'Benedetto Croce', *Revue Internationale de Philosophie*, VII (1952), n. 21.

'B. Croce philosophe de la liberté', *Synthèses*, VIII (1953), 325–32.

MASNOVO, A.: 'Storia e storiografia nel pensiero di B. C.', *Nuova rivista storica*, 1920, n. 6.

MATURI, W.: 'Rileggendo la *Storia d'Italia* di B. C.', *Cultura moderna*, Dec. 1952.

MEGARO, G.: 'Croce on History and Liberty', *New Republic*, 19 May 1941.

MURE, G.: 'Croce e Oxford', *Rivista di filosofia*, July 1953.

PAGUE, G.: 'La pensée politique de B. C.', *L'Arche: revue mensuelle*, Algiers, I (1944), n. 1.

PARENTE, A.: 'La storia come pensiero e come azione', *Nuova Italia*, 1933, n. 6.

PESCE, D.: 'Storicismo e cristianismo', *Leonardo*, 1946.

PREUVES: *Cahier Mensuelle*, II (1952)—December issue dedicated to Benedetto Croce.

Pubblicazioni dell' Istituto Italiano di Cultura di Londra, London, 1953: *Benedetto Croce: A Commemoration*, contributions of Gilbert Murray, Manlio Brosio, Guido Calogero.

Revista di letteratura moderna, Florence, IV (1953), n. 2—issue dedicated to Benedetto Croce.

Rivista di filosofia, Turin, XLIV (1953)—issue dedicated to Benedetto Croce.

SALVATORELLI, L.: 'Uno storico della libertà: B. Croce', *L'Industria*, Milan, 1953.

'Croce storico', *Rassegna storica del Risorgimento*, Rome, XXXIX (1952), fasc. iv.

'Il Mezzogiorno nella storia d'Italia', *Il Ponte*, Oct. 1945, 846–60.

SCHAPIRO, I. S.: 'Croce's History as the Story of Liberty', *Journal of the History of Ideas*, Oct. 1941.

SMITH, D. M.: 'The Politics of Benedetto Croce', *Cambridge Journal*, I (Oct. 1947); II (Feb. 1948).

'Croce and Fascism', *Cambridge Journal*, VIII (March 1949).

STEFANINI, L.: 'Storicismo ed esteticismo', *Logos*, Rome, 1951, 27–39.

Studium: rivista mensile di vita e cultura, Rome, Jan. 1953—issue dedicated to Benedetto Croce.

VEGAS, F.: 'Storia e storiografia nelle più recenti interpretazioni del pensiero crociano', *Rivista di storia di filosofia*, April 1949.

WALL, B.: 'Benedetto Croce', *Twentieth Century*, Jan. 1953.

WELLEK, R.: 'Benedetto Croce: Literary Critic and Historian', *Comparative Literature*, V (1953), n. 1.

APPENDIX C

GLOSSARY OF PROPER NAMES*

ACCETTO, TORQUATO: seventeenth-century poet.

ACHILLINI, CLAUDIO, 1574–1640: critic, poet and historian.

ACTON, SIR JOHN, 1737–1811: naval expert, statesman (first minister to Ferdinand, King of Naples, 1779–1808, with interruptions due to political vicissitudes).

ALFIERI, VITTORIO, 1749–1803: Italian poet, playwright and patriot.

AZEGLIO, MASSIMO D', 1798–1866: Piedmontese statesman and writer.

BABEUF, FRANCOIS-NOËL, 1760–1797: French revolutionary, social thinker.

BAGNACAVALLO, TOMMASO, b. c. 1585: social analyst and essayist.

BAKUNIN, MIKHAIL, 1814–1876: Russian born social thinker and agitator.

BALBO, CESARE, 1789–1853: Italian statesman, historian, man of letters.

BARANTE, PROSPER, 1782–1866: French statesman and administrator; historian.

BARONIUS, CESARE CARDINAL BARONIO, 1538–1607: church historian.

BASILE, GIAMBATTISTA, 1575?–1632: Neapolitan dialect poet; *Muse Napoletane; Pentamerone.*

BELLARMIN, ROBERTO CARDINAL BELLARMINO S.I., 1542–1621: apologist and theologian.

BELLINI, LORENZO, 1643–1704: poet, essayist, literary theorist.

BENI, PAOLO, 1552–1625: moralist and critic; literary theorist.

BISACCIONI, MAIOLINO, 1582–1663: historian and publicist.

BISMARCK, OTTO VON, PRINCE, 1815–1898: Prussian statesman.

BLANC, LOUIS, 1811–1882: social thinker, publicist, historian.

BLANQUI, LOUIS-AUGUST, 1805–1881: French revolutionary thinker.

BOCCOLINI, TRAIANO, 1556–1613: Italian political writer and publicist.

BODIN, JEAN, 1530–1596: French humanist, political and legal thinker.

BOILEAU-DESPRÉAUX, NICOLAS, 1636–1711: French literary critic and theorist.

BORROMINO (or BORROMINI) FRANCESCO, 1599–1667: Italian architect collaborator of Bernini.

BRIGNOLE-SALE ANTONIO GIULIO, 1605–1665 c.: Italian engineer, writer and political figure.

BRIGNOLE-SALE ANTONIO, 1786–1863: Italian engineer and patriot.

BRUNO, GIORDANO OF NOLA, 1548–1600: Neapolitan philosopher and poet.

* This list is intended only to illuminate the text; it contains therefore only names which might be unfamiliar to the reader.

273

CALOPRESO (or CALOPRESE) GREGORIO, 1650–1715: Italian literary theorist and critic.

CAMPANELLA, TOMMASO (GIOVAN-DOMENICO), 1568–1639: Calabrian poet, philosopher, humanist and theologian.

CANNING, GEORGE, EARL, 1770–1827: British statesman and prime minister.

CAPASSO, BARTOLOMEO, 1815–1900: Neapolitan historian and archivist; *Monumenta Napoletani Ducatus; Historia Diplomatica Regni Siciliae.*

CARACCIOLO, DOMENICO, 1715–1789: Neapolitan statesman and diplomat.

CARAFFA-CARACCIOLO, DIOMEDE, DUKE OF MADDOLONI, 1406–1487: states-man, humanist, patron of arts.

CARLO ALBERTO, OF SAVOY, 1798–1849: King of Sardinia.

CAVOUR, CAMILLO BENSO DI, COUNT, 1810–1861: Piedmontese statesman, first minister of United Italy.

CENNI, ENRICO, 1825–1903: Neapolitan jurist, historian and patriot.

CHARLES OF ANJOU, 1226–1285: King of Sicily and Naples.

CHARLES V (Charles I of Spain), Holy Roman Emperor, 1500–1558.

CICOGNARA, LEOPOLDO, 1767–1834: Italian historian of art and sculpture.

COLLETTA, PIETRO, 1775–1831: Neapolitan historian; *Storia del Reame di Napoli.*

CONSTANT, BENJAMIN, 1767–1830: French statesman.

CORNELIO, TOMMASO, 1614–1686: Neapolitan scholar, scientist and arcadian.

CORTESE, GIULIO CESARE, b. c. 1575: Neapolitan dialect poet.

CRISPI, FRANCESCO, 1818–1901: Italian statesman and primier.

CUOCO, VINCENZO, 1770–1823: Neapolitan historian, writer and patriot; *Saggio critico sulla rivoluzione napoletana di 1799.*

DE BLASIIS, GIUSEPPE, 1832–1914: Neapolitan historian; *Chronicon Siculum; La insurrezione pugliese.*

DE DOMENICIS, BERNARDO, 1684–1750: historian of art of southern Italy.

DE PRETIS, AGOSTINO, 1813–1887: Italian statesman and primier.

DE SANCTIS, FRANCESCO, 1817–1883: literary critic and historian.

DI SANGRO: noble family of southern Italy.

ENFANTIN, BARTHELEMY-PROSPER, 1796–1864: French philosopher and economist.

FERRARI, GIANFRANCESCO, 1607–1671: Italian burlesque poet.

FILANGIERI, GAETANO, 1752–1788: Neapolitan jurisprudentialist; *La scienza della legislazione.*

FIORETTI, BENEDETTO, 1579–1642: Italian critic and historian.

FONSECA-PIMENTEL, ELEANORA, 1748–1799: Neapolitan patriot and revolu-tionary; editor of *Il Monitore*, revolutionary journal on Parisian model.

FRANCHETTI, LEOPOLDO, 1847–1917: Italian publicist and political figure.

GAGERN, MAXIMILIAN, BARON VON, 1810–1889: German statesman.

GALATEO, ANTONIO DE FERRARIIS, called il Galateo, 1444–1500: humanist, diplomat, academician, physician.

GALIANI, FERDINANDO, 1728–1787: Italian priest, writer, economist, social critic and historian.

GALILEI, GALILEO, 1564–1642: mathematician and physicist.

GALUPPI, PASQUALE, 1770–1846: Italian philosopher and economist.

GARIBALDI, GIUSEPPE, 1807–1882: Italian soldier and patriot.

GENTILE, ALBERICO, 1552–1608: jurisprudentialist; *De jure belli*.

GIANNELLI, BASILEO, 1662–1716: literary critic and theorist.

GIANNONE, PIETRO, 1676–1748: Italian historian, jurist and publicist; *Storia civile del Regno di Napoli*.

GRAVINA, GIANVINCENZO, 1668–1718: humanist, literary critic and Arcadian; Opico Erimanteo in Arcadia.

GUARINI, GIANBATTISTA, 1538–1612: poet and playwright; *Pastor Fido; L'Idropica*.

GUARINI, GUARINO, 1624–1683: Italian architect and sculptor; Palazzo Carignano in Turin.

GUIZOT, FRANCOIS PIERRE, 1787–1874: French historian and statesman.

HERZEN, ALEXANDER IVANOVICH, 1812–1870: Russian statesman and writer.

KOSSUTH, FRANCIS (FERENC), 1841–1914: Hungarian patriot.

KOSSUTH, LOUIS (LAJOS), 1802–1894: Hungarian patriot.

LANZA, GIOVANNI, 1810–1882: Italian statesman and primier.

LASSELLE, FERDINAND, 1825–1864: German socialist.

LEPOREO, LODOVICO, d. *c* 1650: Italian burlesque poet.

LIGOURI, (S.) ALPHONSO, 1696–1787: Italian saint, moralist and theologian.

LOYOLA, IGNATIUS DE (IÑIGO LOPEZ DE RECALDE), 1491–1556: founder of the Company of Jesus.

MALVEZZI, CRISTOFORO, 1547–1597: Italian historian of literature and essayist.

MARIA CAROLINA, of Hapsburg-Lorraine, 1752–1814: Queen of Naples.

MARINO, GIAMBATTISTA, 1569–1625: Neapolitan poet; founded school named for him, 'marinismo'; *Rime, Adone*.

MASCARDI, AGOSTINO, 1590–1640: Italian historian and publicist.

MAZZINI, GIUSEPPE, 1850–1872: Italian patriot.

MENZINI, BENEDETTO, 1646–1704: Italian poet, literary essayist and critic.

MESANIELLO (TOMASO ANIELLO), 1620–1647: Neapolitan 'popular' rebel; led insurrection called the 'Revolution of Masaniello', 1647.

METTERNICH, KLEMENS VON, PRINCE, 1773–1859: Austrian statesman.

GLOSSARY OF NAMES

MILIZIA, FRANCESCO, 1725–1798: Italian art historian; *Dizionario delle belle arti del disegno.*

MINGHETTI, MARIO, 1818–1886: Italian statesman and primier.

MONTI, VINCENZO, 1754–1828: Italian writer, poet and patriot.

MURATORI, LODOVICO ANTONIO, 1672–1750: Italian historian, literary theorist, Arcadian; Leucoto Gateate in Arcadia.

PANCHIATICHI, LORENZO, 1635–1676: Italian dialect poet.

PELLICO, SILVIO, 1789–1854: Italian writer and patriot; *Le mie prigioni.*

POERIO, GIUSEPPE, 1775–1834: Neapolitan patriot, jurist, diarist.

PONTANO, GIOVANNI, 1426?–1502: (Jovianus Pontanus) Umbrian humanist, resident of Naples, poet; *De amore conjugali.*

ROBERT OF ANJOU, 1309–1343: King of Naples.

ROSA, SALVATOR, 1615–1673: poet, painter, critic.

ROYER-COLLARD, PIERRE-PAUL, 1763–1854: French philosopher and statesman.

RUFFO, FABRIZIO CARDINAL, PRINCE OF CASTELCECALA, 1763–1832: Neapolitan prelate, diplomat, leader of monarchical reaction after revolution of 1799.

SANNAZARO, JACOPO (ACTIUS SYNCERUS), 1456–1530: Neapolitan humanist and poet Latin and vernacular; *De partu virginis; Arcadia.*

SARPI, PAOLO S. I., 1552–1623: Italian historian and theologian.

SCARUFFI, GASPARO, 1519–1584: Italian economist and writer.

SCHIPA, MICHELANGELO, 1854–1940: Neapolitan historian; *Storia del ducato napoletano; Masaniello.*

SELLA, QUINTINO, 1827–1884: Italian statesman and primier; economist.

SERAO, MATILDE, 1857–1927: Italian novelist.

SERRA, ANTONIO, c.1550–1625: Italian essayist and economist.

SETTEMBRINI, LUIGI, 1813–1873; Italian literary historian.

SFORZA-PALLAVICINO, CARDINAL, 1607–1667: historian and philosopher.

SGRUTTENDIO, FILIPPO: 'nom de plume' ascribed by historians to a variety of persons of the baroque period.

SIRI, VITTORIO, 16?–1685: Italian historian and publicist.

SISMONDI, JEAN-CHARLES, 1773–1842: French historian.

SONNINO, GIORGIO SIDNEY, 1847–1924: Italian statesman and economist.

SPAVENTA, SILVIO, 1822–1893: Italian statesman and patriot.

SUMMONTE, PIETRO, 1453–1526: Neapolitan historian.

ST. SIMON, CLAUDE HENRI, COUNT, 1760–1825: French philosopher.

STIGLIANI, TOMMASO, 1573–1671: Italian poet, historian, diarist.

STURZO, DON LUIGI, 1871–: Italian social and political leader; sociologist; founder of Popular Party (1919).

TANUCCI, BERNARDO, 1698–1783: Tuscan diplomat and jurist; became first minister of King of Naples (1752).

TASSO, TORQUATO, 1544–1595: Italian poet.

TESAURO, EMANUELE, 1591–1677: Italian philosopher, rhetorician, literary theorist.

TOSTI, LUIGI, 1811–1897: Italian historian.

TROYA, CARLO, 1785–1858: Italian historian, liberal and patriot.

VERGA, GIOVANNI, 1840–1922: Italian novelist; *I Malavoglia.*

VICO, GIAMBATTISTA, 1668–1744: Neapolitan humanist, jurist, philosopher and poet; Arcadian: Laufilo Terio in Arcadia.

VILLANI, NICCOLO, 1590–1636: Italian historian and critic.

ZUCCOLO, LODOVICO, 1568–1630: publicist, political theorist; *Della ragione di stato.*

INDEX

'abétissement' of man, by Communism, 197

absolutism:

  of Neapolitan monarchy, 23 sqq., 39, 54, 70 sqq., 78–9, 203–4, 228

  post-Napoleonic, 202 sqq.; and Holy Alliance, 202–3; illusory prepotence of, 203–205; intrinsic character of, 205–6; opposition to, 206–10; instability of, 210

  and Catholicism, 192 sqq.

  and liberalism, 193 sqq.

  and Revolution of 1830, 212 sqq.; effect of, upon, 212; retention of power by, after, 213

  and Revolution of 1848, 218 sqq.

  recrudesence of, in France, in 1851, 224

  of modern anti-liberal state, characterized, 196; compared with older forms, 198

academies, in Baroque Age, 142

Acton, Lord John, 73

'Adone', of G. B. Marino, and baroque poetry, 123

Age, The Baroque, 88–166; concept of, analysed, 93–109; and Counter Reformation, 110–18; poetry and art in, 119–40; philosophy in, 140–64; moral tone of, 164–6

  The Liberal, 239–47; genesis of, 239; utopianism and, 239; quality of, 240; in Italy, 240 sqq.; Catholicism in, 241; socialism in, 241–2; weakening of liberal spirit in, in Italy, 245–6; Communism in, 246–7; Croce's vindication of, 249

Alexander, of Russia, 202

Alfieri, Vittorio, and the 'delirium' of the Baroque Age, 122

alienation, in naturalistic historiography, 5

Alliance, The Holy, 202

America, as model for German unity, 222

Andler, Charles, 247

'animo barocco', 119

anti-clericalism, in Italy, overcome in Liberal Age, 241

Arcadia(ianism), 162–3

  correctness, as artistic ideal in, 129

Archivio storico per le provincie napoletane, 13

Ardigó, 246

art: reduction of history to general concept of, 81–2; theory of, in Baroque Age, 154–162; and Renaissance, 154; moral and philosophical instruction as ideal of, in, 154; delight as end of, 155; beautiful form in, 155; autonomy of art in, 155, 158; 'faculty' of taste and criticism in, 156; intrinsic end of art in, 156; 'taste' in, 156; 'ingegno' in, 156; critique of 'genre' in, 156; 'artistic personality' in, 157; progressive character of, 157–8; positive values of, 158; criticism of 'marinism' in, 159; lack of coherence in, 159; 'organon of poetic knowledge' in, 160; unity of the arts in, 160; canons of criticism in, 160–1; cartesian reaction against, 162

'atéliers nationaux', 224

Austria: and Italy, 214; and papacy, 220; in 1848–51, 223; inner unity of, 224; expulsion of, from Italy, 234; and Prussia, 234 sqq.

Balbo, Cesare, 227

Barante, 210

barons, Neapolitan: conflict with Angevine dynasty, 58; power of, 58; political ineptitude of, 60; anarchistic tendencies of, 60; and vassals, 60; and monarchy, 60–1; Machiavelli on, 57; social transformation of, 64 sqq.

Baroque, The (Age): as problem, 93, 101 sqq., 108, 109; as term: significance, 93; genesis of, 94; extension of, 94; as concept, relevance to art criticism, 95; significance, 95; and figurative arts, 95; historical limits of, 95; and 'generalizing fallacy', 97; as programme: formula of Marino, 96; criticism of, by Villani, 96; by Croce, 96; as 'eternal type', 98; positive traits of, 98; and total life of spirit, 99; as 'disposition of soul' ('animo barocco'), 99, 119; spurious positive definitions of, 102–5; authentic positive element in, 106; spiritual character of, 121; 'silence of great poetry' in, 122 sqq.; 'delirium' of, Alfieri on, 122; religious poetry of, 131; satirization of, in dialectal poetry and literature, 135; Crocean

INDEX

'culturalism', 188

Cuoco, Vincenzo, on 'ceto medio', 32, 33; and Luisa San Felice, 32-3 note

Dante, attitude of Baroque Age toward, 122, 154, 161

d'Azeglio, Massimo, 228

de Blasiis, Giuseppe, 13

de Broglie, 210

decadence, meaning of, in history, 108-10

de Falco, Bernardo, and early descriptions of Naples, 17

democracy: jacobin, and Neapolitan Revolution of '99, 29 sqq.; and liberalism, 194; social-, and liberalism, 216; and Communism, 217-19

Depretis, 253-7

De Sanctis F., 254

'descriptivism' in baroque art, 124, 125; in poetry of Marino, 125; 'literary' imitation, consequence of, 124; and 'ingenuity', 125; mistaken for 'realism', 125

de Serre, 210

'devotion' in Baroque Age, and literature, 132

dialect(al) literature, in Baroque Age, 134 sqq.

di Revel, Thaon, 228

Dorsi, 253

dualism: of reason and history, 181; of aim, in Italian unity, 226 sqq.

Enfantin, 217

England: and liberalism, 206; and Revolution of 1848, 222; and imperialism, 264

'ethos' in history, 3-18; 81-5

'exclusivism', social forms of, 188

exiles, Italian political, 30, 31, 228

Fabianism, 244

factor(s), theory of, in history, 52-3

'faculty' theory of art criticism, 155

Farnese, Elisabetta, 24

Fascism: Croce's early optimism toward, 174; transformation of his attitude toward, 174-5; as 'double' of liberalism in Italy, 248; antecedents of, in post-Risorgimento Italy, 248; as problem, 249; as fact, 255; 'adventure' theory of, 249, 255, 263; possibility and necessity of, 256; a 'free choice', 256; Croce and, 256-7

Ferdinand II, of Naples, 27

Filangieri, Gaetano, 72

Fonseca-Pimentel, Eleanora, 23

France: opposition to liberalism in, 207; liberal disillusionment in, 214; liberal retrogression in, 224; and doctrine of liberalism, 209-10; and Liberal Age, 240, 244

Frankfort, Assembly of, 222

Frederick William, of Prussia, 222

futurism, 260

Galateo, and early humanism in Naples, 62

Galileo, on theological and philosophical implications of science, 143

'genre', decline of theory of, 157

German(y): and formation of idea of liberty, 183, 209; weakness of liberalism in, 208; inner freedom vs. outer order in, 208; speculative achievement of, 209; and Revolution of 1848, 222-3; 'little-' proposal, 222; political liberty and nationalism in, 225, 226; unification of, 231-8; and America, 222; contrasted with Italian, 231-2; Bismarck and, 232-3; and Austria, 232, 234; stages of, 234; collaboration of liberal Italy in, 234; opposition to, by France, 234-5; quality of 235-6; significance of, 237-8; as 'lost leader' of liberalism, 246; and imperialism, 264

Giannone, Pietro, 28, 29, 69, 70

Giolitti, 244

Hegel, 3, 183, 209, 239

Herzen, on integral revolution in Russia, 224

historicism, and idea of liberty, 183

history (historiography): place of, in Croce's work and thought, 3; Naples, role of, in Croce's —, 3-4; ethico-political, 4, 6, 7-8, 9, 32, 81-5, 91, 99, 106, 169 sqq., 175-6; as moral drama, 4, 5, 8, 11; 'positivism' in, 4-5; 'alienation' in, 5; nature and, 5, 6, 7, 30, 31; 'laws' in, 5; liberty, as form of, 5; 'factors' in, 6; philosophy of, spurious forms of, 7; universal, spurious forms of, 7; — and special, 7; universality, qualitative, in, 78; 'genres' of, 9; phases of Croce's, 10-14; idyll in, 10; source of, in Croce's —, 12; transition from, 19; tragedy in, 12; positivity of, 102; — defined, 106; — and ethico-political —, 106; negative —, rationale of, 102; ethical will, as dynamic principle of, 107; periodic movement of, 197